# STAGING THE OLYMPICS

One Week
Loan

## One Week Loan

# STAGING THE OLYMPICS

## THE EVENT AND ITS IMPACT

*Edited by*
*Richard Cashman and Anthony Hughes*

This book is published in conjunction with the
Centre for Olympic Studies,
University of New South Wales.

**A UNSW Press book**

*Published by*
University of New South Wales Press Ltd
University of New South Wales
Sydney 2052 Australia
www.unswpress.com.au

Natilia
Cataloguing-in-Publication entry:

Staging the Olympics: the event and its impact.

Bibliography.
ISBN 0 86840 729 1.

1. Olympic Games (27th: 2000: Sydney: NSW) — Planning.
2. Olympics — Social aspects — New South Wales —Sydney.
3. Olympics — Economic aspects — New South Wales — Sydney.
I. Cashman, Richard, 1940– . II. Hughes, Anthony.

796.48

*Printer* Griffin Press Pty Ltd, Netley, South Australia

Cover photograph courtesy of the Olympic Co-ordination Authority.

# CONTENTS

# PREFACE

There are many books on the Olympics but few on the staging of the Games with special reference to the experiences of a particular Olympic city. The books that have been written, such *The Keys to Success*, on the 1992 Barcelona Games, have been retrospective analyses of the Games.

This book is therefore unique in several respects. It is the first book to provide an overview of how Sydney is progressing on many fronts in staging the 2000 Games. It is also the first Games work-in-progress book, reviewing the strengths and weaknesses of the staging of the Games in the lead-up period, while the planning for the Games is still ongoing. It will be first published more than a year before the staging of the Sydney Games. If this exercise was repeated (and further editions produced) shortly before the Games and after the Games have been held, some useful comparisons might appear as to how the staging of the Games appeared at various points along the delivery track.

To some, this might seem exceptionally ambitious and even risky, because such a book will date and revisions will be necessary in a year and maybe again a year later. A chapter written on security before the Atlanta Games would have had to be scrapped and rewritten after the Games: it would change from a discussion of security arrangements and risks, to one about what went wrong with Atlanta's security planning.

Such perspectives overlook some great benefits of publishing a book before the event. Staging the Games in Sydney has generated a dynamic and ever-changing debate among scholars, the media, Olympic organisers and communicators about a wide range of issues relating to the staging of the Games. Researchers, responding to the views of the planners, the politicians and the Olympic Family in

Australia and overseas, will continue to debate many issues about staging the Games.

Contributors to this book include not only academics, but also others involved in the Games planning process. Reg Gratton, of SOCOG, will be in charge of the Main Press Centre (MPC) at Olympic Park in 2000. His role is to ensure that the MPC runs more smoothly and efficiently than the Atlanta MPC. Amanda Johnston works for Lang & Associates, a company involved in Olympic sponsorship. A number of academic writers also have an involvement in the staging of the Games: some sit on Olympic advisory and planning bodies, and others will have a role in the staging of the Games in 2000.

Thus, this book captures some of the process by which the Games were realised and many of the ongoing problems that have to be solved in a short time frame. After the Games, when these issues have been resolved and the Games staged, some of the passion associated with staging the Games will have been removed. There is another practical reason for publishing this book at this time. There is a strong interest among students, scholars and the general public in Australia and overseas about 'how Sydney is travelling' in regard to the 2000 Games.

Each author has been asked to address two central issues: how the Games will be staged from the perspective of a particular theme, such as the environment, security or transport; and what the impact of the Games on Sydney in particular, and Australia in general, will be. The chapter on transport will look at the transport plans for the Games and how they are likely to work; it will also address the impact of the Games on Sydney transport both in 2000 and beyond. There are many other chapters that could have been included, such as discussions on language issues and engineering. These and other topics may be included in a future edition.

This book was written initially for the many undergraduate students at the University of New South Wales in a subject on 'Staging the Games', which will be taught to more than 600 students in 1999. However, the book will also be of use to postgraduate students and scholars who want a starting point for research on one or another aspect of the Games, and who may wish to have an informed opinion on a particular aspect of the Games. It is our hope that the book may also appeal to the general public, which is taking such a keen interest in the staging of the Games.

The views expressed in each chapter are those of each individual author and do not necessarily reflect the views of the Centre for Olympic Studies, or those of the Olympic Movement. One of the positive features of this book is that a variety of opinions are expressed, which will encourage further debate on the staging of the Games, as well as on wider Olympic issues.

# CONTRIBUTORS

**John Black** was the Foundation Professor of Transport Engineering at the University of New South Wales from 1984 to 1999 and was Chair of the Management Committee of the Centre for Olympic Studies from 1998 to 1999. He was a member of the expert panel that reviewed the transport strategy for the Homebush Bay site and advised the Judges of the Olympic Village Design Competition on transport matters.

**Angela Burroughs** has taught subjects on sport, society and the Olympics in the General Education program for a number of years. Her special research interests are the Oympic bidding process and sport and sexuality. Currently she is Executive Officer to the Pro Vice-Chancellor at the University of New South Wales,

**Richard Cashman** has been Director of the Centre for Olympic Studies at the University of New South Wales since 1996. An Associate Professor in History, he has published extensively on sports history in Australia and Asia. He was editor of *Sporting Traditions*, the journal of the Australian Society for Sports History, from 1992 to 1999.

**Mark Duncan** is Professor of Pharmacy at the University of Colorado Health Sciences Center in Denver. He also serves as the Director of the newly established Biochemical Mass Spectrometry Facility located there. His research interests are focused on the ultra-trace quantification of components, notably drugs and drug metabolites, in biological systems. Until recently, he directed the Ray Williams Biomedical Mass Spectrometry Facility at the University of New South Wales and was Associate Professor in the Faculty of Medicine there.

**Kevin Dunn** is a lecturer in cultural and social geography at the School of Geography, University of New South Wales. His main research areas include the construction of place identity, resident activism, the geography of migrant settlement, local government responses to cultural difference, and the politics of heritage and memorial landscapes. He is Secretary of the Geography Society of New South Wales.

**Frank Farrell** is a senior lecturer in Australian history at the University of New South Wales. His specials interests include education, sporting and democratic traditions, and he is author of *Themes in Australian History*, published by UNSW Press in 1990.

**Debra Good** is a researcher on the arts in Sydney. She has completed a postgraduate thesis on 'The Olympic Game's Cultural Olympiad: Identity and Management' at the American University Washington in 1998.

**Reg Gratton** is Manager of Main Press Centre for the 2000 Games. Previously, he was Deputy Bureau Chief and Asian Sports Editor for Reuters International News and Information Agency. Gratton has been foreign correspondent for Reuters in London, Kuala Lumpur, Hong Kong and Sydney. He also worked for the *Rand Daily Mail* in South Africa from 1971 to 1975 and was Chief of Staff of the *Sydney Daily Telegraph* and News Editor for AAP from 1986 to 1991.

**Anthony Hughes**, Executive Officer of the Centre for Olympic Studies at the University of New South Wales, is a sports historian with research interests in the Olympics, along with ethnicity and sport. He is a member of the Chair for Modern Irish Studies Committee, The Ben Lexcan Foundation Scholarship Committee and the Sports Association Blues Committee.

**Amanda Johnston** is General Manager of the Sydney office of Lang & Associates'. She was involved in the managing and implementation of marketing programs for multiple Coca-Cola brands across 27 Olympic sports.

**Pauline McGuirk** is a lecturer in urban geography at the Department of Geography and Environmental Science at the University of Newcastle. Her primary research interest involves investigating the urban impacts of restructuring. She has researched and published widely on changing processes in local governance, planning and public participation; place representation and urban identity; and community responses to urban change. She is Associate Editor of *Australian Geographer* and Vice President of the Geography Society of New South Wales.

**Ron Newman** is Head of School of Design Studies, College of Fine Arts at the University of New South Wales. He has held senior design positions with Philips, Email and Sebel Furniture. He was also editor of *Design in Australia* for six years and has held various executive roles within the Design Institute of Australia.

**Deo Prasad** is the Director of the SOLARCH Group at the Faculty of Built Environment at the University of New South Wales. He has chaired the ANZSES and is a Director of the ISES, Sustainable Energy Industries Council of Australia and the Energy Research and Development Corporation. He been part of the Energy Expert Panel at the Olympic Co-ordination Authority and has written a number of their guidelines for low-energy building design.

**Ray Spurr**, from the Faculty of Commerce and Economics, is Director of the Centre for Tourism Policy Studies at the University of New South Wales. He is a senior policy adviser to the World Travel & Tourism Council and a former Chairman of the OECD Tourism Committee from 1992 to 1996.

**Alan Thompson** is a Senior Defence Fellow at the Australian Defence Force Academy, University of New South Wales, where he teaches management. He was involved in the establishment of the counter-terrorism and dignitary protection structure put in place after the Hilton Hotel bombing in 1978. Thompson collaborated in a review of Australia's counter-terrorism capability for the Commonwealth Government in 1993.

**James Weirick** is Professor of Landscape Architecture at the University of New South Wales where he was Head of School from 1991 to 1995. He held previous positions at the School of Landscape Architecture at RMIT, at Boston Architecture Center, the University of Massachusetts, Boston and the University of Canberra. He is co-author of *Building for Nature: Walter Burley Griffin and Castlecrag*, published in 1994.

A view from the ferry wharf of Sydney Olympic Stadium under construction. (Photograph courtesy of the Olympic Co-ordination Authority.)

# PART 1

## THE EVENT

# THE GREATEST
# PEACETIME EVENT
*Richard Cashman*

Many commentators have referred to the Olympic Games as the world's greatest sports festival and the largest peacetime event. The only sports extravaganza that could perhaps challenge the Olympics as sport's mega-celebration is soccer's World Cup. It could be argued that in some parts of the world, particularly in South America and Africa, the 'people's game' or the 'world game', as soccer is known, has deeper roots than the Olympics and is followed with greater passion.

The popularity of the World Cup in soccer owes much to the fact that the first tournament was played in South America (Uruguay) and won by the host country. The style and brilliance of successive teams from Brazil has done much to enhance the appeal of soccer. In more recent times, the rise in standards and competitiveness shown by teams from Africa and Asia has provided a further boost.

The Olympic Games, by contrast, were born in Europe and, as a consequence, were decidedly Eurocentric in the early years of the modern era.[1] It was not until after the post-1945 era that Third World countries began to make any mark on the Games. Even so, both the Summer and Winter Olympics have mostly been held in Europe and North America (see Table 1.1). The Summer Games have yet to be held in Africa and have appeared only once in Latin America. The Winter Games have moved outside Europe and North America only twice: on both occasions to Japan, in 1964 (Sapporo) and 1998 (Nagano).

Table 1.1
Sites of the Summer and Winter Olympic Games

Olympic Cities (Summer Games) from 1896*

| | |
|---|---|
| Europe (12) | Athens (1896, 2004), Paris (1900, 1924), London (1908, 1948), Stockholm (1912), Antwerp (1920), Amsterdam (1928), Berlin (1936), Helsinki (1952), Rome (1960), Munich (1972), Moscow (1980), Barcelona (1992). |
| North America (4) | St Louis (1904), Los Angeles (1932, 1984), Montreal (1976), Atlanta (1996) |
| Central America (1) | Mexico City (1968) |
| Asia (2) | Tokyo (1964), Seoul (1988) |
| Australia (2) | Melbourne (1956), Sydney (2000) |

*This list excludes Games that were awarded but were not held.

Olympic Cities (Winter Games) from 1924

| | |
|---|---|
| Europe (10) | Chamonix (1924), St Moritz (1928, 1948), Garmisch and Partenkirchen (1936), Oslo (1952), Cortina D' Ampezzo (1956), Innsbruck (1964, 1976), Grenoble (1968), Sarajevo (1984), Albertville (1992), Lillehammer (1998) |
| North America (5) | Lake Placid (1932, 1980), Squaw Valley (1960), Calgary (1988), Salt Lake City (2002) |
| Asia (2) | Sapporo (1964), Nagano (1998) |

Despite the universal popularity of soccer, the Olympic Games have strong claims to be the premier world sporting event. The Olympics involves more sporting countries than soccer, in that all participant countries (197 in 1996 and more than 200 by 2000) will be represented at the Sydney Games. An equivalent number of football countries strive to play in the World Cup, but most of them are eliminated in qualifying rounds. Only 24 countries appeared in the 1994 World Cup and another eight, making a total of 32, at the 1998 World Cup.

While only men played in the World Cup until the 1990s — the first Women's World Cup was held in China in 1991 — the Olympics have become a peak event both for men and women. Although women were excluded from the ancient Games and the revived Games of 1896, they forced their way into the Olympic program and have gradually been accepted. Women have been some of the star performers of the Games. These include Sonja Henie in 1928, Mildred 'Babe' Didrikson in 1932, Fanny Blankers-Koen in 1948, Nadia Comaneci in 1976 and 1980, to name a few. Australian women Olympians such as Dawn Fraser and Betty Cuthbert have achieved more than any Australian man in swimming and athletics respectively. While there is some way to go before gender equity is achieved — women's events now constitute approximately 40 per cent of the Olympic program — women achieve more prominence and greater visibility in the Olympics than in other sporting arenas, where they struggle to gain much attention.

In quantitative terms, the Olympics have several advantages over the World Cup. The Olympics are now held every two years — though organisers of the World Cup are thinking of also staging future Cups every two years — and the Summer Games attract a more diverse television audience than World Cup soccer. More women watch the Olympics than World Cup football — in the Olympics, women constitute more than half the television audience. A cumulative television audience of 37.1 billion tuned into the 1998 World Cup, and the finals were watched by four billion viewers. The global television audience for the 1996 Atlanta Games was an estimated 19.6 billion viewers. However, while the Atlanta Games drew an estimated 1500 million viewers per day, the 1994 World Cup in the United States attracted only 600 million per day.

It is not easy to compare the audiences for these two mega-events, however, since they differ in character — one lasts for just over two weeks, whereas the other continues for five weeks. Can the audience for the opening ceremony of the Games be compared with that for the final of the World Cup? Is it valid to compare the cumulative audience totals for both events, given that the number and range of events are so different?

Another critical difference is that apologists for the Olympics make lofty claims for the Games as something more than a mere sporting event. Also, the Olympic Games have a long history, many traditions, and powerful symbols that add to the meaning of the occasion as a quasi-religious festival. The Olympic Movement has also developed its own 'sacred' sites — at Olympia, where the torch is lit for each Games, and at Lausanne, its headquarters since 1915 and the site of the magnificent Olympic Museum. The Olympics have developed a comprehensive set of ideals, known as Olympism, and cover a wide range of issues, from ethical play to internationalism. To win a gold medal at a world championship does not equate with success at the Olympics, which has a special aura. The *Olympic Charter* also outlines the wider humanistic goals of the Movement: in the 1990s the *Charter* listed the three strands of Olympism: sport, culture and the environment.

The Olympic bribery scandal, which surfaced in December 1998 with revelations about the Salt Lake City bid for the 2002 Winter

Games (see Chapter 3), threatened to tarnish the reputation and undermine the credibility of the Olympics. Because of the lofty claims made for the Olympics, they are more vulnerable than most other sports when it comes to issues of bribery and corruption — the higher the reputation, the bigger the potential fall from 'athletic grace'. It is also true that the sporting marketplace has become more competitive. The organisers of the Olympics cannot assume that their festival will maintain its standing at the pinnacle of world sport as a matter of course. The promoters of rival events are keen to emulate past Olympic success.

Perhaps the gap between the World Cup and the Olympics is diminishing because World Cup matches are followed with great passion and involve threats, resignations, controversies and even deaths. Enhanced World Cup opening and closing ceremonies suggest that the World Cup organisers acknowledge that ritual has an important place in a world festival.

## SOME KEY QUESTIONS

At the outset, six central questions can be posed about the reasons why the Olympic Games have acquired such a pre-eminent status in the 1990s. First, how and why did a relatively minor European sports festival that was revived in 1896 become the largest peacetime event, or what some have irreverently termed, 'the greatest show on earth'? Secondly, how and why were the Games successfully reinvented from a largely Eurocentic event to a world festival? Thirdly, how have the leaders of the Olympic Movement allowed the Games to change from a rigidly defined amateur event to one where commercialism and professionalism are freely accepted? Fourthly, how are the Games able to retain their credibility, and even a semi-religious aura, as a contest that is largely clean and fair, despite continuing problems with drug cheats and allegations of bribery and corruption? Fifthly, how have the Games retained their dignity and credibility despite the 'show biz' and commercialism of much television broadcasting? Finally, it is important to ask: what do the Games represent?

## WHAT ARE THE GAMES?

It is difficult to define precisely what the modern Olympics (and the ancient Olympics as well) represent, because the Olympic festival is complex and evolving. While the staging of an elite sporting competition is the central purpose of the Games, they embrace different cultures, politics, ideologies, identities, arts, religions, commerce and, more recently, environment concerns, among other things. In addition, there is an underlying tension between Olympism and the Olympic Games. Many have argued along the lines of Robert

Paddick that the Games themselves do not always live up to the ideals of Olympism, such as internationalism and fair play.[2]

Staging the Games involves many facets, including planning, sponsorship, tourism, advertising, security, transport, environmental impact, the media, and the costs and benefits to the local economy. Because many believe that the Games are an effective way of showcasing a city's and a nation's culture, there is keen competition among cities to win this prize.

It is difficult to define the Games in any precise sense, and it is inadvisable to attempt to squeeze the Games into a tightly defined framework. John J. MacAloon, biographer of Pierre de Coubertin, the founder of the modern Olympics, has suggested that the Games are truly multifaceted. He stated that the Olympics are 'an immense playground, marketplace, theatre, battlefield, church, arena, festival and Broadway of cultural images, symbols and meanings'.[3]

There is also a great divergence of opinion in assessing the worth of the Games in contemporary society. Apologists for the Games, from De Coubertin to Avery Brundage, an influential president of the IOC from 1952 to 1972, have made lofty claims for what they term the Olympic Movement — that is, those who belong to the 'Olympic Family'. President Brundage stated in 1964 that the Olympic Movement was a religion. He made the following statement at the 62nd Session of the International Olympic Committee (IOC) at Tokyo: 'The Olympic Movement is a 20th Century religion, a religion with universal appeal which incorporates all the values of other religions, a modern, exciting, virile, dynamic religion.'[4]

This view of the Games as a religion is less prominent in a more secular, commercial and professional era. However, it cannot be denied that part of the majesty and mystery of the Olympics is that it has so many symbols, sites and rituals that are quasi-religious. The modern Olympics have links with the ancient Games, which were overtly religious. The five rings, the flame, the torch relay, the flag, the oath and many other symbols, for example, all suggest that the Olympics is something more than mere sport.

The ancient Olympics had a direct link with ancient Greek religion, symbolised by the lighting of the flame at Olympia since 1936, and the modern Games are a coming together of an imagined world community in a global rite. Olympic 'sacred' sites at Olympia and Lausanne have been carefully nurtured. De Coubertin literally gave his heart and soul for the Olympic Movement. When he died in France in 1937, his body was buried in Lausanne, but his heart was removed and buried in a sacred grove at Olympia. The torch relay at each Olympics pauses at this site before setting off on its way to one or another city.

De Coubertin believed that the Games were more than a simple sports event and convened a conference in Paris in 1906 on 'Art, Letters and Sport' to devise ways in which the arts could be incorporated into the Games. De Coubertin implemented a cultural competition and awarded medals in the categories of sculpture, painting, music, literature and architecture, and his *Pentathlon of the Muses*, the Cultural Olympiad, was implemented at the Stockholm Games of 1912.[5] Art and culture — recognising the links between sport and art and that high achievers in both areas develop a champion mindset — have been a part of the Olympics since that date, although culture has remained very much the poor relation to sport (see Chapter 14). The environment was added as the third strand of Olympism in the 1990s, although there has been plenty of debate about whether the Games are truly 'green' or whether they represent a convenient and even cynical 'greenwash' (see Chapter 7). In the 1980s and 1990s, the issue of disabled sport has been integrated into the Olympics, and the Paralympics have gained in stature as an official adjunct to the Olympic festival (see Chapter 15).

By the 1990s, the IOC had very broad-ranging humanistic aims. President Samaranch wrote that the IOC:

> also supports and encourages the development of school and university sport, sport for the disabled, protection of the environment and the fight against scourges such as doping, drugs and violence, through preventive education in order to protect young people.[6]

Critics of the Games, by contrast, have dismissed the Olympics as an overhyped commercial extravaganza and a 'gross mass spectacle' in which corruption and nationalism are more prominent than high-minded idealism. Jean-Marie Brohm, who participated in the student upheavals in Paris in 1968, is one of the more extreme critics of the Olympic Games, which he dismisses as an opiate for the masses. He adds that the Games, and competitive sport in general, produces 'monsters', because 'competitive sport does not educate the body but mutilates it'.[7] In more recent times, two British journalists, Vyv Simson and Andrew Jennings, have levelled their attack on the IOC itself. They created a political furore in 1992 when they depicted the IOC as a secret and self-perpetuating oligarchy, the 'plaything' of the world's leading multinationals, run by an ex-fascist. The IOC was so traumatised by the events, that it took the journalists to court and a Lausanne court sentenced them in absentia to a five-day suspended gaol sentence and payment of US$2000 in court costs.[8] Sociologist Paul Gillen had earlier echoed this view when he suggested that the IOC 'has always been a conservative club and the politics of nearly all its presidents has been distinctly reactionary'.[9] A critique from an opposite perspective suggests that, in practice, the Olympics can fall far short of their ideals. Paddick wrote that the Games should be 'a clear and unambiguous glorification of the athlete' and 'deny their very essence if they appear to use athletics as an excuse for having a party, for selling advertising space, for showing the superiority of a political system, for promoting the tourist industry or economy, or for entertainment'.[10]

However, even those who have been critical of the Olympic Games, such as Australian sociologists Geoffrey Lawrence and David Rowe, admit that, for better or worse, the Games retain genuine popular support, hinting that while the Games have some 'faults', they also has some virtues. They suggest that while the Olympics provide 'a spectacle, much of it grotesque', they also provide 'glimpses of promising possibilities'. There is the opportunity for audiences, which can be critical and even resistant, to be made aware of issues such as 'black power as much as any supposed white supremacy'.[11]

Perhaps the world's sports public wants to continue to believe in the ideals of the Games, that it is a clean and credible competition, despite continuing reminders that cheating and corruption do occur and involve athletes, coaches and officials. However, the crisis over the Salt Lake City bid will test the public's faith in the Games. A lot will depend on how effectively the IOC deals with its greatest crisis in the modern Games.

## EXPLANATIONS FOR THE IMPORTANCE OF THE GAMES
### THE ANCIENT GAMES

The ancient Games, which lasted from 776 BC to AD c. 500, have contributed much to the modern Games. While many modern sporting traditions are of relatively recent origin, the ancient Olympics enhance the legitimacy of the Games by virtue of three millennia of tradition. They link the modern Games with ancient Greece, the first society to give prominence to sport.

Although de Coubertin claimed to 'revive' the ancient Olympics, he actually 'appropriated and recast the symbols of the ancient Games for his own purposes'. 'Dressing the Games in the image of antiquity,' noted Bruce Kidd, 'proved to be a masterstroke of public relations.'[12] Kidd argues cogently that the modern Games were based only loosely on the ancient Games. Ideas about ethics and purpose of play were vastly different in de Coubertin's time, so it is not surprising that some elements of the ancient Games — its violence and its cultic practices — were not incorporated into the modern Games. Sports such as the pankration, a free-for-all mixture of boxing and wrestling, and chariot races were not included in the program of the modern Games. The modern Olympics were associated with new ideals, such as 'fair play' and amateurism, which were unknown in ancient Greece. There were some ancient precedents for some other modern ideals, such as internationalism and the Olympic truce.

While the modern Games didn't flow directly out of the ancient Games, the link with ancient Greece enhanced the status and symbolism of the modern Games, and has been incorporated at many points. Olympic medals include a design of a laurel wreath, which was a core symbol of the ancient Games. The torch for each Olympics is ignited at Olympia, and the words of the Olympic hymn, sung for the first time at the Sorbonne Congress in 1894, were taken from ancient inscriptions rediscovered in the 19th century. The ancient Games provided a rich storehouse of symbols and sporting practices, some of which were appropriate for 19th century Europe and others which were not.

## A GLOBAL MEDIA EVENT

American scholar John Hoberman has suggested that the rise of the mass media encouraged the emergence of internationalist movements at the turn of the century. These included the Red Cross (1863), Marxist internationalism (1860s), the Wagnerian cult (1870s), the Esperanto movement (1887), the Olympic movement (1894) and the Scouting movement (1908). Although the aims of these idealistic movements were radically different, they all appealed 'to deep feelings of Europeans that were rooted in anxieties about war and peace' and offered a form of 'redemptive internationalism'. Some movements, such as the Olympics and Scouting, shared a common ground, both claiming to serve the cause of peace and their founders claiming to be 'educators' and 'mobilisers' of youth.[13] Paul Gillen has added that, by the late 20th century, the Olympics had become a 'premonitory cult of global society'. He added that peak global events like the Olympics are a form of 'civil religion'; 'what holy days and pilgrimages are to religions'.[14]

The advance in media is perhaps one of the most significant reasons for the spectacular growth of the Olympic Games, particularly in the last two to three decades. The idea of the Games as a spectacle appealed to de Coubertin, but for the first few decades relatively few people witnessed this spectacle, directly or indirectly. Since the 1980s there has been a spectacular increase in television broadcast fees (see Table 1.2), which has transformed the way in which the Games are organised and watched, and even what they represent.

Table 1.2
US television broadcast rights fees as a percentage of worldwide fees[15]

SUMMER GAMES

| Year | Place | Network | Cost (US$ million) | % Change | % of worldwide fees |
|------|-------|---------|--------------------|----------|---------------------|
| 1960 | Rome | CBS | 0.394 | | 13.7 |
| 1964 | Tokyo | NBC | 1.5 | 280 | N/A |
| 1968 | Mexico City | ABC | 4.5 | 200 | 46.1 |
| 1972 | Munich | ABC | 13.5 | 200 | 76.7 |
| 1976 | Montreal | ABC | 25 | 85 | 76.6 |
| 1980 | Moscow | NBC | 87 | 248 | 86.1 |
| 1984 | Los Angeles | ABC | 225 | 158.6 | 78.3 |
| 1988 | Seoul | NBC | 300 | 33.3 | 74.4 |
| 1992 | Barcelona | NBC | 401 | 33.6 | 63 |
| 1996 | Atlanta | NBC | 456 | 13.7 | 50.9 |
| 2000 | Sydney | NBC | 705 | 54.6 | 64.1 |
| 2004 | Athens | NBC | 793 | 12.5 | 64.1 |
| 2008 | TBA | NBC | 894 | 12.7 | 63.8 |

WINTER GAMES

| Year | Place | Network | Cost% (US$ million) | Change | % of worldwide fees |
|------|-------|---------|---------------------|--------|---------------------|
| 1960 | Squaw Valley | CBS | 0.050 | | N/A |
| 1964 | Innsbruck | ABC | 0.597 | 1094 | 63.7 |
| 1968 | Grenoble | ABC | 2.5 | 318.8 | 95.7 |
| 1972 | Sapporo | NBC | 6.4 | 156 | N/A |
| 1976 | Innsbruck | ABC | 10 | 56.2 | N/A |
| 1980 | Lake Placid | ABC | 15.5 | 55 | 73.8 |
| 1984 | Sarajevo | ABC | 91.5 | 490.3 | 90.6 |
| 1988 | Calgary | ABC | 309 | 237.7 | 95 |
| 1992 | Albertville | CBS | 243 | −21.3 | 83.2 |
| 1994 | Lillehammer | CBS | 300 | 23.4 | 85 |
| 1998 | Nagano | CBS | 375 | 25 | 73.7 |
| 2002 | Salt Lake City | NBC | 555 | 48 | 82 |
| 2006 | TBA | NBC | 613 | 10.4 | 80.3 |

## THE ROLE OF OLYMPIC SYMBOLS AND SITES

Presidents of the IOC, from the time of de Coubertin, have been keenly aware that symbols and sites add wider meaning to the Games. De Coubertin was a conscious symbol creator who was well aware that symbols enhanced the spectacle of the Games. Table 1.3 lists some of the more important changes in Olympic symbolism over the first century of the modern Games. The list demonstrates the continuing innovation in and formalisation of the Olympic pageant.

Table 1.3
Chronology of the introduction of Olympic ceremonies, symbols and innovations

| | |
|---|---|
| 1896 | Medals first presented. First opening ceremony. |
| 1904 | The practice of awarding gold, silver and bronze medals was established. Some teams appeared in national costume. |
| 1908 | The Australian team first marched in a national uniform. |
| 1913 | The Olympic flag with five rings unveiled. |
| 1915 | Lausanne became Olympic headquarters. |
| 1920 | Olympic oath first introduced. Olympic flag first unveiled at a Games. |
| 1928 | Olympic flame first lit. |
| 1932 | Olympic Village and victory podium first introduced. |
| 1936 | Torch relay first run. |
| 1938 | Olympia, the first Olympic feature film, released. |
| 1956 | Informal closing ceremony introduced. |
| 1960 | First internationally televised Games. Olympics and Paralympics held in the same city. |
| 1964 | First Olympic mascot. |
| 1994 | First 'separate' Winter Games (a different year from the Summer Games). |

Of all the symbols, the flame and the torch are among the most powerful. They provide a link with the ancient Games, as the Olympic flame is rekindled at Olympia some months before each Games. Fire is a powerful symbol of sacrifice, purity and goodwill. The torch relay has become a telling vehicle for community involvement in the Games — communities provide runners and host the torch in their community — and is an extended media advertisement of a coming Games. The lighting of the torch by a local celebrity and its extinction at the closing ceremony are high points of the opening and closing ceremonies.[16]

The *Olympic Charter*, which is revised and republished regularly, constitutes the IOC Bible. It sets out appropriate protocol and procedures for all Olympic ceremonies, appropriate use of symbols, offices with the movement, relationships and definitions. The 92-page 1998 version is a remarkable document because it demonstrates that the IOC recognises the power of Olympic property and is keen to guard it closely.

## THE ROLE OF DOMINANT INDIVIDUALS

The Olympic Games have benefited from the support of powerful and dominant individuals who have been passionate in their commitment to the Games. Since 1896 (following the brief presidency of the Greek Demetrios Vikelas [1894–6]), there have been only six presidents of the IOC, and three of them have been president for two decades or more (see Table 1.4). Pierre de Coubertin (President 1896–1925) set the tone, dedicating his life and much of his money to the promotion of the Olympic Games. While de Coubertin spent much of his life promoting the Games, the American Avery Brundage (1952–72) concentrated much of his effort on protecting the purity of the Games and its symbols. Juan Antonio Samaranch's (1980–) contribution has been to find new avenues to underwrite the Games when they were facing critical financial difficulties in the late 1970s. Samaranch has presided over the greatest expansion of the Games.

Table 1.4
Presidents of the IOC

| | |
|---|---|
| Demetrios Vikelas | 1894–6 |
| Pierre de Coubertin | 1896–1925 |
| Henri de Baillet-Latour | 1925–46 |
| Sigfrid Edstrom | 1946–52 |
| Avery Brundage | 1952–72 |
| Lord Killanin | 1972–80 |
| Juan Antonio Samaranch | 1980– |

While some of the IOC leaders have been controversial, no one can deny that they have provided strong leadership, which has been critical in maintaining the cohesion of a cumbersome international institution that involved continuing and complex negotiations with national Olympic committees and international federations. Brundage was a controversial figure in 1936 when he was accused of anti-Semitism when he thwarted an American boycott of the Nazi Olympics. He was also at the helm in 1972 when, mid-way through the Munich Games, eleven Israeli athletes were killed as a result of terrorist action. He insisted that the Games 'must go on'. However, on occasions, Brundage was able to set aside his extreme right-wing views and act with a pragmatic internationalism in the interest of enhancing the Games. For example, he helped bring the Soviet Union into the Olympic arena in 1952 at the height of the Cold War.

## APPROPRIATION

The IOC cannot claim all the credit for the successful reinvention of the Games and its adaptation to a changing world. The move from a Eurocentric to a world Games occurred, in part, because the people of Asia, Africa and Latin American embraced the Games and made it their own. Countries such as Cuba produced their own heroes, in boxing, and Kenyans excelled in long-distance running from the 1960s.

However, the IOC has assisted this process by introducing sports that are popular in parts of the world other than Europe. When Tokyo was awarded the Summer Games in 1964, judo and volleyball were added to the sporting program. In more recent times, the addition of badminton (1988), table tennis (1992) and taekwondo (2000) has enabled Asian athletes, for instance, to achieve greater success at the Games.

## MEETING CHALLENGES AND REINVENTING THE GAMES

One of the achievements of the leadership of the IOC has been to defend the Olympics from many challenges to the Games as the peak body for sports in the world. Women and workers challenged the Games in the 1920s and 1930s, but threats of alternative rival Games were averted.

Women were so fed up with their lack of recognition in the Olympic Movement that they organised their own highly successful track-and-field championships in 1922 and 1926. The Games were promoted by their organisers as the Women's Olympics. The IOC eventually recognised the threat posed by these alternative Games (and the use of the word 'Olympics') and agreed to the introduction of five track-and-field events for women at the 1928 Games. It has been a long and difficult process for women to approach gender equity in the Games, and by the 1990s approximately 40 per cent of the events of the Games were for women. Adrianne Blue has described the character of this struggle: 'No one wanted women at the Olympics. We cajoled, we argued the case logically, and then little by little, event by event, we elbowed our way in.'[17]

For a time in the 1920s, the Worker Olympics, some official and others unofficial — held at Prague in 1921, Frankfurt in 1925, Moscow in 1928 and Vienna in 1931 — surpassed the official

Olympics, which were viewed as 'bourgeois Olympics' in terms of the number of competitors and spectators and in 'pageant, culture and new sports records'.[18] The aim of worker sport was to make sport truly democratic, to admit women as well as men, black athletes as well as white, and to provide a 'socialist alternative to bourgeois competitive sport, to commercialism, chauvinism and the obsession with stars and records'.

However, the challenge to the Olympic Games petered out by the late 1930s. The Worker Games due to be held in Barcelona as an alternative to the Nazi Olympics of 1936 were not held due to the Spanish Civil War, though they were held in the following year in Antwerp. Although a worker sports movement continued to exist, it lacked the prestige, facilities and funds to compete in the long run with the Olympics. Media coverage of worker sport was another factor that limited its development.

The first Winter Games, held at Chamonix in 1924, which extended the range of Olympic sports, was a less controversial addition to the program. Figure skating had appeared on the Olympic program in 1908 and ice hockey in 1920. The Chamonix Games were a modest event, attracting athletes from only nine countries, and for many years the Winter Games remained in the shadow of the main event, the Summer Games. However, due to the spectacular television footage it provided, the popularity of the Winter Games accelerated spectacularly in the 1980s, and by 1994 the Winter Games had their own time slot, two years after the Summer Games. The Winter Games had become an event in its own right.

The Olympic model has been so successful that it has spawned many other Games for particular regions and communities. Some of these Games, such as the Commonwealth Games (introduced in 1930) and the Asian Games (introduced in 1951), have achieved the status of a lower tier feeding into Olympic competition. Others have not gained acceptance. The GANEFO (Games of the New and Emerging Forces Organisation) Games were a breakaway movement of socialist countries that rejected the Olympics because they believed it was dominated by imperialist countries. Although the GANEFO Games were held in Indonesia in 1963, negotiation and compromise averted this crisis. In more recent times, the IOC was unwilling to include under its umbrella the Gay Olympics, forcing it to change its name to the 'Gay Games'. The Paralympics, by contrast, have been an accepted part of the Olympics since 1960 (see Chapter 15).

## COMMERCIALISM AND PROFESSIONALISM IN THE 1980s

One of the biggest overhauls of the Games and its ideology took place in the 1980s when the ideology of amateurism, which had been so vigorously defended by some previous IOC presidents, was scrapped and sponsors and professionals were fully accepted in the Games. It was the ultimate demonstration that Olympic ideology was sufficiently malleable to admit professional basketball, including the American 'Dream Team' and professional tennis players.

It could be argued that the Olympic organisers had little choice in this regard. By the late 1970s, staging the Games had become so expensive that the future of the Games looked bleak without the engagement of sponsors and the accommodation of television interests. It was also quite evident to the Olympic leadership that it was necessary to accommodate commercial and professional interests — since both became dominant from the 1980s — if the Olympics were to retain their status as a peak sporting event. Just what the long-term cost of this decision to freely accept commercialism and professionalism remains to be seen. Greater IOC wealth and political influence can provide the Movement with greater opportunities, but they can also introduce a new raft of problems.

## CONCLUSIONS

The Olympic Games have become the world's greatest peacetime event because it is an evolving and dynamic festival that has adapted to the needs of a changing society, and world political structure and changing expectations of what sport should be. Past organisers of the Games met challenges from various quarters and creatively redefined the Games to meet the needs of a changing society. The Games have many continuing assets, such as the weight of tradition and the power of the Olympic sites and symbols. The Games have long been etched in the public imagination and there is a fervent desire among the public to continue to believe that the Games are clean and credible, despite some evidence to the contrary.

While there are opportunities for the Games in the next millennium, there are a number of threats that, unless they are dealt with, may jeopardise the future of the Games as a peak sporting event. The operations and structure of the IOC are coming under increasing public scrutiny, and there will be great pressure to make it more open and transparent.

Another problem is that of gigantism; the increasing number of sports and participants threatens to make the festival too unwieldy. There is also the related problem of what constitutes an Olympic sport: should it include dancesport (ballroom dancing), darts and ten-pin bowling? In the 1990s, the twin and related issues of drugs and corruption threaten to undermine the credibility and legitimacy of the Games. (This topic is considered in later chapters.) Finally, while television has transformed the Games and added to its popularity, there is a delicate balance to be maintained between sport as serious play and as entertainment. The once-grand spectacle and pageantry of the Olympic Games, like the institution of the British monarchy, could be reduced to mere soap opera.

## FURTHER READING

Findling, J. E. and Pelle, K. D. (eds) (1996), *Historical Dictionary of the Modern Olympic Movement*, Greenwood Press, Westport, CT.

Guttmann, Allen (1992), *The Olympics: A History of the Modern Games*, University of Illinois Press, Urbana, IL.

Hoberman, John (1995), 'Toward a theory of Olympic internationalism', *Journal of Sport History*, vol. 22, no. 1, pp 1–37.

International Olympic Committee (1997), *Olympic Charter*.

MacAloon, John J. (1981), *This Great Symbol: Pierre de Coubertin and the Origins of the Modern Olympic Games*, University of Chicago Press, Chicago.

# HALLMARK EVENTS
## Kevin M. Dunn and Pauline M. McGuirk

The modern Olympic Games have always been an international event: a celebration of sporting competition between athletes from many nations. In an era marked by the quickening pace of global integration of the world's economic and cultural systems, the Olympics can also be thought of as a globalised 'hallmark event'.[1] Certainly, the Games have economic, cultural and political dimensions that mirror the various processes of globalisation. The impacts of the Games on its host city are similar to the impacts of globalisation processes.

In this chapter we discuss the analogies between the Olympics, as a hallmark event, and the local impacts of economic globalisation. We position the Olympics business — not the sporting aspects, but the bidding and development processes — as an example of economic globalisation. By extension, the responses of localities and local authorities to the impacts of globalisation might be expected to be the same as for an Olympic event. Lessons on how a local community can best capitalise on an Olympic event might be derived, therefore, from examining the broader case of economic globalisation and its impact upon localities. We begin by sketching the major impacts of economic globalisation upon localities, with particular attention to the institutional changes that are commonly associated with localities' efforts to adjust to global economic integration.

## ECONOMIC GLOBALISATION: PLACE-COMPETITION, PLACE-MARKETING AND PLACING THE OLYMPICS

Debates about the nature and extent of economic globalisation and the emergence of a truly globalised economy are rife.[2] However much authors debate the issues, most agree that advances in transportation, communications and production technology, the removal or reduction of international trade quotas and tariffs, and the deregulation of financial flows have fundamentally transformed global economic relations. It is largely conceded that economic activity has been increasingly globalised.[3]

Communications technology combined with financial deregulation has enabled the emergence of an international financial system of trading in a range of financial 'products'. Transnational corporations (TNCs) — major corporations whose trade and production operations span international boundaries — have transformed the organisational form of capitalist firms and forged links around the globe in their quest to minimise the costs of production and the profitability of trade.[4] Though the dominance of truly transnational corporations has been questioned,[5] complex flows of information, financing, raw materials, manufactured goods, services, skilled labour and management expertise between them and their affiliates are an important source of global connections between places. TNCs have been forerunners in creating globally organised manufacturing and service industries. In any case, communications technology enables even small firms to have a global reach, to disaggregate the production process and locate its elements at varied 'least cost' locations beyond the boundaries of the national economy in which parent firms are based. Production processes and capital flows are held together in complex global networks in an economic environment where nationally based regulations (such as limits on foreign direct investment) are much reduced.[6] Technological advances have thus opened up the potential of an enormous array of locations to global capital investment. Capital mobility between nations and regions has been escalated by the drive to exploit this potential and facilitated by the increased permeability of national borders to international investment.[7]

The rhetoric of a 'borderless world'[8] in which capital is 'hypermobile' has been a powerful force in compelling nations, regions and even individual cities to accept a logic of global competition to attract international investment.[9] The global imperative of competition has been a dominant force shaping national economic policies.[10] While the case for 'borderless world' may have been overstated,[11] the realities and the rhetoric of global competition have undoubtedly increased place competition at a range of scales. With potential investors willing to differentiate between investment locations on the basis of the local investment environment, nations, regions and cities compete with each other to offer a combination of favourable conditions that will entice investment into their jurisdictions. A location's investment environment is constituted by a host of physical conditions (for example, infrastructure and telecommunications networks, the availability of development sites, and the quality of the local environment and lifestyle), institutional conditions (for example, the suitability of local labour, local regulatory regimes such as planning regulations, and the availability of investment incentives such as tax breaks) and symbolic elements (for example, the image and aesthetics of a place).

The effects of global competition and capital mobility (and the powerful rhetoric that accompanies it) have resulted in national, regional and local governments becoming increasingly concerned with promoting local economic development within their own boundaries in competition with neighbouring states, cities and regions. Localities attempt to create a combination of investment conditions that will out-compete rival locations in the quest for investment. Many are also involved in active place-marketing to promote their places as investment locations that are cheaper, have the most flexible labour force, are more efficient, more productive, less impeded by regulatory red tape and, therefore, more profitable than other places.

For older industrial regions and cities, the global shift towards the services sector[12] has required them to undertake substantive material changes, as well as a repositioning of their place image, so as to attract new forms of investment. For such cities, the global imperative has tended to produce three related forms of restructuring.[13] First is a physical restructuring of the fabric of the city in which the material legacy of older industry is removed. The emerging landscape must be able to accommodate the anticipated new economic base in activities such as tourism or service industries. Second is a symbolic restructuring in which the location's identity is repackaged. Post-industrial imagery and consumption-based economic activities are often utilised to create a new, more marketable place-image. Third is a restructuring of local or regional governance in which government roles are reoriented towards the entrepreneurial facilitation of economic development and cooperation with the business sector, and a broad range of non-government, often private, organisations are incorporated into government decision-making and policy formulation.[14] A variety of new institutions, such as development corporations, may be formed, forging partnerships between government and private sector interests.[15] Such entrepreneurial governance is part of a broad political shift within industrialised economies towards neo-liberalism,[16] a political philosophy favouring limited state intervention and espousing the logic of the market.

These three reconstructions are, of course, interrelated. For the marketing of a place to be efficacious, the symbolic reconstruction of an industrial place has a co-requisite of physical reconstruction. An image transformation is unsustainable without a corresponding redevelopment of the city's industrial urban fabric. To guide all of this, a more entrepreneurial approach to urban governance is often employed which seeks to remove obstacles (physical, symbolic or institutional) to redevelopment. These interrelated shifts have been identified as occurring within Australian cities like Newcastle and Wollongong.[17] The processes of place competition and the restructurings they promote have distinct similarities to the processes of bidding for and hosting the Olympic hallmark event. The redevelopment of Homebush, in Sydney's west, as the venue for the year 2000 Olympics could be cited as another example in which the material site and place-image have been restructured under the guidance of newly formed, entrepreneurial-driven forms of governance.

## GOVERNING THE LOCAL IN A GLOBALISED CONTEXT

Regions, cities and even localities are increasingly focused upon developing internationally competitive investment environments for investors who possess global reach; indeed, the investment package that constitutes the Olympics cannot be surpassed in these terms. The American geographer David Harvey[18] argued that, in contemporary times, the primary 'task of urban governance is, in short, to lure highly mobile and flexible production, financial and consumption flows into its space'. In the competition to outdo rivals in the global marketplace, the practices of entrepreneurial elected and non-elected governing authorities have resulted in at least four problematic outcomes: subsidising private sector interests at the cost of public concerns;[19] the dilution of local planning powers;[20] the limitation of public participation in the development process;[21] and the homogenisation of community opinion.[22]

We will now outline the problematic dimensions of these outcomes before considering them in the light of Sydney's Olympic preparation. Entrepreneurial forms often have a focus on assisting private sector development that often results in a public subsidising of private development projects. One common example is state provision of infrastructure previously provided by the private sector, such as site preparation for commercial development or transport infrastructure.[23] Another contrasting example is the increased privatism in the provision of user-pays infrastructure, such as tollways.[24] This is associated with a discourse of privatism in which private industry construction and management is presumed more efficient than the public sector equivalent.[25] Urban researchers have found, however, that the balance of capital risk in part- or fully privatised public service provision tends to be borne still by the public purse,[26] while private exposure to risk and to absorbing non-profitable elements of development is decreased. Such public subsidisation of private interests has the effect of reallocating government expenditure from other areas, particularly from social welfare expenditure.

Internationally, entrepreneurial urban governance has been found to involve the relaxation of local planning requirements in order to 'fast-track' urban development.[27] In innumerable instances, special planning agencies have been instituted to hasten particular developments deemed to be of significant status. This is the case too for developments necessary to host major urban spectacles or hallmark events that can be used as vehicles for economic growth and urban redevelopment.[28] In Australia, as elsewhere, state and local planning systems have been streamlined to become enablers rather than regulators of development.[29] In 1998, for instance, the state government of New South Wales introduced major reforms to its development approval system through amendments to the *Environmental Planning and Assessment Act*. The reforms introduced private certifiers and assessors for building and development applications, and will further centralise planning control of larger developments, regardless of their location, to the central planning authority within state government. This privatisation and centralisation of planning control is posited as a response to 'persistent calls for streamlining and fast-tracking'.[30]

One common strategy of entrepreneurial urban governance is to remove 'obstacles' to development. Public scrutiny and participation in development appraisal are often positioned as obstacles by prospective investors. Many city administrations, in their attempts to respond to the rhetoric of global competition and produce a globally competitive investment environment, have instituted attempts to limit public participation in planning and development processes, or to restrict the stages at which participation is accommodated. New methods of participation are being trialed which allow intensive community consultation about broad policy dimensions but for strictly limited periods and under controlled conditions.[31] Recent research[32] on various forms of public participation in local government planning in Sydney revealed that many local governments were making sincere and legitimate attempts to meet statutory requirements on public participation, and some were attempting to expand and improve participation. However, the state government reforms may well further confine the public input into the latter stages of the development process. The reforms follow a series of state government initiatives over the last decade which have attempted to rein-in both public participation and local planning powers.[33]

Tensions between the agendas of state and local government become apparent. State governments' pursuit of globally competitive investment environments, including hallmark events, can be somewhat removed from the impacts of these pursuits on specific localities. Local governments are more directly concerned with place-specific impacts and with representing local communities' concerns for their own locality and for their rights as local citizens. Ironically, the importance of LOCAL governance is highlighted, rather than obliterated, by processes of globalisation,[34] as it is at this scale of governance that democratic principles of representativeness, public involvement and accountability regarding development and planning are the most accessible.

Contemporary large-scale development projects, such as those associated with hallmark events, have often involved the silencing of divergent voices opposing development or aspects of it.[35] Public reception of development and investment projects is an important component of the investment environment. Governing bodies wish to present their locations as having a homogenised, unified voice in support of investment, rather than fragmented voices expressing resistance to development.[36] Even opposition to specific components of a development may be branded as contrary to legitimate 'public interest' and as endangering the ability of a location to attract global investment. Place-competition, inspired by global capital mobility and the deployment of its rhetoric in the discourses of governance, has worrying implications for local accountability.[37]

## THE OLYMPICS LOCALLY

The processes of place-competition and place-marketing are partially brought into play by capital mobility and are partially a product of the powerful discourse of a globalised world. Local differentiation is reduced by the multiplicity of locations all marketing themselves — often in identical ways — and offering similar incentives in order to capture investment. Such tactics leave localities vulnerable to exploitation by global capital. What are the lessons then that can be learned from a comparison of the local impacts of these processes of economic globalisation and the process of bidding for and developing Sydney's Olympics event? The parallels between them are striking.

Place-competition and place-marketing are not unlike the process of bidding to host an Olympics event which witnesses cities competing in a place-marketing exercise that seeks to capture the enormous potential investment and economic benefits of hosting such a global hallmark event. Hosting an Olympic Games represents the opportunity to attract enormous investment and consumption spending, both during and after the Games. It can also generate significant ongoing local development, particularly in the tourism and retail sectors. The Atlanta Games in 1996, for instance, drew US$4 billion into the Atlanta state economy between 1991 and 1996.[38] The exposure a city receives globally on hosting such an event can result in positive image projections that differentiate that city in the minds of investors and tourists.[39] A locality's capture of the jewel in the crown of hallmark events becomes a mechanism for driving material and symbolic transformations of place and, as we will explore in relation to Sydney's development of the Olympic site, has profound implications for governance at a local and regional scale.

The Olympics are a significant global event and place-competition. The International Olympic Committee (IOC) has purposefully enhanced and encouraged a bidding process for the Olympic Games. In a critical analysis of Manchester's failed bid to host the 1996 and 2000 Olympic Games, British geographers[40] concluded that the IOC was purposefully fostering a sense of competition:

> Bidding for the Olympics means submitting to the competitive rules laid down by the IOC ... The IOC takes steps to ensure that a vigorous — and ever more elaborate — competition is fostered amongst the bidding cities.

Heightening the competitive process has enabled better leverage of subsidies for the Games from the potential hosts. Indeed, the allegations of corruption in the bidding process that emerged in early 1999 suggest that other corrupt 'incentives' have also been leveraged by increased competition. Host cities must pledge higher levels of financial support, servicing and infrastructure provision than they have had to in the past. These subsidies are often paid from public funds — although the Atlanta Games was largely a privatised affair[41] — and this has direct implications for public spending in other portfolios such as education and social welfare, both areas in which Australian public spending has been cut in recent years. Crucially, hosts have had to trade more concessions to the IOC in terms of television broadcasting rights and merchandising, both important sources of spin-off consumption spending for Games' hosts. They have also had to bestow expensive 'gifts' upon IOC members[42] and offer higher levels of subsidy to visiting athletes — the Sydney Organising Committee for the Olympic Games (SOCOG) will pay the return transportation costs of all teams through the private sponsorship of Team Millennium Olympic Partner Airlines. The Australian Olympic Committee (AOC) president John Coates talked of having to 'play the rules': of supplying subsidies, of lavish hosting, and 'leveraging' the voting system.[43]

## RESTRUCTURING HOMEBUSH

The preparation of the sporting venues at Homebush, and of the adjacent Showground pavilions, has involved a large-scale rehabilitation of what was abused and disused land (see Figure 2.1). This piece of western Sydney has been undergoing a profound physical and symbolic restructuring. The prior land uses of the Homebush Bay area can fairly be described as noxious industrial. The area was dominated by an industrial complex of chemical manufacturers, brickworks and abattoirs. The Olympic Village will be sited over what were a landfill garbage tip and an Australian Navy ammunition dump. The area was, and still is, badly contaminated by industrial, chemical and household wastes. The Minister for the Olympics announced that more than A$137 million will be spent on rehabilitating polluted sites in the area.[44] There are concerns, however, that the rehabilitation will not be adequate. Indeed, it is unlikely that the Homebush Bay water body itself will recover ecologically for many decades. The long-term environmental impacts of the operations of such firms as Union Carbide, ICI and Berger Paints, which were located in the Rhodes industrial estate, are now becoming painfully clear to the NSW government, which is funding the rehabilitation. Nonetheless, it is difficult to imagine how the physical problems in Homebush Bay could have even begun to be addressed had it not been for the preparation for the Olympic hallmark event.

Other physical restructurings to western Sydney include the provision of new sporting, showground and transport infrastructure (Figure 2.1). Likewise, it is highly unlikely that, in different circumstances, western Sydney could ever have had facilities of the range and quality that will be the legacy of the Games. This legacy is one of the major long-term local benefits that results from the hosting of such an event. Harvesting other forms of direct social benefits for the immediate local community (such as improved housing) from the impetus of the Games has proved much more difficult.[45]

The Olympics site preparation has also initiated a symbolic restructuring of the Homebush area. There is little doubt that Homebush will become associated with both the 2000 Olympics and other smaller hallmark events such as sporting finals, and the annual Easter shows. The benefits anticipated from such investment in sports and event-related tourism are typically optimistic and have tended to gloss over significant differences between the local elites and those others in the locality who are less likely to benefit.[46] Nevertheless, the symbolic transition to become a site of hallmark events marks a positive shift from its previous identity as a noxious industrial and dumping area. As a result of the associated image-shift, office development has been attracted into the area, including the national headquarters of TNCs such as Daewoo, and firms like Quality Semi-conductor of Australia and Akai. The recognition gained by the site has clearly raised its profile in the view of international investors. An important part of this symbolic restructuring is the representation of Homebush

Figure 2.1
Past, present and proposed land uses, Homebush Bay, New South Wales

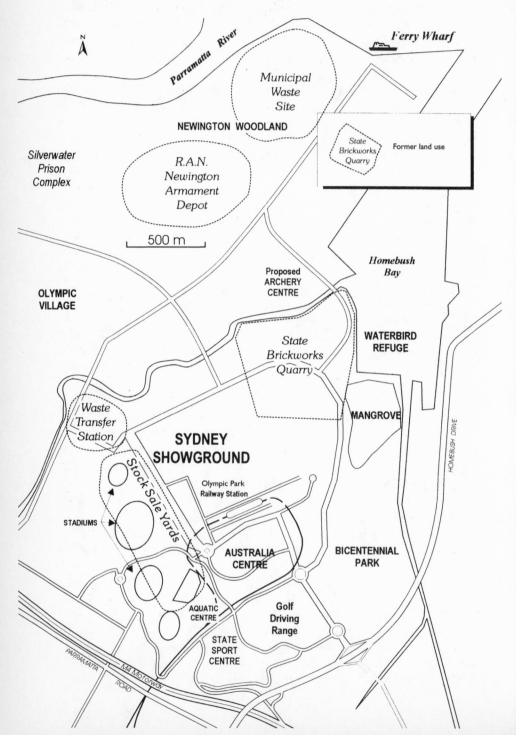

as a 'clean and green' venue. The incorporation of environmentally sound building products, and the use of solar power and energy-conscious design in the Olympic Village are well intended to foster this image. The success of symbolic restructuring at Homebush will undoubtedly affect the broader image of Sydney internationally as a potential growth centre with the capacity and capability to host perhaps the most significant global hallmark event.

In terms of institutional restructuring, the process of staging the Sydney Games and providing the facilities has seen the creation of two new state government agencies, SOCOG and the Olympic Co-ordination Authority (OCA). SOCOG is composed of both government officials and corporate leaders. In recent times, a number of ex-politicians have also been included. Total costs to the NSW state government for the Games were estimated in early 1999 at A$2.3 billion, which is one billion more than was anticipated during the bidding process.[47] Sydney 2000 sponsor partnerships have been established with international and national private interests, named the Team Millennium Olympic Partners. This will ensure considerable privatisation of some aspects of the Games with over A$828 million pledged in sponsorship from Team Millennium and TOP sponsors including Coca-Cola, IBM, McDonald's, Kodak, News Limited, Fairfax, Panasonic, BHP and Pacific Dunlop.

The Atlanta Games were to have been run with no public subsidy, but significant public subsidy was necessary for the less profitable aspects such as security, access and infrastructure provision. This public subsidising of a supposedly 'private-funded' event mirrored the public/private partnerships in other forms of global development.[48] Lessons from the Atlanta Games revealed that extensive private funding resulted in removing discussion of the opportunity costs of policy priorities from the public realm.[49] Limiting the funding role of the public sector, or at least the pretence, relinquished opportunities for democratically accountable decision-making processes and reduced public means of directing the financial resources of the Games towards public priority areas.

The planning and development of the Games have been highly centralised. As with most hallmark events, the final nature of development deadlines and the high price of any public failures to meet those deadlines have meant that the scope for any widespread public involvement has been limited. The non-negotiable nature of the deadlines for Olympic preparations pose the very real threat that public consultation and participation, for which there is provision in the planning and development phases, could be tokenistic and superficial.[50] This raises the question of whether local dispossession results from the process of hosting a global hallmark event.

## OLYMPIC DISPOSSESSION?

Much like globalisation-inspired place-competition, hosting an Olympics can involve changes in how cities are governed. Hosting an Olympics can permanently impact on the geographic and planning framework of the host city.[51] As with other forms of entrepreneurial public/private sector development partnerships, the Olympics bidding and hosting process threatens to stifle local community input and to discourage public dissent. This is a serious concern given that the positive and negative impacts of the Olympics will be felt most keenly by local communities long after the Games have been held. With place-competition, discouraging dissent is driven by the perceived need to present a united welcoming voice to prospective global investors. With the Games' preparation, it is driven by the immovable deadlines and the unsubstantiated notion of regional and national 'public good' being served by the Games. Greenpeace was portrayed as 'unpatriotic' for bringing public attention to the toxic substances in the soil at the old Union Carbide site.

Master planning for developing the Games' sites was carried out by the OCA, under State Environment Planning Policy (SEPP) No. 38, Olympic Games, which produced site development guidelines. The NSW Minister for Urban Affairs and Planning acts as the consent authority for all developments. As with all 'designated' or significant developments in New South Wales, most of the Olympics projects have been exempt from the requirement for preparation of Environmental Impact Statements (EIS). Six major consulting or advisory panels were set up to liaise between SOCOG, stakeholders and experts on various aspects of the Games. These panels involve representatives from community organisations such as the NSW Council of Social Services and the Public Interest Advocacy Centre. The panels have been the major sources of public consultation and input and could have had the potential to be mechanisms for demonstrating best practice in public consultation, scrutiny, participation and accountability. However, in their assessment of public participation in the Games for Green Games Watch, Albany Consulting[52] concluded that the Environment Advisory Panel (EAP) had been ineffectual 'in drawing into the Olympics preparation process the range of expertise that was available' and had instead been a marketing or public relations exercise. The EAP was disbanded and its replacement body has lacked the weight even to demand briefings from government agencies involved in Olympics preparation. It has subsequently lost credibility with community and environment organisations.

In planning and executing the Games' preparation, a minimal role has been granted to local government. Representatives from the

Local Government Association (rather than specific local councils) are present on only the Environment and Social Impacts advisory committees. The NSW Local Government Association's president[53] has publicly stated his opinion that:

> The avenues for local government involvement have been tokenistic at best. Local government has not been given any real say in the decision-making process; in many instances it has been blatantly excluded.

Local government, the most accessible avenue for local public representation, has been largely locked out of the significant decision-making stages. Even those whose jurisdictions will encompass Olympic sites have received little information on key issues like anticipated transport flows, which are crucial to the formulation of local transport plans. The mayor of Mosman City Council complained about the 'apparent lack of commitment to putting in place mechanisms for an effective ongoing two-way flow of information between SOCOG and local government'.[54] Similarly, the executive officer of the Inner Metropolitan Regional Organisation of Councils (IMROC) stated that local government officers were frustrated by the lack of detail that Olympic authorities were providing about developments, and he noted the refusals to supply documentary materials.[55] SOCOG has delayed the dissemination of the results of prior research on the impacts upon local communities hosting previous Olympic Games,[56] leaving councils to undertake their own reviews of the local impacts of previous Olympic Games.

Only in the latter stages of development, rather than in the planning stages, was a Local Government Liaison Committee formed. It is comprised of representatives from the five councils surrounding Homebush Bay (Auburn, Concord, Parramatta, Ryde and Strathfield). In late 1998, SOCOG, the OCA and the Olympic Roads and Transport Authority (ORTA) were in consultation with Waverley Council where the beach volleyball competition will be held. Though such consultation is commendable, it also represents involvement at what Albany Consulting[57] has termed the 'therapy end' of developments, assisting with the 'big-sell' rather than influencing policy formulation phases. SOCOG sees its main public participation initiatives as being the affordable ticketing strategy and the Volunteers 2000 program. Indeed, this latter program is planned to involve 50 000 specialist and general volunteers, each of whom was being offered 'the chance to be part of the Australian team which will stage the biggest sporting event in history'.[58] Direct involvement or attendance at hallmark events has been found to be one of the best ways to ensure long-term public support. This involvement also cultivates a widespread sense of possession of the event. However, the provision of 'crowd atmosphere' for the international telecast, and other free labours, are all at the 'easier end' of public involvement.

The matter of public representation has serious implications for public support for the Games, and for all authorities whose jurisdictions encompass Olympic venues. Public faith in the integrity of planning instruments and processes, termed 'social capital',[59] may well be put at risk by any widespread sense of disenfranchisement or dispossession of local citizens resulting from SOCOG's degree of openness, transparency and accountability. Reports from SOCOG indicate that polling figures on public support remain notably high (75 per cent approval in late 1997), though this is likely to differ by locality and by class and perhaps even ethnicity.[60] Equally, it is likely to be reassessed when the distribution of costs and benefits from the Games becomes apparent rather than hypothesised.[61] Any Olympics-derived loss of social capital would produce a long-lasting residue of public mistrust in Sydney's planning system. That will have impacts not only upon SOCOG and the NSW government, but will also threaten the social capital of local residents in the areas proximate to Olympic venues.

## CONCLUSIONS

One of the problems with place-competitions for global investment flows is that the costs of participating, of playing the rules of the game, can be quite high. The same is true of bidding for and hosting an Olympic Games. In the rush to win these competitions, important democratic principles can be flouted. These considerations include public accountability and participation.

Sydney's civic leaders did not just agree to an offer to host the Olympic Games; Sydney was — as Juan Antonio Samaranch himself said — 'the winner'. Political leaders gain undoubted kudos and benefit from capturing global investments and hallmark events. But the public in any city that competes for and wins a global investment, or indeed a hallmark event, has the right to demand comprehensive assessments of the costs and benefits involved. This includes a measure of the balance and distribution of benefits, such as environmental rehabilitation and sporting legacies (in both participation and infrastructure provision). Many of these are 'real' benefits that could not have been achieved without the impetus and resources of the Games (for example, new public housing stock or rehabilitated industrial sites). The Barcelona Games in 1992 were the catalyst for US$8.1 billion in infrastructure and housing that significantly revitalised the city's seafront.[62] However, the accounting of the chase and capture of global investment and hallmark events is too often one-sided. A limited set of benefits are postulated, and sometimes enumerated, but the costs (especially those beyond direct government expenditure) are rarely so readily available. For example, broader assessments of the opportunity costs of spending on the bidding and hosting need to be publicly available and debated. Can these expenditures be justified in a period of shrinking health care budgets? Is it legitimate to spend these public monies when there are critical political and financial constraints upon almost all public social services provision? The distribution of the benefits and costs must also be critically assessed. The benefits may be unfairly skewed towards business and the costs towards the average taxpayer, or they may favour the rich and middle class over the less affluent. Who among us has won, and who is going to pay? The public has a democratic right to be informed about, and be able to debate, exactly what they have supposedly won.

Local authorities that are compelled to put together plans for the 2000 Olympic Games require advice from, and access to, the central planning bodies responsible for the Sydney Olympics. Both local and central authorities must not only protect existing public participation mechanisms, but they should aspire to expanding and improving public involvement. Councils in those localities where events are planned should bargain hard with SOCOG to get the best possible deals for their locality. Notions of civic duty or patriotism could prove costly. Local councils and their communities should ensure that they do not pay while other areas or private interests gain at their expense. In most cases, local governments and communities have a distinct competitive advantage and they should use it. The potential costs for SOCOG to move events to more remote venues are immense. It is rare that localities have such bargaining strength with regard to global investment and they should always seize and capitalise upon it when it occurs.

A mega-event can potentially achieve many results for a city beyond economic benefits. These could include an increase in public participation in civic affairs, an enhanced a sense of community (spirit of the Games) and increased cross-cultural interactions. The hosting of the Olympic Games should have been a way of further entrenching and expanding community participation in planning in Sydney. Olympic Games preparations could enrich our planning systems, which are facing the entrepreneurialist pressure of economic globalisation. There is little doubt that the Olympics preparation has involved some important physical rehabilitation. However, the criticisms by Greenpeace and other green organisations suggest that the 'Green' in the 'Green Games' is superficial rather than structural. There is a symbolic change happening in Homebush too. The area is shifting from industrial to post-industrial. Sydney's international exposure and image will also be enhanced. But questions remain as to whether the institutional restructuring involved will be progressive or regressive. Will Sydney's planning processes be made more transparent and accountable, and can social capital be enriched as a result of Olympics preparation?

## FURTHER READING

Cochrane, A., Peck, J. and Tickell, A. (1996), 'Manchester plays games: Exploring the local politics of globalisation', *Urban Studies*, vol.33, no. 8, pp 1319–36.

Harvey, D. (1989), 'From managerialism to entrepreneurialism: The transformation in urban governance in late capitalism', *Geografiska Annaler*, vol. 71B, pp 2–17.

Ley, D. and Olds, K. (1992), 'World's fairs and the culture of consumption in the contemporary city', in K. Anderson and F. Gale (eds), *Inventing Places: Studies in Cultural Geography*, Longman Cheshire, Melbourne, pp 178–93.

Ritchie, B. and Lyons, M. (1990), 'Olympulse VI: A post-event assessment of resident reaction to the XV winter games', *Journal of Travel Research*, Winter, pp 14–23.

# PART 2

## WINNING AND DESIGNING THE GAMES

# 3

# WINNING THE BID
*Angela Burroughs*

In December 1998 there were serious allegations of corruption in the Olympic Games bid process which again placed it under the spotlight and brought into question the way in which the International Olympic Committee (IOC) members select host cities. It was revealed that the organisers of the successful Salt Lake City bidding team for the 2002 Games offered inducements to IOC members — for instance, the tuition fees of six IOC members' children at United States' universities were paid.[1] By January 1999 the scandal had claimed two Salt Lake City victims: Frank Joklik, chief of the city's Olympic committee, and Alfredo La Mont, of the US Olympic Committee, had both resigned.

These revelations encouraged a senior member of the IOC to reflect on some of the problems associated with the current bid system. Marc Hodler, Swiss IOC member and IOC executive member, alleged that corruption had been a feature of the successful Salt Lake City bid for the 2002 Games and may have been a factor in many Summer and Winter Games since 1996, including the Sydney Games. Hodler was reported as saying that four agents, including an IOC member, solicited bribes of up to US$1 million to vote for bid cities and that 'the agents then charged the successful bidder "something like $US3 million to $US5 million"'.[2]

Although Hodler retracted his comments in regard to the Sydney Games, his allegations about corruption in the bidding process for the 2002 Games prompted IOC president, Juan Antonio Samaranch, to establish a committee to investigate the bidding process for the Salt Lake City Winter Games. Separate investigations were also called within the United States.

As the investigations proceeded, bribery and corruption allegations escalated. In addition to providing cash payments, university scholarships, free medical treatment and a real estate deal, the Salt Lake City Olympic bid committee was rumoured to have hired prostitutes to help sway the votes of IOC members.[3] The publication of these allegations gave others the confidence to expose further incidences of unethical behaviour, as the Olympic bidding scandal spread internationally. Nagano, which bid successfully for the 1998 Winter Games, and Amsterdam, which made an unsuccessful bid for the 1992 Summer Games, became implicated in the corruption scandal.[4] The draft report on the Salt Lake City bribery allegations prepared by Canadian member and one of the IOC's vice-presidents, Dick Pound, confirmed that corruption was not confined to the one bidding round, stating that, 'inappropriate activities of certain members of the IOC did not commence with the candidacy of Salt Lake City'.[5] The IOC indicated that up to 13 members faced possible expulsion because of their implication in the bribery scandal but later revised the figure to 16 members.[6] By January 1999, Finland's Ms Pirjo Haeggman had resigned when her links to the Salt Lake City scandal and to Toronto's unsuccessful bid for the 1996 Summer Games were revealed. In what appeared to be minor misdemeanours amid rumours of million dollar vote-buying claims, Ms Haeggman submitted her resignation as her former husband had worked briefly for the Salt Lake City and Toronto bid committees, and the couple had had their rent paid for 18 months while living in Canada.[7] The escalating scandal claimed further victims, when Bashir Mohamed Attarbulsi of Libya, David Sibandze of Swaziland and Charles Mukora of Kenya resigned soon after. Samaranch called an emergency meeting of the IOC full membership for mid-March 1999 to consider whether any members should be expelled and ways of cleaning up the bidding process.

For some time, but particularly since the bidding round which resulted in Atlanta hosting the Games in 1996, both supporters and critics of the Olympic Games have aired concerns that the modern bid system is flawed: it is too cumbersome and expensive and open to corrupt practices. Sydney's successful bid in 1993 cost A$25.2 million, and current estimates by the NSW Auditor-General have placed the cost to government for staging the Games at $2.3 billion.[8] Clearly these costs place hosting the Games out of the realm of possibility for developing countries, and the enormity of the event in terms of infrastructure, facilities and security rules out many others. With calls for major reform to the bidding process coming from those inside and outside of the IOC, the corruption scandal exposed in late 1998 provides a unique opportunity for significant changes to the existing process.

## THE BID PROCESS

Every two years, IOC members meet to select which city from a number of vying cities will be awarded the right to host the next scheduled Winter or Summer Olympic Games. For many IOC members, this accounts for much of their membership obligations — in addition to selecting the host city for the Olympic Games, IOC members have the final say about which sports and events are included in the Olympic program.

The IOC has been viewed an exclusive club of well-connected, self-selected members, appointed for life,[9] whose members are often royalty, previous political or military leaders, and members of the aristocracy. Sports sociologist Jennifer Hargreaves describes the IOC as 'an undemocratic, self-regulating and male-dominated institution' which began its existence with all members being 'upper-class Anglo-Saxon men, many of whom had strong aristocratic connections, and for almost a century the IOC remained elite and exclusively male'.[10]

While there was some truth in these perspectives in the past, the IOC has reformed itself in the 1980s and 1990s. Women became IOC members in 1981 and numbered 12 out of the 111 IOC members in 1997 — still a comparatively small proportion. Outspoken US IOC member, Olympian Anita DeFrantz, who has risen to the status of a vice-president of the IOC, represents a new voice in the organisation who may play a crucial role in the future as the IOC attempts to remake itself as a more open and transparent organisation. It is also true that while the IOC numbers royalty among its members, the current IOC includes an increasing number of ex-Olympians.

It is evident that IOC members have a good life — enjoying first-class travel, fine food and wine, and being lavished with gifts is all part of the inducement process bidding cities use to secure a member's vote. The culture that surrounds the bid process includes gift-giving, inducements and even bribes.

Allegations of bribery and corruption in the bidding process are not a new challenge confronting the IOC. As the bidding process which led to the award of the 1996 Summer Games to Atlanta got out of control, the IOC tried to curb the potential for vote-buying by limiting gifts to IOC members to the value of US$200. To understand how the selection of a host city became synonymous with the indulgence and pampering of IOC members, it is necessary to examine two turning points in the recent history of the Olympic Games.

## THE MODERN BID SYSTEM

Montreal in 1976 represents the first point of significance. Staging these Games left the city with a C$1 billion debt, due in part to the construction costs of new facilities, increased security following the terrorist actions that occurred in Munich in 1972 and a boycott by 20 African nations in protest at the IOC's inaction against New Zealand who continued to engage in sporting contest with South Africa. At best only a small number of competing countries can afford to stage an Olympic Games, but the debt incurred by Montreal left the IOC with only Los Angeles and Teheran expressing an interest in staging the 1984 Games. Ultimately, Teheran withdrew from the bidding process, leaving the IOC with no choice but to award the Games to Los Angeles.

With no competition in the bidding process, Los Angeles had considerable bargaining power with the IOC. The IOC agreed to the organisers' plans that the Games be staged not by the city but by a private company, the Los Angeles Olympic Organising Committee (LAOOC). Further, as the citizens of California had passed a resolution forbidding the use of government funds to support the Games, the IOC agreed to financially guarantee the Games in a three-way partnership with the United States Olympic Committee and the LAOOC.

Under the guidance of Peter Ueberoth, the chief executive officer of the LAOOC, the Los Angeles Olympic Games set the direction for all future Games. Ueberroth recognised the marketing value of the five Olympic rings and masterminded exclusivity in sponsorship. Rather than numerous opportunities for sponsorship, LAOOC offered very few, but very expensive sponsorships. This in turn drove up the cost of television rights to the Games, which sold for US$310 million. Figures vary on the exact profit generated by the LA Games, but estimates have put it between US$150 million and US$215 million. The realisation that the Olympic Games had the potential to generate profits obliterated the memory of Montreal and has led to a bidding frenzy where competing cities spend millions in both private and public funds trying to outdo one another. Not surprisingly, bidding to host the Olympic Games has become a much more elaborate and sophisticated process.

The bid system before Montreal was far less elaborate and expensive. When Melbourne won the bid in 1949 to stage the 1956 Games, it was on the basis of an attractive bid book and a set of promises. In 1949, Melbourne hadn't even settled on the site of the Main Stadium. It was not until three or four years later and after much controversy that the bid organisers settled on the Melbourne Cricket Ground.

National Olympic Committees (NOCs), which control Olympic teams in individual nation states, are responsible for indicating an expression of interest to the IOC that a city within their nation wishes to host the Olympic Games. NOCs are able to put forward only one city from their country, and often the role of the NOC is first to determine the selection of the city. Before Sydney entered the Olympic race for the 2000 Games, it had to win the Australian bid race, with Brisbane and Melbourne the other contenders. Previously in 1988, when the Australian Olympic Committee (AOC) decided to make a bid for the 1996 Games, these three cities had lobbied hard to win the AOC's support. In making a bid for the 2000 Games, the AOC wanted to avoid the intense internal lobbying that had emerged in the previous round, and its executive board was able to arrive at a consensus to put forward Sydney.

Having made an expression of interest, at a later date the bidding cities submit a candidacy file to the IOC. This is then evaluated by the IOC's Commission of Inquiry, using a number of criteria including technical merit, environmental considerations, transport, media facilities, security, health and cultural support. In March 1993, Sydney received a five-day visit by the IOC's Commission of Inquiry, which reported on the city's technical capability to host the Games. Bidding cities strongly encourage visits by all other IOC members on the basis that these members can also assess the technical merits of the bid.

After IOC members have had the opportunity to visit bidding cities, a meeting of the IOC is held to select the successful city. The bid announcement has become a major event in its own right. When Sydney was announced as the successful city at the IOC's meeting in Monaco in 1993, the ceremony was watched there by an audience that included many dignitaries, including a number of prime ministers. The ceremony included elaborate protocol, the Olympic anthem, and a promotional film by one of the leading Olympic film-makers, Bud Greenspan, all of which added to the suspense and excitement.

Allegations of bribery and corruption add an extra dimension to the formal bidding process. Marc Hodler's comments might be most recent, but in 1992 Andrew Jennings and Vyv Simson made even more sweeping criticisms in their book *Lords of the Rings*.[11] Jennings and Simson claimed that a handful of IOC members corruptly solicited bribes and accepted lavish gifts from bidding cities in return for their votes. This publication was widely condemned by the IOC, and Jennings, an award-winning journalist and visiting academic at the University of Brighton, claims he risks gaol if he returns to Switzerland, as the IOC has taken out a criminal libel action against him for being critical of the Olympics and the IOC. While assertions made by Jennings have been steadfastly denied by the IOC, they continue to taint the legitimacy of the bidding process, and indeed the image of IOC members. As Helen Lenskyj, from the University of

Toronto, points out:

> Even if only 10% of the exposes currently circulating in books such as *Lords of the Rings* by Vyv Simson and Andrew Jennings, and Jennings' New *Lords of the Rings* are valid then people should be able to recognise that it is clear that money and power, rather than merit, dictate who wins and who loses.[12]

Even if the selection process is not rife with corruption, it is clear that bidding cities must not only demonstrate the technical merit of their bid, but are also required to 'laud, indulge, coddle and pamper IOC members'.[13] So how did Sydney do it?

## SYDNEY'S BID SUCCESS

Sydney's success can be explained through meticulous planning and learning from and building on experience. Sydney's bid was the third consecutive bid by an Australian city. (Brisbane and Melbourne bid for the 1992 and 1996 Olympic Games respectively.) Sydney inherited a wealth of knowledge and experience in over ten years of the AOC planning Olympic bids. In addition, the Sydney bid committee modelled its strategy on Atlanta's experience, as, in winning the right to host the centenary Games in 1996, Atlanta had defeated the sentimental favourite, Athens. They added some attractive features of their own: the environmental dimension that became known as the Green Games, and the inclusion of an Olympic Village, capable of accommodating all the athletes, at the main Olympic site, Olympic Park.

As well as preparing a technically superior bid, the Atlanta organisers lobbied IOC members at every available opportunity. Similarly, the Sydney Olympics 2000 Bid Limited set about an exhaustive two-year program of lobbying support for its bid. The strategy involved realistically assessing the merits of staging the Games in Sydney, accentuating the positive elements during 1991 and 1992, and tackling the perceived weaknesses later in 1992 after the Barcelona Games had been staged.

The strengths of Sydney's bid were considered to be the compactness of Sydney's Olympic geography, the support from the state and federal governments for the bid, and the advanced state of Sydney Olympic facilities preparation. The bid committee estimated that 80 per cent of sports facilities would be completed by the time the IOC decision was taken. Other positive aspects to Sydney's bid included the stability of Australia's security and political systems, Sydney's attractive climate and Australia's Olympic record. Historian Harry Gordon, in researching a book on Australia's involvement in the Olympic Games, uncovered evidence confirming that Australia and Greece were the only two countries to have competed in every Summer Olympic Games.[14] Up until this time, Great Britain had staked a claim in this club. As this evidence came to light during Sydney's bid campaign, the organisers took great delight in its announcement, particularly as Manchester was one of the bid competitors. The bid committee was also hopeful that, as this was Australia's third bid, there might be a chance of 'third time lucky'.

Sydney's geographic location, in terms of its isolation and the distance and cost involved in travelling to Australia, were considered to be the major weaknesses of the bid. A hang-over from 1956, when Melbourne hosted the Olympic Games and Australia's strict quarantine laws forced the equestrian events to be held in Stockholm, was perceived as the only other threat to what was thought to be a technically superior bid. These weaknesses were strategically addressed, first through the announcement that Sydney would cover the travel expenses of athletes and officials. The cost of equipment was later included in this offer. The country's quarantine laws were relaxed so that the equestrian events could be held in Sydney.

No expenses were spared in the lobbying to gain support for Sydney's bid. The bid committee was well aware that the corporate sector and government would not again provide the level of support needed to finance a bid. Current and former politicians and corporate leaders, as well as sports stars, were sent around the globe to secure votes from the influential IOC members. Gough and Margaret Whitlam, for instance, lobbied the African members, as the former prime minister was well regarded in Africa for his stance against apartheid.

Booth and Tatz consider that the Sydney organisers engineered some of the support for the city's bid, particularly the NSW Department of Education-backed project involving school children lobbying IOC members.[15] However, while Booth and Tatz and Lenskyj have argued that the Sydney organisers attempted to 'manufacture consent', others such as Farrell have argued that Australia has had a long 'love affair' with the Olympics and that the Olympics are taken more seriously and followed more avidly here than in most other countries.[16] Unlike cities such as Toronto, where there is an active anti-Games coalition entitled 'Bread not Circuses', there was virtually no organised opposition within Australia to the Sydney Games before the bribery scandal of early 1999.

Garnering support for the bid was not limited to IOC members; the Sydney committee ensured that it had a noticeable presence at any influential sports events, especially at meetings of the all-powerful international federations, the governing bodies of sports.

There is no doubt that part of the strategy to 'win' the Olympics for Sydney involved indulging members of the IOC when they visited Australia. Some IOC members were treated to holidays on resorts in far north Queensland. Through an arrangement with Sydney's traffic controllers, normally only used in emergency situations, the president of the IOC, Juan Antonio Samaranch, was whisked from Sydney Airport to the Homebush Olympic site without ever coming across a red traffic signal!

Chief executive officer of the Sydney Olympics 2000 Bid Limited, Rod McGeoch expressed no apologies about engaging in blatant lobbying, explaining it as just that which is required to secure the result. It was only the concern of members of the bid committee that Australia's trade relations with China might be jeopardised that led them to veto McGeoch's brash idea to leak a report on Beijing's human rights record and so eliminate Sydney's major bid competitor.

The allegations revealed in December 1998 point to the urgent need for greater clarification about what is acceptable bid behaviour. Is it appropriate for a wealthier sporting country to provide athletic scholarships for a developing country that has far less sporting infrastructure? Amid all the controversy, those involved in Sydney's bid have repeatedly claimed the bid was 'clean'. However, during January 1999, some of Sydney's bid practices attracted debate and criticism. The 'clean' practices involved justifying paid holidays for IOC members to the Great Barrier Reef as part of the 'promotion of the country', assistance in securing jobs for the relatives of IOC members and providing last-minute cash 'inducements' to shore up wavering votes.[17]

Although Sydney and Beijing were reported as the two main contenders, it was clear that Sydney had a technically superior bid. Sydney's official submission of its bid document was made on 1 February 1993. It contained 550 pages, 1500 photographs and over 80 technical drawings. The IOC's Commission of Inquiry evaluated the bids over five days in March 1993. In its report issued in July of that year, Sydney was rated very favourably and Sydney's main rival, Beijing, was listed fourth.

It was widely acknowledged that Sydney would be a better location for staging the Games. However, rumours circulating raised the stakes for Beijing, as it was suggested that bringing the Games to China would advance the IOC's chances of winning a Nobel Peace Prize. Other rumours centred on the commercial desirability of exposing Olympic sponsors to the huge Chinese market.[18]

At 4.27 am on Friday, 24 September 1993, thousands of Sydneysiders gathered at Circular Quay and Homebush to celebrate the announcement that Sydney (pronounced 'Syd-en-ey' by President Samaranch) would host the 2000 Olympic Games. It has been suggested that the selection of Sydney as the 2000 Games host has restored some credibility to the bidding process and that the 'winner' was sport over political or commercial interests. While sport might be the winner in this instance, the closeness of the final outcome does little to instil confidence in the bidding process.

Table 3.1 indicates the bid voting in 1993. The table reveals how Sydney was rewarded for its lobbying efforts, especially for third- and fourth-round preferences, which it ultimately relied on to defeat the clear front runner, Beijing.

Table 3.1
IOC voting for the year 2000 Olympic Games[19]

| Round | Votes | Istanbul | Berlin | Manchester | Beijing | Sydney |
|---|---|---|---|---|---|---|
| 1 | 89a | 7(0)b | 9 | 11 | 32 | 30 |
| 2 | 89 | | 9(7) | 13 | 37 | 30 |
| 3 | 88c | | | 11(8) | 40 | 37 |
| 4 | 88 | | | | 43 | 45 |

Notes:

a   There are currently 91 members of the IOC. The president votes only in the event of a tie, and Bulgarian Ivan Slavkov was under house arrest, charged with misappropriating sports funding during the Zhivkov regime.

b   Numbers in brackets redirected to Sydney in the following round.

c   David Sibandze (Swaziland) left midway during the vote to return in time for his country's general election two days later.

## REFORMING THE BID SYSTEM

Continued allegations of bribery and corruption place the whole Olympic selection process under question. Supporters of a more transparent process, and one in which the IOC members would become more accountable, call for IOC members to 'publicly rank cities according to strict, unambiguous criteria'.[20] It is hard to see how this would curtail the lobbying, but at least it would reveal IOC members' voting patterns and suggest what elements of a bid proposal influence their assessment. Other suggestions to improve the process include allocating the host to a specific region and only inviting bids from that region, or establishing a permanent host city. The latter could perhaps be maintained by applying a pro-rata levy on competing countries that took account of the size, and hence resource consumption, of a country's Olympic team.

As part of a radical revamp of the Olympics, Jay Coakley of the University of Colorado proposes the use of multiple sites for each Olympic Games. He says that:

This would make it possible for additional countries, especially those without massive economic resources, to submit bids to be hosts. Poorer nations that hosted only a portion of the events could benefit economically from hosting the Olympics. Multiple sites would enable media spectators to see a wider range of cultural settings, while still seeing all the events traditionally included in the games.[21]

Juan Antonio Samaranch has even mooted that the selection of host cities become the responsibility of the executive of the IOC, rather than the full body of members. But Samaranch is well aware that such a move would take away much of the reason for IOC members' existence. The suggestion seems, however, to be gaining support as the IOC's image has been tarnished with allegations of corruption. Australian IOC member Kevan Gosper is advocating a more 'transparent' and 'streamlined system for selecting host cities' and the introduction of 'due diligence and compliance business processes to guard against corruption'.[22] A former Australian Minister for Sport, Andrew Thomson, has even called for the 2004 Olympic Games to be the last, as the bid system in particular, and the Olympic Games in general, had become too unwieldy and lost sight of its original purpose, though such a view was unsupported by his federal colleagues.

## CONCLUSIONS

Winning an Olympic bid is regarded as the ultimate sports prize, and many cities vie with each other to use the Games to showcase their city. As the Games have become bigger and have attracted greater sponsorship and media coverage, so the bid system has become more elaborate and complicated.

Even the staunchest defenders of the Games believe that there needs to be some reform of the bid system. There is no easy or obvious solution to a range of problems, but there will be much attention focused on the IOC's response in March 1999 to the corruption scandal currently surrounding the bidding system. It became abundantly clear by the end of January 1999 that the cumbersome, cosy bid system that had spawned a culture of inducement would never be the same again.

*Postscript:* By March 1999, the IOC reacted to the growing public outcry about bribery associated with the bid system. The IOC expelled six members and strongly reprimanded another nine, including Australia's Phil Coles. Over 40 IOC members had been implicated in various bidding scandals. President Samaranch announced the establishment of an IOC 2000 reform commission which, among other things, would review the future of the bidding process.

## FURTHER READING

Booth, Douglas and Tatz, Colin (1994), 'Swimming with the big boys'?: The politics of Sydney's 2000 Olympic bid', *Sporting Traditions*, vol. 11, no. 1, November, pp 3–23.

Gordon, Harry (1994), *Australia and the Olympic Games*, University of Queensland Press, St Lucia.

Lenskyj, Helen J. (1996), 'When winners are losers: Toronto and Sydney bids for the Summer Olympics', *Journal of Sport and Social Issues*, vol. 24, November, pp 392–418.

McGeoch, Rod with Korporaal, Glenda (1994), *The Bid: How Australia won the 2000 Games*, William Heinemann, Melbourne.

Simson, Vyv and Jennings, Andrew (1992), *The Lords of the Rings: Power, Money and Drugs in the Modern Olympics*, Simon & Schuster, Sydney.

# DESIGN
*Ron Newman*

While excellence in sport is the primary rationale for the modern Olympics, the scale and complexity of the festival also require the services of many professionals to design the communications and the products used, and to create a suitable and appropriate environment for the event. Design covers a wide range of issues, from logos, symbols and letterheads, to the layout of Olympic Park and its venues. It also covers the context of the Sydney Olympics, from the wetlands of Homebush Bay to the look of the city itself.

What is the input of designers? I will focus in this chapter on the management framework of Olympic design, using graphic elements as the main example. Such comments will have wider application across the entire design spectrum.

Some key questions can be posed at the outset. What is design? How is it done? Designing an Olympics is not a simple task, because, unlike even a major corporation that hires a designer, provides a brief, and evaluates and realises the design, a movement like the Olympics is multifaceted. It does not have a single face that can deal with a design profession.

Design can also be a commercial — even a political — tool that can be used by the International Olympic Movement, the Australian Olympic Movement, the Olympic organising committee and the state government. The Berlin Games of 1936 were a good example of how the Games were politically exploited from a design perspective. In one sense the Nazi Olympics were the first Olympics of the modern era — the first fully designed Olympics — because the athletic imagery in carefully designed posters and publicity suggested a link between Nazi Germany and ancient Greece.

Money is a powerful factor in the organisation of the modern Olympics and affects the character of the design. Because design is linked with sponsorship and marketing, many believe that the design process is caught up in the 'rough and tumble' of the contemporary Olympic Movement. There is almost as much competition and controversy in the design Olympics as the athletic events of the Games.

## WHAT IS DESIGN?

It is useful to start with the following questions. What is design, and what is good design? Who are the designers? It is important to develop our own understanding and evaluation of design and design processes.

Q: What is your definition of 'design'?

A: A plan for arranging elements in such a way as to best accomplish a particular purpose.

Q: Is design an expression of art (or an art form)?

A: Design is the expression of the purpose. It may (if it is good enough) later be judged as art ...

The well-known furniture designer Charles Eames spoke these words when he was interviewed on the issues facing designers. Neuhart reported in his book *Eames Design*[1] that Eames also said:

Design depends largely on constraints ... The sum of all constraints. Here is one of the few effective keys to the design problem — the ability of the designer to recognise as many of the constraints as possible; the willingness and enthusiasm for working within these constraints: the constraints of price, of size, of strength, of balance, of surface, of time, and so forth. Each problem has its own particular list.

The above definition is at odds with what Eames's practice indicates and brings us back to a notion of normal design, the designer as a planner. Two other definitions are of interest. 'Design is anything that doesn't happen by accident' — a definition coined in 1990 by Peter Miller, the then president of the Australian Academy of Design — and 'Design is the concept which links human ingenuity to selected activities in order to meet challenges and find solutions. Designing may begin with an original thought or develop from existing design' — a definition taken from the current NSW schools Design and Technology syllabus (in my view, a political statement).

These two definitions do not indicate anything about the creative process, about innovation of ideas, about the designer stretching the parameters in the brief development process; they simply talk about the act of designing, not the professional practice of design. This process requires a 'good design' result and we need to learn how to manage the design process to ensure this result.

'Don't give us that good design crap! You never hear us talk about that. The real questions are: does it solve a problem? Is it serviceable? How is it going to look in ten years?' Once again our friend Charles Eames, who is, I believe, undervalued in his descriptions, and his creative and visionary input into the design process.

Eames fails to discuss directly the feelings of the end user, or the cultural or emotional relationship the end user will have with the product. However, he does raise issues about sensory effect and sustainability. These processes enable the end user to develop a relationship with a product and a design — to develop an emotional response.

Further questions are worth posing. Can we measure good design? How do we manage to attain good design? In my view, good process equals good design: the two cannot be separated.

## TWO DESIGN PROJECTS

In our quest to identify good design, let us consider the tale of two projects: first, Jorn Utzon's Sydney Opera House; and secondly, Charles Eames's bent plywood chair. Both have been judged by posterity as examples of good design. In fact, I consider them works of art!

If they are good, what makes them good? We know that if it were not for Utzon, the Sydney Opera House would be a box — a nice sandstone box — but a box just the same. When we talk about what makes that building exceptionally good, we necessarily use words like 'vision', 'belief', 'passion' and 'philosophy'. Utzon's constraints were not only satisfying the program of an Opera House, but also a response to context, a belief in natural systems as a structural device, mathematical order, the perception of harmony that lies within emotional relationships, the idea of a sculptural form-in-the-round with the harbour as its viewing platform.

Without searching for references or even the designers' pronouncements, I believe the same is true of the Eames's chair. There is no doubt that within the Herman Miller furniture company of the 1950s and 1960s under the control of Hugh de Pree,[2] the design process was a focus, resulting in an extraordinary group of furniture products. We therefore come to the role of design management.

Both of these examples are about the individual as primary creator. But not all of us are an Eames or an Utzon. Design practice cannot wait for the individual, nor can good design. We must invent and use systems of managing the design process to get what we want from it! How can Utzon's vision and Eames's complexity of constraints be injected into the design process by design management? What are the tools for realising such objectives? Peter Gorb, when defining design management, wrote:

> Design management as an idea has been around for over a quarter of a century. The Royal Society of the Arts made its first design management awards in 1966. Since then the two words have been used to convey a multiplicity of meanings ... Design management is not the process of managing a design consultancy or practice, either within or outside a corporation. It is not the education of designers about the importance of the management world or the education of managers about the importance of design. All these are important activities: indeed they are relevant, preliminary and necessary to the effective practice of design management. But they are something else. They are only aspects of the whole.[3]

Gorb went on to define what he believed was the central essence of design management:

> Design management is the effective deployment by project managers of design resources available to an organisation in the pursuance of its corporate objectives. It is therefore directly concerned with the organisational place of design and with the identification of the specific design disciplines which are relevant to the resolution of key management issues and with the training of managers to use design effectively.[4]

The key words in my mind are 'effective deployment by project managers of design resources available to an organisation in the pursuance of its corporate objectives', not just designing projects and managing that design, but understanding the objectives of the organisation and understanding how design can be utilised across all activities to achieve those objectives.

Within the Australian context, much has been said about design and its place within the community. But does it have a secure and an understood place? Do we recognise what design can achieve for us? Stephano Marzarno, the design director of Philips Electronics, reflected on the significance of the design process:

> In today's complex world, it is no longer possible to tackle a design problem from a single skill: a multi disciplinary team approach is required. The answer to 'High Complexity' is what I call 'High Design'. By High Design I mean an integrated process incorporating all the skills on which design has historically based itself, plus all the new design-related skills we need to be able to respond to the complexity and challenges of the present and anticipate those of the future. The High Design process is one which continuously adopts more advanced cultural and technical criteria ... High Complexity Design is no longer a case of clever individuals creating products in splendid isolation, but of multi disciplinary organisations or networks creating 'relevant qualities' and 'cultural spheres'.[5]

We can then add the thoughts of lawyer, Dr Alberto Alessi, who has a lot to say about design management. In a letter written by Alessi to Philippe Starck in 1990, Alessi wrote that:

> For years I have been sick of the attitude of the international producers of utilitarian cars: I find them increasingly tired, boring, without spirit or emotion. I wish to show them how it would be possible to escape from the vicious circle of pure manufacturing technique (and from copying from each other) and leave more room for creativity. I wish to conceive and realise a car which is entirely new, poetic, full of emotion![6]

Alessi wrote elsewhere that:

> I also had some convictions, some philosophical thoughts, on the role of objects in our actual society, the consumer society. We live in a society where all relevant material needs are fulfilled by the production of objects, but the big mass production industry didn't seem to have understood this — I believe — that in most cases, mass production industry goes on working simply to satisfy people's needs, instead of paying more attention to their wishes, to their desires.[7]

These, in my view, are the issues that separate normal design, the planning process, from good design, or high design as Marzano called it.

So, in design management, we need to consider the issues of managing the process rather than the practice. Don't hire a designer and allow them to control the process independently. Hire a designer and immerse yourself, as the client, in the process; force the process to consider all the issues, and place among them the issues of creativity, emotional response and poetry, as Alessi would call it. Truly consider the broad objectives of the organisation. To attain good design, we will also need to observe the following precepts:

1 Establish a corporate vision for both the entity and for design within the entity.

2 Empower those working within the system to influence it.

3 Delineate the role of the players, and avoid non-designers designing.

Within the above framework, we then will need to ensure the following arrangements are made:

1 Make a realistic time allowance for design to take place.

2 Provide adequate funding.

3 Bring to bear appropriate and quality design capability. Understand the limitations of the entity and the designers.

4 Provide a framework for the realisation of the design.

## DESIGNING THE OLYMPICS

Good process equals good design. Now that we understand what design is, or are on our way to determining our view, we can move back to the Olympics and examine the design processes and the resultant projects. The task of designing for an event such as the Olympics is large and multifaceted: it involves graphic design, visual communications, urban design, architecture, product design and interior design. Design covers a range of issues, from designing the torches and the uniforms, to the venues and graphics.

I will not discuss in detail all of the processes that have taken place; rather, I will provide a considered commentary. The design process for the Sydney Olympics is neither concerted nor well organised. No real authority existed early in the process, and even at the time of writing the real control is constantly moving. Two design committees exist to overview the process in two broad spheres, one for communications and another for the built environment. However, neither committee has any real approval authority because both merely advise the various authorities, from the Sydney Organising Committee for the Olympic Games (SOCOG) to the Olympic Co-ordination Authority (OCA) and many others.

So how does the design of the Olympics fit within the notion of good design that we have developed, and what role does indecision, often caused by fear of the media or of making the bold decision, affect the quality? The design process for the Sydney Olympics began with the design of the bid logo. Rod McGeoch, the chief executive of the bid company, recalled in his book *The Bid*:

> The first step in the creation of our image was the selection of our logo. By the time I arrived at the Olympic Bid Office, a competition for the logo was underway. About eight firms had been invited to send in an entry. Some companies sent in three or four entries and others not on the list sent one anyway. We ended up with about 50 to 60.[8]

McGeoch fails to mention that the eight experienced major graphic designers in this area were paid for their efforts, while the others provided professional design services at no cost. One of the eight chosen designers refused to take part in the process, noting that he was prepared to design the logo if asked but that a competition was not necessarily the best way to gain a successful design solution.

You may recall that the 1988 Bicentennial logo was also the result of a competition. Because the winning entry could not be reproduced in print, it had to be redesigned. The Bicentennial logo began as a compromise that was not improved in its redesign. In fact, it never worked.

McGeoch went on to say:

> As the new chief executive I was added to the judging panel which includ-
> ed Leo Schofield, Greg Daniel, Andrew Andersons and David Churches.
> Famous people like Ken Done, Ken Cato and Michael Bryce had all sub-
> mitted entries ... I looked at them all [and] I was bewildered. There seemed
> to be 20 winning entries. I sat in the judging panel thinking: 'I hope they don't
> ask me'. There was a lot of deep consideration and milling around. All of a
> sudden Leo Schofield said 'it isn't here, it simply isn't here!' There were dis-
> cussions about how there was no Aboriginality in the designs and that
> nothing just jumped off the page. So the firms were asked to resubmit
> designs by the end of the week.[9]

After resubmission the design produced by Michael Bryce assisted by Aboriginal artist Ron Hurley was chosen. 'The logo was further developed by our own in-house design people, ISIS/FHA
Design Company, which we used,' added McGeoch.

Emery Vincent of Emery Vincent Design stated to a gathering of
Australian designers: 'In our experience, developing design work
based on inadequate information (which usually goes hand in hand
with a free pitch), is seldom productive or rewarding for the client or
the designer.' Vincent went on to state that: 'Clients who are inca-
pable of preparing an adequate design brief often use competitive
design submissions to assist them in defining the particular project
requirements and to help them gain an understanding of the design
process and in order to determine costs.'

At the time of the competition, Bryce was arguably the most
experienced designer in the country in terms of sports communication design. In 1982 there was no thought of holding a competition
to select the best design and designer. Bryce was commissioned to
design the graphics for the 1982 Commonwealth Games in Brisbane.
This was a better process of securing the best design result for the
Brisbane Games. No judging panel — no non-experts on a committee deciding on design solutions.

Can we expect design excellence if the design process is decided
by a committee? Do we stage a competition when we seek medical
expertise? The question is a rhetorical one, but one that should be
considered. Competitions are often used for political reasons: it
leaves the choice open, and the notion of the winning entry relieves
those involved of an administrative and decision-making role.

## THE SYDNEY OLYMPIC LOGO

We have all seen the current Olympic logo which was designed by a
single design firm but with a myriad of design criteria not related to
excellence or vision, and with Michael Bryce managing the process.
The process has been fraught with controversy — some people have

even contemplated legal action. We all have our own view of the logo's suitability. A core issue relates to the rights to some of the core imagery, such as the boomerang.

We have all seen the development of the Olympic mascots, and read the press releases about their creators. The design review committee chaired by Bryce saw them for the first time when they were released to the media. Olympic graphics are now everywhere, even appearing on Visa cards. But what do they communicate? How do they extend the Olympic message?

There are a number of ways in which designers are commissioned to take part in a public project. These include the organisation of a design workshop to develop a design solution. Other options are to invite responses to an open design competition, to solicit responses to a professional design competition, to develop a public tender purely on a most competitive fee basis and, finally, to hire what is considered to be the 'best designer' for the project at a competitive fee. The first option is preferable every time.

Designers have been involved in all the above processes, producing more and more graphics for the Olympics and the Paralympics, including mundane matters such as stationery, business cards and letterheads. In mid-1997, many designers believed the graphics of the Games were in trouble. The management of the design process seemed out of control, producing many and varied cards and graphic designs. Public criticism often plays a part, and the pictograms, considered so important for non-English-speaking visitors, have now been much criticised. They were the result of a doubtful design process. I believe the design review committee had no effective review role prior to adoption and release.

In April 1998 the entire graphics department, which had been built in SOCOG, was disbanded and the work was once more placed in the hands of consultants. The overall management of the communications design was brought under tighter control under the leadership of Michael Bryce.

## THE DESIGN OF THE HOMEBUSH BAY SITE

The design process used for the Homebush Bay Olympic site is little better than what has been achieved in communication graphics. The site, which is 760 hectares in Sydney's mid-west, requires significant remediation. Parts of it are wetlands and are extremely sensitive from an environmental perspective. Once again there was a bid design, the bid masterplan undertaken by Cox, Hassal, Rice, Daubney and others. The Masterplan Mark 2 was undertaken by Coneybeare, Nield, Andersons, Choong and others. Criticisms of both these designs can be read in the press and in professional magazines such as *Architecture Australia*.

Government intervention has been rife. The decision to under-ground the power cables and to build a railway station and loop was taken relatively late in the planning process, allowing a limited role for those interested in best practice design. Contracts for the design and construction of the Main Stadium and the Olympic Village left any design role in the hands of developers.

A building process led by the developers and involving a pletho-ra of authorities does not usually lead to innovative structures. There is also inadequate community consultation and involvement in such a design process. The more likely result is that many buildings rely on separate economic viability for their design brief. This has also been the case with many of the graphic products and merchandise pieces.

In a project like the Olympic Games, the will, desires and needs of the community should be paramount. That is more important than assuring profitability for one or another developer. The design process, like most other professional practices, is extraordinarily sen-sitive to the environment under which it is forced to exist.

And then we believe that we have lost control and direction, and arrive at the belief that no Australian can achieve the design task — so we hire an American; we bring in foreign expertise.

With all the Australian design expertise, which is clearly world class, being applied to the site, we read in a *Sydney Morning Herald* article written by Anne Susskind:

> Landscape architect George Hargreaves was puzzled when he first saw the Olympic site three months ago. It was full. All its structures had swollen by over 20% since the original masterplan, and there was no space, no room to breathe. It needed a void but where to put it? Now the Harvard Professor, who is one of the world's leading landscape architects, has recon-figured the site, cutting a huge hole in its middle.[10]

The remainder of the article lavished praise on Professor Hargreaves' vision, but the last short paragraph was telling, indicat-ing that even this eminent designer could not truly affect the com-mercial reality of the Olympics. It added that 'the one thing Professor Hargreaves was not able to achieve was the removal of a 14 storey hotel from the plaza'.

## CONCLUSIONS

So we arrive back at the earlier statement, that the design of the Olympics Games is often controversial and even political and may lead to much gnashing of teeth and controversy. Design is a para-mount issue and is just as controversial as any other aspect of staging the Games. There is a need to do it well and to produce an end result that will not be an embarrassment. Because design is intensely political, there is a need to get the politics as well as the design process right. Community involvement is desirable. If the community cannot identify with the design, it will fail.

Consider how Hitler used the Games in 1936. It was a design spectacular in terms of the graphics, the built environment and the communications.

These are the second Australian Games and they are important, so I will put my cynicism aside and call on my colleagues in the design profession to be vigilant about the design process and the design outcomes. Observe the design quality of the Sydney Olympics: its communications and its built environment and where they overlap. Are they of the highest standard that can be produced? If not, why not? If the design processes are flawed, the end result will be flawed. Design is a sensitive discipline that can serve a project well if managed well.

## FURTHER READING

De Pree, Hugh (1986), *Business as Usual*, Herman Miller Inc., Zeeland, MI.

Gabra-Liddell, M. (1994), *Alessi: The Design Factory*, Academy Editions, London.

Gorb, P. (1990), *Design Management Papers*, Architecture design technology Press, London, p 745.

Marzano, Stefanno (1993), 'Flying over Las Vegas', unpublished conference paper, September.

McGeoch, Rod and Korporaal, Glenda (1994), *The Bid: How Australia Won the 2000 Games*, William Heinemann, Melbourne.

Neuhart, John, Neuhart, Marilyn and Eames, Ray (1989), *Eames Design*, Thames & Hudson, London.

# PART 3

## STAGING THE GAMES

# 5

# AUSTRALIAN IDENTITY
## *Frank Farrell*

Australia has had a long love affair with the Olympics. The Olympics are probably taken more seriously, and watched more avidly, in Australia than in any other country. The love affair dates from 1896, when Australia's sole representative, Edwin Flack, won two track-and-field events and was one of the stars of the Games. Australia, along with Greece, is one of only two countries that have attended every Olympic Games. Although some of the early Australian teams were small, they were among the most dedicated participants at the Olympics.

No country of the size of Australia can match its record as well in securing the Summer Games in the second half of the 20th century, when Australia hosted the Games twice in a period of just 44 years. To do so, Australia had to convince sporting administrators from the Northern Hemisphere that the Games should be in Australia despite the extra cost of travel, and its different time and seasonal context.

The Australian reverence for the Games is one reason why Australia has been the host city for two Summer Olympics. Australia has been regarded as a safe haven for the Olympics because the Games are taken seriously, no effort is spared to make them a success, and there is an absence of any organised opposition to the Games. Both Games have enjoyed a remarkable bipartisan support.

Why do Australians have this special relationship with the Games? Why are Australians so passionate about the Olympics? Let us begin with an exploration and analysis of Australian identity, via the images of identity in Australian society and its media.[1] Such a discussion is no more than a sketch or a map, more like that in an explorer's journal than a well-worn guide or tour. Naturally, sport assumes a prominent place in any such analysis of modern identity, and it turns out that Olympism is particularly relevant to some of the more recent trends in Australian 'character'.[2]

## THE 'FOUNDING' THEORY OF LOUIS HARTZ

Four approaches will be outlined as a way of exploring Australian identity. First, it can be seen as a product of the 'founding' of Australia. Louis Hartz developed, and following writers popularised, a theory that goldrush and predominantly Chartist (working-class radical) immigrants, thrown off by the developing industrial system of an emerging modern Europe, and especially Britain, were the 'founding' influences on society. Just as 18th century America drew unto itself the liberal ideas of Europe in an emerging national consciousness, Australia also was a product of its 'founding' times: a 'radical fragment' of 19th century Europe.

As a fragment of Britain, Australians indirectly inherited the British passion for sport. At the time when Australia was colonised, Britain was undergoing the beginnings of a sporting transformation. Britain was at the forefront of a 19th century sporting 'revolution'.

Originally expounded in the context of American political science, the Hartz thesis is a complex set of ideas defining the modern 'national' ideals of the 'new' or colonial settler societies into the eras or stages of growth in the evolution of Europe. The Australian identity it produced can be characterised in famous figures such as Henry Parkes (often referred to as the 'Father of the Australian Federation') or Peter Lalor (leader of the diggers at the Eureka Stockade), both of whom, in their highly individual ways, gradually shifted over time from radical protesters or reformers into symbols of the colonial establishment. As this idea began to percolate into a distinctly national consciousness with the development of an Australian Commonwealth, this vague Chartist program moved over into federal politics, or was developed in interesting ways by the labour agitator, William Lane, or deepened into culture by Henry Lawson, Australia's great short story writer and a poet of those social and cultural tendencies resulting from that important attempt to break away from the old order and try one's luck on the gold fields. Unable to finance an overseas tour to the 1900 Paris Olympic Games, the sprinter David Strickland rejected the amateur tradition and won the Stawell Gift, a prize that had evolved out of goldrush Victoria. His daughter, Shirley, is one of the great Australian Olympians.[3]

How does all this translate into an Australian identification with sporting traditions? The willingness to try one's luck obviously overlaps with the sort of society that emerges from the gold fields experience. When gold was discovered in eastern Australia in 1851, the first 'open' sprint race was held in Melbourne and resulted in the acknowledged sprint star of colonial Australia being left behind by an Aboriginal runner, Manuello. Constitutional change accompanied the gold fields experience, and responsible government led on to the absorbing democratic drift described in the Hartz theory as a product of the Chartist program of reform absorbed by goldrush immigrants in their earlier political socialisation in England. In 1856, when the first Victorian parliament under responsible government was convened, the first inter-colonial cricket match between New South Wales and Victoria also took place. Both developments eventually helped in breaking down the barriers between the colonies and influencing the growth of Australian nationalism, though they were initially a focus for inter-colonial rivalry. By 1890 the first inter-colonial cricket match for women was staged in Sydney and, although it attracted limited publicity, it was very much in tune with appropriate voting and electoral changes soon under way to elevate women in the emerging Commonwealth.

The 'founding' notion of Australian identity offers a clear explanation for the sporting traditions and the reverence for the Olympic Games. Both sport, and the defining social phenomena of the goldrushes, are based on chance and require discernment and skill in the management and use of change and opportunity. They also share their greatest appeal in 'open' competition for the 'prize' or win, and the difficult battles to establish or maintain such a principle are a common source of pride in achievement. They both are also in the tradition of the 'great outdoors', which has seen the development of games and competitions that have come to be associated with the modern Olympics.

The gold fields experience similarly shaped the Australian political scene, which is recognised by its expert commentators as analogous to an 'open air theatre', a 'big picture' or simply a game. Its participants are seen as 'actors', and even some of its recent rhetoric is rather like a dead-pan rerun of mature gatherings of discontented diggers. So also the sporting life of Australia has simply intertwined with the gold fields experience, in much the same way that outdoor barbecues, tents, camping, and public and backyard pools highlight a fundamental tradition which provided freedoms and opportunities based ultimately on a sluicebox, a shovel, and a secluded, shady stream.[4]

## A 'CONTINUOUS' DEVELOPMENT APPROACH

One problem for the supporters of the 'founding' theory is the survival of cultural tendencies from the pre-goldrush era. Cricket, for instance, had earlier cultural origins. Cricket is recorded as first being played in Sydney by ship's officers in 1803. Others have pointed to the obvious convict legacy and the environmental effects of the peculiar frontier, emphasised by Russell Ward, author of *The Australian Legend*.

If the gold fields tendency has its bards and writers and theorists, the earlier traditions were maintained intact by some or adapted slightly. In sport, this fed directly into some of the enthusiasm in the 19th century for a 'Pan-Britannic Festival' to revive Olympic ideals before the modern Olympic Games, and, in the 20th century, for the British Empire Games and the idea of continuous development.[5]

Even the idea of 'open' competition in running was in fact established before the actual gold discoveries in Australia. Geoffrey Blainey has pointed out that the most famous runner in early Australia was 'The Flying Pieman', who in 1848 raced the Brisbane-to-Ipswich coach and beat it soundly, though he carried a long and extended pole on his journey. It is true that the Californian gold-rushes were soon under way, but Blainey suggests that this era in Australia dramatically increased the interest in spectator sports, in which 'The Flying Pieman' had earlier specialised, sometimes handi-capping himself by wearing a top hat and even running while holding a live goat as his theatrical and self-imposed handicap.[6]

Consequently, the origins of sporting competition in Australia are neither clear-cut nor 'pure'. If cricket began as a game for ship's officers to play, it later grew on the gathering complexity of local culture. Canvas and crewmen's pursuits were anyway soon more popular. Two-up began in 1804, with prize-fights established a decade after, the familiar sports scene of the modern era discernible already by 1824 when the local 'Young' Kable knocked out a visiting Englishman in a ten minute encounter. Boxing was formally illegal until the usage of gloves encouraged its popularity with all classes, and it emerged as a mass-entertainment and media phenomenon in the 20th century.[7]

The Sydney and Launceston turf clubs also appeared as early as the 1820s, and, like football and rowing, combined with a betting culture to produce a society still readily recognisable today. On a trip to Parramatta in 1836, Charles Darwin counted 17 of the 198 hotels or licensed premises in Sydney and he recognised that government was already quite dependent for its revenue on the colonists' consumption of spirits. The long-term trend in such a society, he thought, would produce a mix of people not unlike the Americans.[8]

## THE FRONTIER THEORY

Russell Ward's differentiation of the Australian and American frontiers is also relevant to a discussion of national identity. Both countries have similar but different frontiers and social identities, still influenced by the formative past. In Australia, cricket evolved over time and in 1868 a team of Australian Aborigines toured England. If Australian cricket later succumbed to a greater influence of rising colonial respectability, it has clearly maintained its appeal, while in America it lost out to baseball.

The Australian frontier, with its abundant space and its opportunity for innovation, provided the stimulus for the development of 'national character', in which sport played a prominent role. Some of the sports of the frontier, such as roughriding and woodchopping, were masculine and individual, and represented a local response to frontier life.[9]

Both Australia and America have a significant exposure to climates similar to those of the Mediterranean regions, where the cultivation of physical excellence helped to inspire the ancient Games. When gold had induced significant European populations to settle in these 'new' regions, the sports that attracted a minority of enthusiasts in the 'old' countries of the Northern Hemisphere now developed a mass following and participation. At the turn of the century, the extent of settler-country influence was still becoming clear. Professional sprint carnivals, such as the one that attracted David Strickland away from an Olympic career, continued to maintain some of the world's fastest athletes outside the amateur traditions still prevalent in Europe. A series of boxing bouts throughout eastern Australia also culminated in the perfection of the modern formula for media sports promotion, based on film rights for the 1908 world title fight in Sydney between the Canadian Tommy Burns and the American Jack Johnson. It has recently been hailed as the fight that 'changed the world' and projected the epic struggle beside the bullrushes at Rushcutters Bay on to film screens overseas.[10]

Australia's greatest contribution to world sport has been the staging of the Olympics in Melbourne in 1956. It was a remarkable juxtaposition of the ancient and modern influences of the classical tradition. The fable of a mature, yet still prospering 'Marvellous Melbourne' had been unravelled as if straight out of the goldrush era, like a welcoming mat unrolled for the advancing Olympians; the ill-timed death of Frank Beaurepaire, who had symbolised the creativity in the national culture that was still maintained into the 20th century, presenting a darker side of affairs over the months before the actual welcoming of the visitors. Emerging out of this respectably well-worn carpet, Australian female athletes rescued a reputation of radical innovation in the development of the modern Olympics. The 1956 Games remain vivid in sporting memory for the numerous youthful swimming champions, some of whom would help to revive the 'golden girl' imagery developed earlier by Fanny Durack and Mina Wylie and the more photogenic Claire Dennis and even, in due course, a brother and sister duo in the traditions established by Frank and Lily Beaurepaire, much earlier in the century.[11]

Similarly in the field of athletics, Australia assumed some prominence. The postwar dominance of European track stars like Fanny Blankers-Koen had already been eclipsed by Marjorie Jackson, popularly known as 'the Lithgow Flash', after a small town west of Sydney, not far from the first find of gold at Bathurst in 1851.[12] Shirley Strickland starred in the hurdles in the 1952 and 1956 Games, and Betty Cuthbert repeated Jackson's sprint success in 1956.

Thus the men and women of Australia had displayed a national identity in Olympic competition that is easily recognisable today. It is certainly possible to see Australian identity in the modern Olympic Movement as the unwinding of the rights of 'man' and 'woman' discussed or proclaimed as ideals at the end of the Enlightenment. Australian sporting traditions have provided a mechanism for the realisation of these ideals within the emerging 'theatre of the masses'. What is not so well understood is the continuity that marks out this symbolism of the Enlightenment as itself set more deeply into the wider history of humanity. Thus, for example, in the world title fight of 1908 the great skill of Jack Johnson, the giant African-American from Galveston, and the dexterity of his nimble 'white' opponent, little Tommy Burns, also stirred memories of an enduring mystery, concerning two of life's battlers in the convict era in that very same arena. This intriguing allegory in the history of geographical expansion remains a mystery because of the intervention of a third party able to deliver a deadly blow, which left behind no discernible cause of death! So, like quite a lot of 'Western' cultural history, that tiny natural stadium at Rushcutters Bay resembled a natural theatre of life and provided a much larger perspective on the greater human zoo. Close by the Rushcutters Bay 'theatre' lies Point Piper, named after John Piper, who in 1818 stroked a winning ship's gig in a first race across the harbour from Bradley's Head to Sydney Cove.[13]

## THE OUTFLOW THESIS

A dynamic relationship of past and present that I have advanced is a fourth approach to identity called the outflow thesis. While the Hartz theory suggests an indirect and even unconscious fragmentation from the mother country, the outflow theory argues that there was a more conscious and even deliberate cultural 'outflow'. Despite their straightforward ideals and attachment to freedom, Australians are well aware also of the continuities that bind them into the outflow from Europe. Their identity is based upon the notion of the 'practical man' (or woman) whose traits were defined over several centuries of Empire and expansion. Consequently, many discordant or contradictory aspects of modern cultural and political life are resolved by theatre and illusion, rather than in the straightforward way that the founding legends might imply. So there is a continuity between Australia's sporting tradition and its outdoor theatre with what I have described as the symbolic or 'psychiatrical theatre', a way in which apparent contradictions are played out and resolved. The very notion of theatre still connotes Shakespeare in our culture, and a passing acquaintance with his plays brings to mind allusions to Italian or Continental ideas, or ancient Mediterranean tensions or philosophies, as well as entertainment based on the popular themes of Elizabethan times. The great Elizabethan blossoming which succeeded Renaissance culture ended symbolically in a live performance on stage at the Globe Theatre in London when a cannon fired at a bale of hay set alight the whole complex and burnt Shakespeare's famous 'Wooden O' to the ground. Thus the transformation of ideas through the outflow society into Australia's modern-day sporting theatre of the masses would be readily recognisable to an intelligent observer of Elizabethan times. There is a symbolic continuity in sport and society.[14]

The European-derived concept of an Elizabethan theatre extending beyond the stage-show and into real life is thus fundamental to the eventual emergence of sport as a 'theatre of the masses' in Australia. If Shakespeare was playing on stage when the Globe burnt down, it was the more anonymous figures in the audience who would build on to the earlier achievements of the two Iberian powers who 'trod the boards' in earlier Renaissance times in a closely similar culture of world theatre. The reputed author of the term 'the British Empire' had a recent biography published about him simply entitled, *Theatre of the World*. And there was little provision for leisure or culture to evolve in the continuing wars and battles that followed the first British Empire into the second (of which Australia was an important part). So there was a continuity maintained in every cusp of the outflow.

The old world behaviour pattern of the first British Empire simply outflowed into the settlement of Australia. Australia's founding was also a part of a long-term strategic structuring of the world by the European powers. Thus, a vast historical 'baggage' of ideas had accompanied the first settlement of Australia, some of which left its traces in mundane tasks and activities of the 'practical man' of legendary fixations; all of which determined the circumstances in which any 'founding' of a new society could take place at all, and so set into an orderly outflow progression the particular processes of any nationalist development. Earl Grey suggested the form of a Commonwealth as appropriate to Australian circumstances half a century before its fruition as a national project, and the name was in part adopted because the future Lord Bryce had depicted the United States as such a form of development in his book *The American Commonwealth*, which appeared slightly before the national convention debates in Australia. So the intellectual powerhouse of the practical man was not in his own domain, and the psychiatrical theatre of the old world simply determined his behaviour and activities.

The outflow society that emerged in the settler communities both in America and many regions of Empire came to be characterised by the 'practical man', who was a natural product of the era of exploration and expansion. The pragmatism of the 'practical man' became a factor in Australian sport. In 1902, William Gocher defied a long-standing law that restricted daylight bathing at surfing beaches. Gocher was a journalist, as well as a pioneer bather, and the issues of freedom tumbled out of the surf beside him as he rode the wave of defiance on to those golden sands at Manly. Surfing and swimming became a big social issue in young Australia.

Out of such defiance of the cold disciplines of European heritage the substantial significance of Australia as a swimming nation was to proceed. The surfing culture developed rapidly out of the earlier colonial and restricted 'hideaway' harbour sites like the Fig Tree Baths at Woolloomooloo Bay. Debate raged on, of course, but there was a declining audience for that once respectable assumption of colonial society that a 'flogging' was in order for 'white' people who responded to climate in a way that resembled past Aboriginal 'shame'. It was directly out of this social turmoil around surfing and swimming that early Olympic champions like Durack and Wylie were propelled into public prominence and sporting 'stardom'. The famous Wylie's Baths at Coogee were opened in 1907, and several competing attractions developed around that beach which, by the inter-war years, had firmly established surfing culture's place in Australian social history.[15]

Many old ideas remained in force, however, and the surveillance society's enthusiasts and 'wowsers' soon turned their attention to the personal standing, habits and morality of sporting champions who had eluded the restrictions of the past. Their personal lives and doings were minutely examined for any faults or failings. Frank Beaurepaire, the acknowledged champion of personalities in this new era of mud-wrestling in public 'character' and golden swimming achievements, did not overcome controversy until he wrestled a surfer from out of the jaws of a shark at Coogee Beach and a fund was established for this great swimmer whose career had earlier been interrupted by the controversy over amateurism in Olympic sport.

Even so, he judged it prudent to withdraw from the arena of New South Wales, and begin anew in Melbourne. After an impressively successful business career, he later played a crucial role in securing the Olympics for Melbourne but died shortly before the Games.[16]

Like the modern Olympic Movement itself, Australian identity is an evolving set of ideas. In each case, the great outdoors and a concentration on peaceful physical activity is central to the process of evolution. In each case, the ideals being promoted are modern notions of a straightforward or practical kind, and largely pragmatic in application. The special historical connections between Australia and modern Greece have undoubtedly helped these tendencies to evolve. The very beginnings of democratic advance in colonial Australia are often dated to 1824 when William Charles Wentworth and Robert Wardell started *The Australian* and the official censorship of the *Sydney Gazette* was brought to an end. In the same year, Lord Byron (1788–1824) died in the cause of Greek independence, and these two countries have had a long history of what might seem to be merely 'coincidental' attachments, recognisable in the classic tradition as more interesting than one might suppose. There was, of course, an expanding matrix of Grecian revivalism accompanying developments in the social history of the second British Empire that was common to white dominions in the 19th century. Along the Parramatta River, in Sydney, suburbs such as Rhodes appeared nearby stately homes like Yaralla in Concord; registering long-time cultural connections with the British Empire. Rhodes was positioned between Bray's Bay and the recently beautified Olympic site at Homebush Bay.

The formal participation of Australia in the Olympic Movement began in 1896. The athlete Edwin Flack's observations indicated something of the bemusement of modern enthusiasts of the Olympic Games with the museum-like attempts to revive the past in older countries. The famous Panathenean stadium was the centre of events; one had to be cancelled because the turns were now too sharp to be negotiated by modern athletes. The rapid widening of perspective on sports and social issues, such as coloured or female participation in the Games, was thus accompanied from the beginning by numerous minor or technical adjustments, or changes in rules, which produced a cumulative effect. As much as Australians took pride in the thoroughly modern setting of the Melbourne Games of 1956, developments after that were even more rapid in moving away from ancient templates and precedents. Although television had just begun in Australia in time for the Melbourne Games coverage (though negotiations for worldwide television coverage fell through), the media coverage later transformed the Games. The changes in Australian identity have been a step along the way to this overall achievement of a spectacle, which in Marshall McLuhan's terms, is likely to become a media occasion in 'tactile time'.[17]

## CONCLUSIONS

The passionate attachment to sport noticeable in many Australians is clearly an important aspect of their emerging national identity. Like the Olympic Movement itself, the Australian identity is a shifting spectrum of influences, ideas and innovations. Sporting traditions connect with a variety of perspectives on national identity and help to shape the course of social history and the relevance of different approaches to understanding what has transpired.

There may also be specific sporting reasons for Australia's love of the Olympics. For Australians to succeed at the Games, they have had in the past to overcome many obstacles: competing out of season and on the other side of the world; a lack of international competition; and the heavy cost of international travel. Such obstacles have been less of a factor since the 1980s when the government has underwritten much elite training and specialist sport. Australians admire the achievements of athletes who succeed against the odds.

Australia's long history of success in swimming is another reason why the Games are so popular. With its outdoor climate and abundance of waterways, swimming has always been a popular sport in Australia. The Games are the peak event for world swimming. Some of Australia's greatest and most admired sports champions are swimmers, such as Dawn Fraser, Murray Rose, Shane Gould, Kieren Perkins and Susie O'Neill. Such accomplished modern champions represent the successful adaptation of Australians to the great potential of the 'Lucky Country': the climate and environment of which allows the sports enthusiasts to enter both the Summer and Winter Games, and to enjoy other sports or the 'great outdoors' year-round if they so choose. Swimming, in particular, represents the triumphant adaptation of the European outflow to the modern conquest of Australia's earliest 'frontier', the sea which surrounds it, after finally overcoming the inhibitions of 'wowserism', which had cluttered the 'psychiatrical theatre' of the 19th century scene.

Australia's success in the Olympics and its positive experience of a home Olympics in the 1950s is another crucial factor. Australians remember the 1950s as a golden era of Australian sport when our swimmers, track and field team, and tennis players dominated the world. The 1956 Olympics came to be regarded as the jewel in Australia's crown in this glittering decade. The 1950s have become the stuff of legends, even to the point of overlooking the fact that Australia had some sporting failures in the 1950s as well —

Australia's cricketers, for example, were humbled by Jim Laker who took 19 wickets out of 20 in a memorable Test in the same year as the Olympics. Romance and nostalgia are always important elements in sport. One factor behind the push to secure the Games again in the 1990s was undoubtedly a deep desire to experience another golden era in Australian sport. Many Australians have a yearning to experience again the halcyon sporting days of the 1950s when an Olympic 'goldrush' added to a sense of national self-esteem.

## FURTHER READING

Cashman, Richard (1994), *Paradise of Sport*, Oxford University Press, Melbourne.

Davison, Graeme (1997), 'Welcoming the world: The 1956 Olympic Games and the re-presentation of Melbourne', *Australian Historical Studies*, no. 109, October, pp 64–77.

Farrell, F. (1990), *Themes in Australian History*, University of New South Wales Press, Sydney.

Gordon, Harry (1994), *Australia and the Olympic Games*, University of Queensland Press, St Lucia.

Hartz, L. (ed.), (1964), *The Founding of New Societies*, Harvest, New York.

Howell, Reet and Howell, Max (1988), *Aussie Gold: The Story of Australia at the Olympics*, Brooks Waterloo, Melbourne.

Phillips, Dennis (1992), *Australian Women at the Olympic Games 1912–1992*, Kangaroo Press, Sydney.

Vamplew, W. and Stoddart, B. (eds) (1994), *Sport in Australia: A Social History*, Cambridge University Press, Melbourne.

Ward, Russell (1965), *The Australian Legend*, Oxford University Press, Melbourne.

# 6

# URBAN DESIGN
## James Weirick

In this chapter a number of major issues will be raised. The first challenge is to look at the Sydney Olympics in terms of the form and structure of the metropolis itself. A second objective is to explore the history of the sports facilities, in particular the process which saw Homebush Bay selected as the principal venue for the Olympics. Some of the earlier design interventions at Homebush Bay, including the first competition for the Olympic Village, will then be examined briefly. Finally, there will be discussion of the urban design issues arising from the site.

The Sydney Olympic experience is only partially to do with sport and the Olympic Movement. The main impulse behind the Games is to promote Sydney as a 'global city'. A discussion paper prepared by Dr Glen Searle for the NSW Department of Urban Affairs and Planning[1] in the mid-1990s clearly identified Sydney's ambition to attract the attention of the world in terms of investment opportunities. There is no question that the state government wants Sydney integrated with the major financial centres of the world. Although Sydney may not be able to emulate the great centres of international finance such as New York, Tokyo, London or Frankfurt, it offers significant advantages for regional headquarters and middle-management operations in finance, media, information technology and tourism.

Sydney's great ambition is to challenge Asian cities such as Singapore and Hong Kong as the financial leader in the region. Sydney has certain natural advantages. It is in the same time zone as Japan and Korea, so the stock exchange opens at the same time. It is a city with an attractive character and lifestyle. It hopes to encourage international business or TNCs to locate, if not their head offices, then at least their middle-range offices, there. This process has already started: Cathay Pacific has relocated many of its facilities from Hong Kong; and American Express has moved many of its Asia-Pacific facilities. It is likely that in the next 20 years, some head offices might be in New York, the mid-offices in Sydney, marketing will take place in Europe, while manufacturing in the region will probably take place in Southern China and other parts of Asia. This is the way in which global capital investment, and manufacturing and tertiary sector functions are being globally disaggregated through the whole revolution of information technology.

Sydney offers much that appeals to a middle-management view of the world. Its quality of life, in terms of its climate, schools, infrastructure, resident accommodation and recreational opportunities, and its status as an English-language city enhance this attraction. The image and identity of a city is a factor in the location of TNCs there.

## IMAGE OF THE CITY

Media and telecommunications play an important part in the global city, not only as a burgeoning industry sector but also as a constant generator of images. Media includes more than television and print; architecture and signage also promote the way in which a city is presented locally and internationally. The images selected for the cover of Glen Searles' report show not the harbour and the Opera House, but the heart of the CBD as viewed from the Pyrmont Bridge. Here are the high-rise commercial towers occupied by IBM and the Fairfax media group, along with international insurance companies and the Hotel Nikko — icons of the transnational experience.

Nevertheless, the image of the city and its harbour is central to the selling of Sydney. There is no question that Sydney presents itself as a cultural dream. The city includes the fabulous harbour, the Opera House, the great natural reserves that have been left to us from the 19th century (the military reserves and the Botanic Gardens), the new housing opportunities in convenient areas such as Pyrmont, and the transformation of other major former harbour-side industrial sites.

When Sydney decided to enter the bidding process for the Olympic Games, either consciously or unconsciously it was trying to put itself into the stakes of being a world city. However, some important questions need to be posed. How much will Sydney gain in return for its considerable investment in particular facilities and infrastructure? What are the costs and benefits of this ambitious exercise in global marketing?

## ENVIRONMENTAL PROBLEMS

Sydney at the new millennium has three major environmental problems. First, there is the problem of air quality. The city occupies a basin that experiences the effects of air inversion. Because it is a disaggregated, low-density city with a large car-based population, there is quite considerable daily air pollution generated by traffic movements. Each day, air sheds or cool air drainage develop; and at night, the cool air sinks and proceeds down the valley of the Hawkesbury River and out to sea. The following day, around midday, the north-easter arrives and the sea breeze blows all of the previous day's pollution back towards western Sydney, where more pollution is in the process of being generated. The air quality in western Sydney is extremely poor.

There has been some improvement in Sydney's air quality, however. Sydney does not have the heavy industry in the inner city that it used to have in the 19th and early 20th century. Cars are using less lead-based petrol. Nevertheless, the problem of air quality will only be solved in the long run by technological changes in the way people move around the city.

The second problem relates to the city's water quality. Sydney occupies peculiar terrain: there is a subtle divide in the middle of the Cumberland Plain, just west of Parramatta, between Parramatta and St Marys. All the rivers to the east flow into the Pacific Ocean — Middle Harbour Creek, Parramatta River, Lane Cove River, Cooks River, Georges River and the Hacking River. This was where the city grew from the 19th century, the urbanised settlement occurring within the catchments of many rivers. There was some ecological resilience in this system.

However, once you cross this divide — and the city has been moving in this direction since around 1965 — all the urban development in the Cumberland Plain loads into one river, the Hawkesbury–Nepean, which rises under Wollongong escarpment, near Goulburn, and in the Blue Mountains. The river then journeys in a great arc around the city, with all of these streams flowing into the Hawkesbury–Nepean, particularly in the stretch between Richmond and Windsor. In 1998, the Environmental Protection Agency (EPA) issued health warnings advising that the waters of the Hawkesbury system had developed algal blooms and were deemed dangerous to health. There is no easy solution to the problem of water quality in the region. The only real solution is to have high-quality water cycle management for any urban development in the western Sydney area. Another possible strategy is to try and restrict further development in western Sydney.

The third problem in Sydney is its lack of biodiversity. Although we have great reserves of bushland at Ku-ring-gai Chase, the Royal National Park and the Blue Mountains, almost all the indigenous vegetation has been removed from the Cumberland Plain. As a result, there are few natural resources to clean the system, to provide movement corridors for native animals and birds, and to create diversity in all living things, including insects and plants. All of this has implications for the sustainability of the open-space and natural areas and those pockets of vegetation that remain.

Will the Olympics address any of these problems? Although by my calculations we are spending around $15 billion in the city, we are not addressing any of the real problems of our metropolis. One of the more recent plans for Sydney, produced by the Greiner–Fahey governments about the time they were planning the Sydney bid in the early 1990s, is confused in terms of planning and fails to address the issue of where Sydney might expand in the future.

The Olympic 'city' is predicated on an east–west axis: it starts with the sailing off Sydney Heads and in the harbour; it has facilities in Darling Harbour; then it jumps to Homebush Bay, and then west to Penrith Lake for the rowing. The equestrian and shooting facilities occupy some regional parks which the Carr government has established in its constituency in western Sydney — perhaps the only gesture so far that has aimed at dealing with Sydney's real current problems.

## THE OLYMPICS AND URBAN PLANNING

When the Olympics open on 15 September 2000 at Homebush Bay, the main transport movement will be east–west. But the large infrastructure investment that is currently taking place in the city is in the north–south corridor. The Eastern Distributor, built in 1998 and 1999, will occupy a tunnel that passes beneath Taylor Square and exits at Anzac Parade and South Dowling Street. There is also a proposal to extend the M5 East,which currently ends at King Georges Road at Beverley Hills, down the Wollai Creek Valley to the airport. At the same time, an earlier proposal funded by the Keating government, to build the Sydney Orbitel — a road that was to go further westward, was cancelled by the Howard government. The government then changed the investment laws to make infrastructure investment a more attractive proposal and introduced taxation laws to encourage people to invest in privatised infrastructure investments. That development made the building of freeways as private corporations under a build–own operate–transfer (Boot) scheme on a 30-year lease — quite a proposition. It is in the interests of those private infrastructure companies to have as many cars as possible go through their toll plazas. At present, the Melbourne–Brisbane connection, the north–south connection along the east coast of Australia, is being channelled through the centre of Sydney. This is a short-sighted solution that adds to the problems generated by the city's car-based transportation system.

The other development is a railway to the airport, thus locking investment into Kingsford-Smith as the major airport for Sydney. This means that aircraft movement across the inner suburbs will continue to impact on the quality of life of residents there. It is clear, therefore, that Sydney's current large-scale infrastructure projects are not being built according to any Olympic agenda — of moving people across an east–west corridor; nor are they being built to an environmental agenda aimed at solving the inherent problems of Sydney in its metropolitan setting. Rather, the commercial advantages of the inner-city investment, tourist and finance capital functions of the city are the driving imperatives.

## HISTORY OF THE HOMEBUSH SITE

The selection of Homebush Bay as the Olympic site is an interesting case study of local concerns having an impact on the major decision-making structure of the city and state officialdom. The story goes back to the early 1970s when the then Liberal–National Party government hoped to generate a bid for Sydney to stage the 1988 Olympics in conjunction with the Bicentennial celebrations. The Minister for Lands, Tom Lewis, commissioned a study by a leading firm of consultants, Edwards, Madigan, Tresillan and Briggs, to nominate where the Games should be staged. The consultants opted for the Moore Park–Centennial Park area: the proposal involved building the Olympic Stadium across Robertson Road and Martin Road and encroaching on half of Centennial Park. Construction of the Main Stadium in that location would have led to the demolition of a whole neighbourhood which included the home of the then Leader of the Opposition, Pat Hills, and that of the prominent author, Patrick White. The consultants suggested that the stadium be connected to the CBD with a two-storey elevated concrete freeway, which would require the removal of all the fig trees along Anzac Parade.

This proposal caused a storm of protest in 1970 and 1971. A resident action group (RAG) was founded, and the well-connected residents of Centennial Park area mounted a very sophisticated and well-funded campaign against the proposal. RAG formed an alliance with the Builders Labourers Federation (BLF), then under the control of Jack Mundey, and put a brake on the proposal. Members of the BLF — the labourers who would be working on the building jobs

— decided that the quality of life of the city was as important as the industrial issues of their wages and conditions. They wanted to build a city that was both attractive and on a human scale, and were happy to ally themselves with middle-class activists in placing a ban on demolition or construction of specific projects around the city. A number of important sites in the city were saved as a result, including The Rocks and Woolloomooloo, which was slated to have high-rise towers. Kelly's Bush, a 'Green Ban' site in the middle-class suburb of Hunter's Hill, was one of the first battles fought to keep the harbour foreshore as a public open space.

In the meantime, the activists from Centennial Park persuaded the government to hold an inquiry into the whole idea. This occurred before the current *Environmental Planning and Assessment Act* was introduced. Under the planning legislation in place at that time, it was very difficult to intervene in these decision-making processes and so a special one-off inquiry was held in 1973, chaired by the architect Walter Bunning. The residents of south Paddington and Centennial Park commissioned their own consultants to develop a better plan than the state government's proposal. The consultants included traffic engineers, Professor Blunden from the University of New South Wales, and recreation consultants. I played a role in this consultancy. I was involved in writing a history of the area that was in danger of being demolished. These consultants, who sought a large parcel of state-owned land close to public transport at the geographic centre of the population spread of Sydney, identified Homebush Bay as an appropriate Olympic site.

From the 1890s to 1961, trams had been a highly efficient mode of public transport from the city to Randwick Racecourse, the Sydney Cricket Ground and the Showground. Once trams were removed from Sydney's streets, these regional sporting facilities became dysfunctional in the metropolitan region, because getting there involved using bus or car transport, parking in the parks, or walking from Central Railway. For much of the Sydney population, it just became too difficult. Since 1970, it has not been appropriate to put metropolitan-scale facilities in this area.

The land at Homebush Bay was originally granted to William Blaxland and some other early figures in the colonial history of Australia. It was resumed by the state government in the early part of the 20th century, principally to provide a site for the state abattoir. That in itself was an expression of the public health issues of having a properly controlled supply of fresh meat for a metropolitan population. The government moved the abattoir from a very degraded and highly polluted site at Glebe Island, on the harbour, into a very efficient abattoir that was one of the largest and most modern in the world at that time. The process involved transporting sheep principally, plus cattle and some pigs, from the rural hinterland of New South Wales to the Flemington stockyards where they were sold at auction. Then they often went on the hoof, or sometimes by train, to holding paddocks until they were slaughtered.

The other state facility located at Homebush Bay was the state brickworks, based on the shale resources of the Cumberland Plain. Other parts of the site were used progressively to create industrial sites and a series of great waste dumps, as we have since discovered, of metropolitan refuse and industrial waste. At Homebush Bay itself from the 1950s, a whole series of industrial and chemical plants were built. Some of these dumped their pollutants straight into the harbour, under lease from the former Maritime Services Board (MSB); other solid wastes were dumped on the site to create more industrial land. In fact, the MSB planned to fill in the whole area, including the wetland area, and to create a man-made wetland and bird habitat of extraordinary diversity. By that time almost every mangrove site on Sydney Harbour had been destroyed. However, by the mid-1970s there was the beginning of a real understanding of the ecology of rivers and harbours. It was recognised that the mangrove system was of great value to the health and diversity of the water systems: trapping silt from the catchment and providing all sorts of habitat environments for fish and birds in the area.

This whole area of Homebush Bay looked like a very simple site, but it turned out to be extremely complex. It has been filled and refilled over time, so that it has become a highly modified environment, but there are no accurate records of what actually took place. The Bunning Inquiry of 1973 decided that Homebush Bay should be the site for the future sporting facilities for Sydney and that no more intensive development should take place at Moore Park and Centennial Park.

When the Labor government came to power in 1974, it made the first move to establish sporting facilities recreation facilities in this area. One of their first projects was to create Bicentennial Park. This provided an early experiment in remediating this highly polluted area and conserving the wetlands. The government also built some initial sporting facilities, creating the State Sports Centre, which included a hockey field.

The government soon discovered, however, that many of the potential sites for a major sporting structure were unsuitable for development. For example, the area of land fill didn't provide an appropriate foundation on which to build. The existence of the brick pit also limited development possibilities. Instead, it was decided to build on the ridgetops.

Bicentennial Park — like Centennial Park, completed a century earlier in 1888 — was an important gesture to celebrate a milestone of European settlement in Australia. It has some attractive qualities, like a boardwalk through the mangroves, which helped to change attitudes towards these fascinating ecosystems. However, the area lacked essential services.

Between 1988 and the early 1990s, when Sydney's 2000 Olympics bid was lodged, Technology Park was built at Homebush Bay and the waterfront sold off. To enhance the bid, the Greiner–Fahey government built some preliminary facilities on the site as a gesture of good faith, notably the Aquatic Centre and the Betty Cuthbert Stand at the Athletic Centre. These facilities, designed by Philip Cox, one of Sydney's best-known architects, provided important and much-needed facilities for Sydney. The Aquatic Centre has proved a popular and democratic resort, attracting people of all ages and from all over the city. The Betty Cuthbert Stand, built on the crown of the ridge, is exposed to the prevailing wind; when the north-easter comes up each day, the flags thrash on the flagpole. Because wind issues are important at an athletic field, a variety of mounds were built in the hope that they could create a sort of air-foil condition over the top of the running track. Sydney was building something to prove that it could put on the Games and have a major facility of international standing.

At the same time, the Sydney Olympics 2000 Bid Limited (SOBL), which was a public–private consortium putting the bid together, organised a competition for the design of the Village, located on the other side of Haslam's Creek at an industrial site called Newington, next to the suburb of Silverwater. The land had been used since the 1890s as the armament depot for the Royal Australian Navy, which stored shells and missiles, dating from the 1890s to the Second World War, in various bunkers which became a green area.

## THE VILLAGE

The winners of the competition to design the Olympic Village included a team that had been supported by Greenpeace. This created world news because, until that time, Greenpeace had been known for its direct action and its environmental activism, and for building sustainable environments for the future. SOBL quickly realised the international benefits of developing a green image for the Sydney Games. The International Olympic Committee had begun to embrace environmental issues beginning at the Lillehammer Winter Games in 1994. Although the green measures at Lillehammer were relatively small-scale, they featured some appropriate use of recyclable materials in the design of its facilities. Sydney decided to promote an environmental image, and the idea of the 'Green Games' captured the imagination of the world. A consortium of young designers developed the concept of an eco-village which was incorporated into the bid books. The eco-village was to be aligned so as to maximise solar energy. Water would be recycled through the wetlands so as not to create pollution, and the Village would be linked to public transport.

Tragically, when Sydney won the competition, the government decided not to proceed with this design. The reason given was that SOBL was a public–private consortium, which ceased to exist after the bid was won. It is an interesting comment on what a city promises in its bid and what it does after it gains the Olympics. This occurs in part because host cities want to avoid what happened to Montreal in 1976, when the city experienced enormous financial problems by over-investing in infrastructure for the city, including a very elaborate and rather unworkable stadium. It took decades for Montreal to pay off its Olympic debt. Then various political events overtook the Olympics. After the 1980 Moscow Olympics boycott, few cities were interested in putting on the Games because of the cost and the political implications of staging the Games. However, there was a dramatic revival in the fortunes of the Olympic Movement at Los Angeles in 1984. Los Angeles delivered a minimalist, privatised Games, which was highly effective. It proved that private investment could deliver a world-standard event.

The Seoul Olympics were important because, once again, politics came to the fore. The world attention on the South Korean political system helped to weaken some of its more authoritarian structures and open up democratic opportunities. In 1992, Barcelona was highly successful because it showed once again that design could change the image of a city. Finally, the 1996 Atlanta Games showed that public and private enterprise could sometimes deliver, but sometimes it could also go wrong. Sydney's Olympic dream was really conceived in terms of the Atlanta-type model of a public–private alliance, and the Olympic Village was to be one of the major facilities to be funded entirely by the private sector. Although the design had been formulated with some important private sector advice, the developers were not committed to all the ideas laid out in the bid. The private sector told the Fahey government that they weren't prepared to proceed with the Village design. When the Carr government came to power, it discovered an embarrassing blowout in the cost of the Village. It appeared that the state government would have to pay up to $700 million for something they hadn't budgeted for, so it abandoned the eco-village concept..

The state government then ran a second competition — a

developers' competition — to see what could be built that would meet minimal green standards. From the time of the first competition, there have been around 150 complete designs for the Village — a totally inefficient use of the city's design talent. Instead of deciding on a master plan, then getting designers to work on the detailed design of each area, much time and effort was wasted in developing the master plan.

So what was the final resolution of this whole imbroglio? A consortium of our best and most experienced developers, Lend Lease and Mirvac, with Philip Cox and Andrew Andersons as the design team, along with a number of other young architects involved in designing individual buildings, developed a project scheme that operated on a slightly different principle from the first design. The Village now covers more land, so the development is not as dense as the original scheme. Secondly, the developers dealt with some of the negative aspects of the site, such as the fact the Village was to be located in a region that did not have high-status residential marketing. Nearby are humble worker suburbs such as Auburn and Silverwater that feature the great Australian fibro house and a backyard. Also located nearby is Silverwater Prison, and across Duck Creek are the Camellia oil refinery, a major freeway and a major liquid waste treatment facility. Power lines surround the site, although some of these will be buried before 2000. Looked at in objective terms, it is not the most ideal real estate on which to locate an upmarket development.

One of the developer's proposals was to create a world within itself, so the Village turns its back on the existing suburb. It consists of a series of neighbourhoods in a buffer zone between the prison and the town centre. The first neighbourhood was constructed in 1998, and this housing will be sold off before the Games. Those who buy a unit there have the opportunity to lease their property during the Games. Pre-Games sales will assist the developers with cash flow for further development. It is also a way of recouping the considerable investment tied up in the infrastructure costs of roads, water supply and so forth. Only parts of the development will represent permanent buildings; the majority of dwellings for the athletes will be demountable units that will be moved off-site after the Games and sold. Over time, the fully serviced vacant land will be sold on the market. This will overcome the problem of releasing all at once, after the Games, a large amount of housing that can accommodate perhaps 5000 people under normal conditions and 15 000 under Olympic conditions. This would have a major effect on Sydney's real estate market.

The Village will have local electricity generative capacity from solar energy — an attractive feature. There will be a minimal use of

PVCs and preference for environmentally appropriate materials such as recycled plantation timbers. There will be some selective recycling of waste water, treated through the wetland system before it goes into Homebush Bay. Recycled grey water will be used to water residents' gardens, wash cars and flush toilets. There will be a dual water supply of drinkable water from Warragamba Dam, along with recycled water for other uses. While there will be some innovative technological features in the Village, overall the project is not as exciting as the young, original design team imagined it could be.

## THE MAIN STADIUM PRECINCT

Designing the main Olympic precinct at Homebush Bay has been a major challenge. At the time that Sydney won the bid, there was no master plan for the site. Many quite bizarre ideas were floated, most of them dealing with the fundamental problem that Homebush Bay is located in an inner-west industrial area, a sort of New Jersey-type landscape. The reality of Homebush Bay contrasts with most people's mental image of Sydney: blue water, beaches and the Opera House. So how will this disjunction between image and reality be confronted?

One idea was to bring the harbour into the site itself by flooding the brick pit at Homebush Bay to create a Darling Harbour-type environment. A number of schemes were under serious investigation in 1993 before the full impact of the pollutants on this sort of proposal was realised. Large amounts of heavy metals, dioxins and PVCs had been simply dumped into a very shallow bay, where they mixed with the sediments at the bottom of the bay. Ferries venturing into Homebush Bay would churn up these sediments, which would be unacceptable under international health standards. For this and other reasons, Homebush Bay could not be used to ferry large numbers of people.

It was realised that there had to be a careful mapping of where the pollutants were so that a risk management assessment could be devised. Research indicated that the development had to be pushed back from the waterfront and over to the area marked for the aquatic and athletic centres. The master plan was not produced until September 1995. This master plan concept is based on a grid plan surrounded by green space, including some remnant original areas that are fortunately intact. One idea was to create the same sort of ambience at Homebush Bay that exists in south Paddington: having a little urban core adjacent to the sporting facilities.

As a result, the original plan had grid streets and buildings built to demarcate streets. The major stadia stand as sculptural elements in a sports park located along a tree-lined boulevard— similar in some respects to Anzac Parade — where buses ply up and down delivering spectators to the sports facilities. This was preferred over a modern design that would include freeways, car parks and bus interchanges, in the style of Bondi Junction.

Important elements of Olympic Park are the existing Aquatic Centre, the Betty Cuthbert Stand and the Athletic Centre (the much earlier hockey centre, which had been built in the 1970s and early 1980s — it was one of the first sports facilities on the site), the Main Stadium and a multi-use arena. The railway station, serviced by a loop, is the principal transport mover. Nearby is the Showground with its show ring, exhibition halls and animal pavilions. All of these sports facilities had been completed by 1999. They are surrounded by the parklands of Millennium Park, which includes the former brick pit and Bicentennial Park.

## PROBLEMS

The development of Olympic Park represents a very ambitious plan that has some inherent problems. Because of the fast tracking of the whole process, the design of the master plan proceeded at the same time as the private consortiums were invited to design the stadium. The master plan designers thought the stadium would be a certain size, but it turned out to be much bigger. As a result, there was no longer space for one of their side streets and the grid planning had to be redefined.

The master plan then had to be rethought and reconceptualised from its September 1995 configuration. Another consideration was to avoid the problems experienced in Atlanta, where crowd and transportation management became controversial international issues. The Minister for the Olympics and others involved in the site planning realised the need to rethink the design of the public space of the master plan and to create much more space around the Main Stadium itself. American landscape architect George Hargreaves was commissioned to undertake the task of reviewing the master plan and suggesting ways in which there could be greater integration of the site. Hargreaves persuaded local Olympic authorities to move the hotel site to another area and build it as a tower, to retain more permanent open space, and to use the wide, tree-lined boulevard as an integrating link.

## CONCLUSIONS

Olympic Park is an impressive and very substantial achievement. Most of the sports facilities, including the Main Stadium, have been completed a year before the Games. Despite some lost opportunities and continuing problem areas, Olympic Park will contribute markedly to Sydney's urban design. A former wasteland has been transformed into a state-of-the-art sporting precinct in a place where it is most needed.

It is less clear whether Olympic-driven changes in Sydney's urban design will provide any long-term benefit or whether they represent just another chapter in ad hoc planning that has been the history of Sydney's urban design. The Games may also not lead to any marked improvement in Sydney's ongoing environmental problems: air and water quality and a lack of biodiversity. Only time will tell whether Sydney's investment in the Olympics will advance its claims as a 'global city' and will enable it to challenge rival Asian cities for financial pre-eminence in the region.

## FURTHER READING

Buzacott, S. (1996), 'Planning Homebush: A potted history', *Architectural Bulletin*, 16 March.

Jackson, Daryl (1992), 'Olympic Village competition', *Architectural Bulletin*, August, pp 5–12.

Towndrow, Jennifer (1993), 'The sites that got the Games', *Australian Business Monthly*, November, pp 120–3.

Ward, Peter (1996), 'Have we blown it already?', *Australian Magazine*, 21–22 September, pp 10–18.

Weirick, James (1996), 'A non event? Sydney Olympics', *Architectural Australia*, vol. 85, no. 2, March/April, pp. 80–3.

# ENVIRONMENT
*Deo Prasad*

The 'Green Games' is a tag that is closely associated with the Sydney Olympics. A 'green' response was part of the promise made by the Sydney Olympics 2000 Bid Limited. Organisations involved in the delivery of the Games and the other interested community groups are working towards a good 'hue' of green in the final outcome. The general discussions and investigations emanating from attempting to deliver the 'Green Games' have helped bring the issues under the microscope. It has also helped the environmental industry and the professions to gain a better, but by no means complete, understanding of many wide-ranging considerations.

Many questions can be posed about the 'Green Games'. What is it to be green? What are the imperatives, costs and benefits of the 'Green Games'? How green is green enough? How can greenness be measured at Homebush Bay or in other environmental projects in Australia?

There clearly has been an increasing global concern about the changing quality of our environment. Despite the wide-ranging debates between the different views on the subject, it is now accepted that there is a minimal moral responsibility to leave the environment in no worse a state for our future generations than we inherited ourselves. In case of varying levels of uncertainty about how bad the global warming and climate change problem might be, we should, if at all, be erring on the side of least negative impact. Hence, the promise to deliver the 'Green Games' was very timely, opportunistic and globally significant as a model.

In keeping with broader community perceptions, the International Olympic Committee (IOC) has now also accepted the environment as a third dimension of Olympism. President Samaranch at the 1996 Centenary Conference in Paris noted that 'environmental responsibilities must become a key tenet of the Olympic Movement'. This is due largely to the efforts of the Sydney Olympic organisers who have put 'green' on the Olympics agenda. This chapter discusses the promises and responses of the 'Green Olympics' and tries to highlight some of the changes in building industry practices as a result of the Games.

## HOMEBUSH BAY: THE SUBURB

Projects at Homebush Bay are the largest developments of mixed-purpose buildings in Australia or New Zealand. As a result, it was recognised by many as having the potential to bring about significant cultural and other changes within the construction industry in Australia. The buildings and other developments will be part of the urban infrastructure of Sydney, but practices and changes to the building industry culture will be part of a lasting legacy as well.

The developments will have a long-term impact. A whole new green suburb is being created, and many people will live and work there after the Games. The Games in this context is a couple of months of 'peak load' from a number of points of view — people, energy, water, waste, noise, pollution and so forth. Therefore, in delivering the short-term outcomes (that is, the venue for the Games), we should not be inconsiderate of the long-term issues. The suburb is potentially a blueprint for sustainable urban development and its urban scale impact, both visually and environmentally, is very important, as are the sociocultural aspects.

The overall site area at Homebush Bay is approximately 760 hectares and includes the Newington area that contains wetlands. One of the first tasks on achieving bid success was to undertake detailed scientific studies identifying the site's environmental values and development constraints. Figure 7.1 summarises the site values and their level of significance.

As part of the site was known to be cleared for use and other parts were contaminated through past use, there was an identified need for major remediation of those parts of the site. Human health and ecological risk assessments were undertaken in 1992 and this led to site-wide remediation works. Most of the remediation work has now been largely completed. The chemical remediation has been undertaken with as much care as possible, given the budget and available scientific knowledge at the time. On the balance of probability, we hope that there are no avenues for contaminants to escape; for, if this happened, there would be considerable risk to the new inhabitants. Details of the works have been discussed in the State of the

Figure 7.1
Site values at Homebush Bay

| VALUE | INTERNATIONAL | NATIONAL | STATE | REGIONAL | LOCAL |
|---|---|---|---|---|---|
| SITE AS A WHOLE | ● | | | | |
| FLORA | | | | | |
| Saline wetlands | ● | ● | ● | ● | ● |
| Freshwater wetlands | ● | ● | ● | ● | ● |
| Forests | | ● | ● | ● | ● |
| Shrub/grassland | | | | | ● |
| FAUNA | | | | | |
| Mammals | | | | ● | ● |
| Waterbirds | ● | ● | ● | ● | ● |
| Woodland birds | | | ● | ● | ● |
| Amphibians and reptiles | | | ● | ● | ● |
| Fish | | | | ● | ● |
| Visual environment | | | | ● | ● |
| Heritage | | ● | ● | ● | ● |
| Open space | | | | ● | ● |

Source: *Homebush Bay Development Guidelines,* vol. 1, p 3.

Environment Report produced by the Olympic Co-ordination Authority (OCA) in 1996.

The water-ways and wetlands in the area have been considerably damaged or depleted over the years. However, there still remain pockets of original wetland ecosystems. The overall site contains about 250 hectares of remnant natural ecosystems with a variety of vegetation types and animal species. There is a positive effort being put into rehabilitation of these areas. Whereas there remains room for greater attention, the current effort shows a level of commitment by the OCA to improve the natural habitat.

Considerable attention has also been put into maintaining air, noise and light quality at the site and for surrounding residents. It is expected that there would be temporary compromises during construction time, but in the longer term the developments should, if anything, improve the benchmark conditions.

In addition, research has been conducted into the Aboriginal and non-Aboriginal heritage values of the site. The Sydney Regional Environmental Plan (SREP 24) had identified three heritage conservation areas — the State Abattoir, the Royal Australian Navy Armaments Depot and the wharf area. Plans have been developed for conservation of both the Aboriginal and non-Aboriginal heritage values.

## LOCATION AND CLIMATE

Sydney has a mild, temperate climate. Average air temperatures at Homebush Bay are slightly more extreme than those of central Sydney, and the effect of north and north-east cooling sea breezes is less evident. During the Sydney Royal Easter Show, which is held annually for a few weeks in autumn, the mean maximum temperature is 23.3°C with a mean minimum of 15°C. Winds are mostly westerlies, but at this time the prevailing wind speed is at its lowest. During the period of the Olympics 2000 (September–October), rainfall conditions are at their lowest and mean temperatures range between 11.2°C and 20.1°C. However, August and September are also among Sydney's windiest months. This relatively mild climate implied that there were considerable opportunities for 'smart' building designs that do not require year-round indoor climate control by mechanical means. This allows for much greater opportunities for energy efficiency.

## THE PROMISE

The Environmental Guidelines for the Summer Olympic Games were prepared by the Environment sub-committee of the Sydney Olympics 2000 Bid Limited. They were presented to the IOC in September 1993 and have been incorporated into the State Environmental Planning Policy (SEPP No. 38). This policy now applies to all Olympic developments.

The 'green' promises were part of the original bid, and the eventual memorandum included specific calls for consideration of issues such as energy conservation, use of renewable energy, passive solar buildings, appropriate material selection, density of developments, and appliance and equipment selections. The main areas included issues such as conservation of species (flora and fauna, and people and their environment), conservation of resources (including water, energy, waste materials, open space and top soil) and pollution control (air, noise, light, water, soil and waste).

It is not clear whether the broad range of 'green' issues were fully understood in terms of what they constituted — that is, how to achieve those goals at justifiable cost, how to measure success and what benchmarks were available. The broad-ranging issues included planning and construction of all projects. Since winning the bid, a lot has been learned about what we know and particularly what we don't know. Benchmark data for performance is one area on which little information has been available, and in the absence of such data one could argue about 'how good is good enough'. As discussed below under 'The response', considerable research was required to document guidelines for developers to facilitate implementation of all environmental concerns. It was acknowledged that successful delivery on such grounds will require a holistic approach to dealing with the environmental issues.

## THE INHERITANCE

Having won the bid, it was evident that the constraining factors, other than cost, quality and time, also included the condition of the site and the state of the industry. On the first point, a lot has been said about the remediation work in terms of its importance, success and potential future problems. Critics from the green left, such as Sharon Beder and Helen Lenskyj, have been critical of the remediation process at Homebush Bay. Beder argued that the media had failed to report on the extent of contamination at the site and dismissed the remediation process as 'cheap, dirty, quick and convenient'.[1]

On the second issue, we have not had any regulations in Australia requiring energy performance of buildings (probably the only OECD country in this group). In asking for energy-efficient and passive solar buildings, though the knowledge was available in literature and research institutions, the building industry had to be educated about its means, costs and benefits. In the last three to four years a lot has happened in this area, including a national drive for codes and performance ratings. The industry has clearly been made aware of the benefits of an environmentally benign approach. I believe that this will be one of the most lasting legacies of the Games for the industry.

Knowledge of emerging technologies with improving economies has become more common. Directories of innovative technologies have been developed and are now widely available. There has been a particular emphasis on energy technologies such as photovoltaics, solar thermal and co-generation. These are all serious considerations in the Olympic projects leading to effective demonstrations.

## THE RESPONSE

It is now evident that the 'green' issues have been given serious attention in terms of the overall planning and landscaping, individual building designs and other infrastructure developments. The 'processes' that have been put in place to ensure success provide important support for this view. The OCA set up to deliver on the projects established an environment division at an early stage and this led to the development of a consultative-based environment strategy and specific guidelines for achieving the goals. The use of expert panels for the various areas has provided a good balance of inputs and much-needed consultations on such issues. The 'green' groups have also been well represented and have contributed significantly to ensuring that the promises made in the bid documents are followed.

A number of documents have been produced to guide developers. These include:

Volume 1 Environment Strategy
Volume 2 Homebush Bay Area Structure Plan
Volume 3 Homebush Bay Masterplan
Volume 4 Transport Strategy
Volume 5 Landscape Strategy
Volume 6 Design Codes
Volume 7 Management Plans

The environmental monitoring process is illustrated in Figure 7.2.

Figure 7.2
Environmental monitoring processes

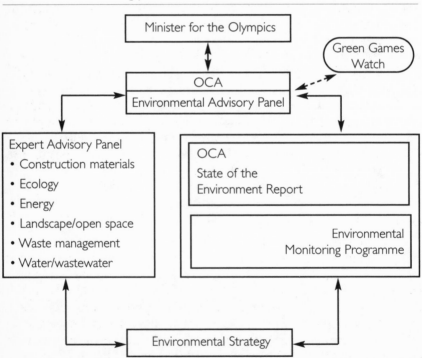

Source: *Homebush Bay Development Guidelines*, vol. 1, p 11.

This process was abandoned in 1997 when it was considered by the OCA that the expert panels had served their purpose. One important element that was the victim of this decision was 'independent monitoring' by expert groups. The Green Games Watch 2000 (GGW) was considered the sole group to provide this monitoring, and an occasional report by the Earth Council was commissioned to ensure monitoring success. (These are discussed below under 'Monitoring reviews'.)

The guideline and strategy documents have a much wider potential use now and the OCA should ensure their availability to the community (another legacy). The processes put in place to deliver on 'green' promises are in themselves a good model, because they inform the building community on approaches to achieve such goals.

The building briefs on the projects included requirements that force environmental consideration. The guidelines developed for energy-efficient buildings can be used effectively as part of building briefs on most building types. The process of negotiating on contracts that include environmental considerations (that is, balancing cost and environmental considerations) is particularly interesting and can be of educational value to the building industry. The approach by OCA to negotiate and let the tenderers exceed performance, rather then be prescriptive, has been a contributing factor in gaining a high level of commitment from them. (Prescriptions tend to be limiting in design flexibility.)

A key factor in employing 'cutting-edge' technologies has been the need to 'showcase' local technologies. It has been acknowledged from the start that the Olympics provided significant opportunities for demonstrating local skills and technologies to the world. The use of PV (photovoltaic cells) on village roofing is a good example of this. Clearly, a lot can be achieved in this regard and we are hopeful that much more is done to demonstrate such technologies at the highly visible sites.

## KEY PROJECT SUMMARIES

### OLYMPIC VILLAGE

The village has been designed not only to provide highly energy-efficient dwellings (80 per cent of houses are to be minimum five-star energy rated) but also to accommodate 665 kilowatts of photovoltaic output. This allows for 1 kilowatt per dwelling on 665 dwellings — all grid-connected systems generating approximately 1 million kWh of electricity per year. The village, including PV and energy-efficiency measures, should save about 4500 tonnes of carbon dioxide emissions per year, and the commercial support buildings another 2500 tonnes per year, compared to current practice.

## THE MAIN STADIUM

The Main Stadium has been designed to optimise daylight and natural ventilation. The lighting energy savings would approximate to around 20 per cent compared with existing energy requirements and an airconditioning load reduction of 40 per cent is expected. Five hundred-kilowatt gas fuelled co-generation engines will produce heat for water heating and power savings, with estimated total carbon dioxide reductions of approximately 500 tonnes per year. The 19 lighting pilons will each house 6.5 kilowatts of grid-connected PV.

## THE SHOWGROUND

The Sydney Showground (venue for many indoor sports) has been designed for passive mode operation with daylighting and natural ventilation being used effectively to achieve 20 per cent reductions in energy use compared to other similar projects.

## THE AQUATIC CENTRE

The Aquatic Centre has incorporated a number of passive design concepts, including an innovative air flow control requiring only 20 per cent of the volume to be cooled and an air distribution system which is more effective in cooling the occupants at occupant levels. Studies are being conducted to choose between a 750-kilowatt co-generation or heat pump system to supply on-site energy.

## THE HOMEBUSH HOTEL

The Homebush Hotel is also aiming at setting benchmarks for energy efficiency. It will purchase 100 per cent 'green' energy from off-site sources. It has a 400-square-metre solar hot water collector system supplying 60 per cent of total needs. It uses natural lighting and other passive solar design concepts. It has a 50 per cent waste reduction target and a carbon dioxide reduction of 1200 tonnes per year.

Whereas at the individual building level a lot is being achieved in terms of efficiency, there is not as much evidence of a site-wide approach in aspects such as energy supply and on-site generation. Some projects offer great potential for co-generation or roof areas for solar collection. A site-wide approach can allow for the use of the excess supply in these areas for other projects. An overall energy management system can optimise on energy use.

The OCA had an overall initial budget of approximately $2 billion, of which 25 per cent is for dealing with environmental issues. This may seem a considerable proportion. We hope that the environmental performance reports reflect this input.

## MONITORING REVIEWS

The 'Green Games' have been monitored primarily by two agencies, which have provided regular progress reports. The Green Games Watch 2000 was set up as an official and independent watchdog of 'green' progress. Maurice Strong, on behalf of the Earth Council, has also made regular progress reports. While Strong's assessment of the 'green' achievements has been for the most part positive, GGW2000 has been more critical of Sydney's performance. While the Games have scored well in some areas, such as energy, GGW2000 has been less impressed with performance such as waste treatment, remediation and communication.

Other 'green' interests have criticised individual aspects of Sydney's 'Green Games'. While Greenpeace was included within the Sydney bid — and continues to work within the Olympic Movement supporting the 'Green Games' — it made public its concerns about dioxin on the Homebush Bay site. Ian Kiernan, of Clean Up Australia, is another critical supporter of the 'Green Games'. He expressed disappointment that the waste treatment process at Homebush Bay was too limited.[2]

While some of the scorecards provided by the independent reports and the state-of-the-environment reports are positive, the final test will be the effectiveness in the long term of the remediation of the site and the educational impact of the 'Green Games'. And will the advanced solar practices of the Olympic Village encourage other local communities to adopt more 'green' practices?

## BUILDING INDUSTRY IMPACT

The building industry in Australia has historically paid little attention to issues other than construction cost, quality and time. The whole issue of performance has been given minimal importance except where it has a short-term bearing on cost. Given such a background, it is not surprising to find that there have not been any energy, greenhouse gas emissions or environmental impact-related codes within the building codes. The lack of these also implies the added problem of lack of user awareness and concern for additional compliance requirements.

In the face of the rising government push for voluntary codes and standards for energy efficiency and greenhouse gas (GHG) reductions, it required a large-scale project to demonstrate interest in following that path and, to a large extent, to show that it can be done without too much cost penalty. (That is, the market can bear it.) In building environmental performance criteria into the project briefs and allowing the designer-builder-financier consortia to find ways of delivering on 'green' grounds, the OCA has set but minimal benchmarks for performance. An increasing number of project briefs now seek environmental performance to be considered and delivered on; in some cases, environmental performance is also being used by designers as value-adding to outcomes without the briefs explicitly asking for such considerations.

More recently, studies have been commissioned by the Australian Greenhouse Office (AGO) to determine the baseline GHG emission from the building sector nationally. Arising from these, and in keeping with the Prime Ministerial Statement of 20 November 1997, a wide-ranging policy initiative will be considered to achieve targeted sectoral reductions. The Master Builders Association of Australia (MBA) has taken a proactive approach to forming the Australian Building Energy Council to coordinate initiatives in this area with the government.

With the industry and the professions now already accepting environmentally sustainable development as an important new criterion, or more appropriately 'quality', in building developments, the path is set for environmental codes and standards to be adopted as part of normal practice. The Olympics projects should take some credit for driving the market to this stage of acceptance.

## CONCLUSIONS

The Games are clearly acting as an agent for change in a number of ways. The introduction of 'green' criteria in building projects has helped bring a change in thinking which should be a legacy. The IOC itself is now adopting the environment as a key factor in decision-making about future Games. The release of information on processes, environmental strategies/guidelines, benchmarks, and environmental measurement and reporting will be of great value to the professions and the industry. The Games will have left a better-informed community about environmental issues.

## FURTHER READING

Beder, S. (1994), 'Sydney's toxic Green Olympics', *Current Affairs Bulletin*, vol. 70, no. 6, pp 12–18.

Cashman, R. and Hughes, A. (eds) (1998), *The Green Games: A Golden Opportunity*, Centre for Olympic Studies, Sydney.

Earth Council (1997), *Sydney 2000 Olympic Games, Environmental Performance of the Olympic Co-ordination Authority*, Review 1.

Kiernan, Ian (1998), 'Opportunities for education', in Cashman and Hughes, *The Green Games*, pp 71–6.

Olympic Co-ordination Authority (1995), *Homebush Bay Development Guidelines: Volume 1 Environmental Strategy* (working document).

Olympic Co-ordination Authority (1997), *State of the Environment 1996*, Sydney.

Lenskyj, Helen (1998), 'Green Games or empty promises? Environmental issues and Sydney 2000', *Global and Cultural Critique: Problematizing the Olympic Games*, Centre for Olympic Studies, University of Western Ontario, pp 173–9.

# 8

# TRANSPORT
## *John Black*

The operation of Sydney's transport system will come under close scrutiny during the Games. How well will Sydney cope with the additional road, train, ferry and air traffic in 2000? What plans have been developed to deal with the increased traffic? Can Sydney do a better job than Atlanta? There is also the question of whether transport innovations developed for the Games, including the railway station at Olympic Park, will be of long-term benefit to the city. And will the Games generate any change in the culture of transport, encouraging more people to make use of public transport, for instance?

A Sydney sports fanatic — who had attended the 1956 Olympic Games in Melbourne and then settled there — returns for the 2000 Olympic Games. Once through the upgraded Sydney (Kingsford Smith) Airport terminal building and on the New Southern Railway to the city centre, she reflects on the changes over 40 years to Sydney's transport infrastructure and its management of transport services. The evolution of the transport system (to support a doubling of population at ever-decreasing residential densities) has passed through (a) a period in which public transport was the dominant passenger mode (trains, trams and buses) and shipping dominated international travel markets; (b) a period when private transport became dominant; (c) a period at the end of the 'long postwar boom' of tightening financial and environmental constraints; and (d) a period where the jet aircraft has driven passenger ships from the high seas.

The transport institutions of today, compared with those in the immediate postwar period, are dramatically different. Institutional histories of the major players — the Department of Railways (1955) and the Department of Main Roads (1975) — have been published, but these are very different corporate organisations today (the Rail Access Corporation, State Rail, City Rail and the Roads and Traffic Authority). There are new players. The Olympic Roads and Traffic Authority (ORTA) was established in 1997. Major Australian airports have been privatised — except those providing regular passenger services and general aviation in the Sydney Basin. The ports have been corporatised and wharf services provided by the private sector. In addition, the private sector operators of transport services have emerged since the late 1980s with the encouragement of state government policies — TNT Monorail, Sydney Light Rail Company, the Sydney Harbour Tunnel Company and various tollway operators.

## PLANNING FOR THE GAMES

Given this institutional fragmentation in the provision of transport infrastructure and its associated passenger and freight services, how has the Olympic transport infrastructure been planned? How will the multifarious transport services be provided in the year 2000? The Olympic and Paralympic Games will create the highest continuous demand for passenger movements ever witnessed in Australia. Superimposed over the normal requirements of Sydney going about its daily activities and businesses (whatever way they may be modified during the Olympics) will be periods during which over 500 000 spectators and workers are expected to travel to the Homebush Olympic site on the busiest of days, plus a further 100 000 movements to the other major venue at Darling Harbour. (This does not include the minor destinations such as Bondi Beach for beach volleyball or Penrith Lakes for rowing.) That is, over 1.2 million passenger trips in addition to the daily trips made routinely by Sydneysiders. Even with some reductions in travel demand resulting from school holidays and universities in recess, for example, the rail system will need to handle 80 per cent more people, and the bus system as least 50 per cent more people, than normal.

What are the likely traffic impacts? This is a major question of social impact given the adverse media publicity given to transport at the Atlanta Games. (A 'post-mortem' on the Atlanta Games at the Transportation Research Board Annual Conference in Washington DC in January 1997 suggested that the major transport problem was the volunteer bus drivers — many of whom were not from Atlanta and were therefore unfamiliar with the road system and event locations.) Can Sydney do better? Or are traffic problems an inevitable fact of life when large crowds are concentrated in time and in space?

Somewhat paradoxically, we will find the answers primarily with land-use planning — the revitalisation of derelict industrial land and an ammunitions storage and supply site. Unlike the three previous Games held in Seoul, Barcelona and Atlanta, the major sporting venues and athletes' village in Sydney at Homebush Bay were constructed on a purpose-cleared site some 15 kilometres to the west of the CBD. This story reflects the deindustrialisation of the state, the promise of Japanese investment in a city for the next millennium (the multi-function polis, or MFP), opportunities for the practical demonstration of ecologically sustainable development (ESD) and the promise of environmentally friendly Games. The transport task is a secondary one. Transport is a derived demand. Transport infrastructure planning follows in a logical way — capacity being provided, consistent both with engineering performance measures in mind and with a political imperative that public transport should form the backbone of passenger movement. Transport services, operations and logistics during the Olympics will resemble 'a command and control' strategy — to strike a military analogy. We will not be embarrassed in the year 2000 with the negative perceptions of 'traffic chaos' that plagued aspects of the Atlanta Games.

This chapter also addresses, in addition to the planning and operations of transport, the wider implications of the aftermath of the Games on Sydney and on Australia. This will take us to the crucial nexus involving land use, transport and the environment. ESD becomes a distinctly Australian government response to global initiatives on the environment, and the 'Green Games' as an agent of social change will be assessed. Speculations will be offered on the wider significance of the planning experience and technology being developed in Sydney. But first we must describe the characteristics of the site before explaining the planning of transport infrastructure.

## THE HOMEBUSH BAY SITE

In 1948, the Maritime Services Board commenced reclamation of a large area (210 hectares) of mangrove swamp on the upper reaches of the Parramatta River at Homebush Bay in response to the general shortage of waterfront industrial land. Around the time of the Melbourne Olympics, plans were afoot to expand a plywood factory into the largest single-storey building in the Southern Hemisphere. Here was a prime location near to one of the important centres of heavy industry in Sydney. However, by the era of the Munich and Montreal Games, the manufacturing base of Sydney had collapsed.[1] The State Abattoirs and State Brickworks at Homebush both closed in 1988. The impetus for transformation of this disused and degraded site came, somewhat surprisingly, from a perceived 'pot of gold' dangled by the Japanese government as overseas financial investment to Australia.

In January 1987, Japan proposed building a centre for 'future-oriented high-technology and leisure facilities' in Australia. The Commonwealth government announced a joint feasibility of the project coined by the Japanese as the multi-function polis — described as an 'exciting opportunity for Australians to . . . take control of our national destiny in the twenty-first century'. The project's chronology, and the saga leading to the final site selection in June 1990 of Gillman, in Adelaide's mangrove swamps, is told in a lively fashion by the ABC journalist Walter Hamilton.[2] That the NSW government's bid to attract the project to Sydney in a highly enthusiastic, national inter-state competition failed is of paramount interest in our story of the Olympics. Its initial proposal was centred on a 660 hectare site at Homebush Bay, with complementary housing and industrial activities in South Creek Valley (close to the second Sydney airport site proposed at Badgerys Creek) and at Pyrmont–Ultimo. Although subsequently modified, with more focus out west, when the influential report on MFP urban development concepts was released by the National Capital Planning Authority in 1990, the multi-nodal strategy was disqualified immediately because it proposed to divide the city into three.[3] Sydney's planning efforts were not wasted: they provided the springboard to capture a more glittering international prize.

The Homebush Bay site and the contiguous land to the west of Haslams Creek provided a unique opportunity in the recent history of the Olympic Games to spatially integrate new sporting venues and the athletes' village. Planning and implementation commenced in 1989 when the NSW Property Services Group (PSG) was established to implement asset management throughout the state. A master plan was unveiled in July 1992 for the revitalisation of Homebush Bay. The Homebush Bay Development Corporation was created within the PSG to coordinate land-use planning and site development. The non-Olympic plan had the prudent flexibility that would accommodate additional facilities, such as a velodrome, a baseball centre, tennis courts and an entertainment centre, should Sydney's Olympic bid prove successful. It did. Therefore, the original plan costing $807 million (of which the transport elements described below cost $140 million) had additional facilities and an implementation schedule dramatically collapsed from 20–30 years to seven years.

## TRANSPORT PLAN

Within this master plan the transport strategy was flexible in order to address the different requirements of large sporting crowds and of residents and commuters. Extensive consultation with a myriad of government agencies further refined this strategy. Engineering consultancy services simulated the traffic implications of alternative transport modal plans using sophisticated computer models. The key features of the transport strategy for Homebush Bay are a new heavy rail loop and station; regular bus services to existing rail stations at Lidcombe and Strathfield; external road connections to the surrounding freeway and arterial road network; restricted supply of on-site parking; new ferry wharves at Bennelong Road and at the mouth of Haslams Creek (primarily for ceremonial occasions); and extensive networks of pedestrian and cycle paths.

Three aspects of this strategy demand attention. One, the environmental imperatives permeate. Two, a closely related issue: planning and design of the athletes' village are underpinned by principles of ecologically sustainable development. Three, the special event strategy developed by the NSW Department of Transport to address peak needs is being refined operationally by all transport service deliverers. The institutional response to create the ORTA is one important example explored below.

First, the environment dominates the agenda. The Environmental Guidelines for the Summer Olympic Games (September 1993) have been translated into legal obligations with State Environmental Planning Policy No. 38, which applies to all Olympic projects. Thus, the Olympic Co-ordination Authority (OCA) is guided by this policy (SEPP 38) in all developments at Homebush Bay, and must also adhere to 'at least 16 pieces of relevant environmental legislation'.[4] In addition, the environmental policy adopted by OCA in October 1996 makes a commitment to the principles of ESD.

Extracts are summarised here and reproduced from 14 categories in the Environmental Guidelines that have direct relevance to transport.

A  Planning and Construction of Olympic Facilities

. . . 8. all Olympic sites being accessible by public transport . . .

B  Energy Conservation

1  the use of ferries to provide transport operators, VIPs, athletes and media between Sydney Olympic Park and the Sydney Harbour Zone

2  establishment of satellite parking areas at major bus and rail interchanges

3  provision of cycle ways and pedestrian walk ways linked to public transport interchanges . . .

F Protecting Significant Natural and Cultural Environments

. . . 8. use of low wash ferry transport to minimise impact on mangrove ecosystems

I Ticketing

1  ticketing systems integrating event admission with public transport . . .

There is one category in the Environmental Guidelines devoted exclusively to transport, with the commitments spelt out as follows in their entirety:

L. Transport

Sydney is committed to:

1   the successful implementation of transport strategies to ensure efficient movement of the Olympic family and spectators

2   selection of specific Olympic transport systems which minimise energy use and reduce pollution

3   public transport being the only means by which spectators will be able to directly access events at major Olympic sites

4   satellite car-parking venues being established so people can transfer to trains, buses and ferries for access to Olympic sites

5   special concession transport tickets being available allowing spectators to use all forms of public transport for a defined period

6   sale of admission tickets and public transport tickets being at the same outlets.

## ENVIRONMENTAL PERFORMANCE

It appears that OCA is meeting, or is well on target to meet, the vast majority of its environmental commitments in this list. A detailed evaluation of performance relative to the guidelines as of December 1996 has been compiled by The Earth Council[5] using a qualitative rating scale of 1–10 (where 10 is total 'compliance') against each line item issue unless it is too premature for them to form an opinion. Suffice to note here that all other generic environmental issues have been rated '8'; transport is '7'; and public consultation and community relations is '6'.[6]

A different review is a little more critical of OCA's performance. Green Games Watch 2000 Inc. is obliged under its funding conditions by commonwealth and state agencies to review and report on progress for the 2000 Olympic Games. Peggy James[7] has attempted to determine whether OCA's planning and development activities comply with the Environmental Guidelines for the Summer Olympic Games. Categories are judged 'good performance', 'fair performance' and 'poor to very poor performance'. A low level of compliance in the OCA's transport plans with respect to provisions for off-site public transport interchanges and connecting cycle and pedestrian paths has been identified,[8] but there were nearly three years to rectify these deficiencies in meeting the guidelines when the criticisms were raised in the public domain. ORTA commenced a major study of bus–rail interchanges in 1999.

As a public statement, the Environmental Guidelines for the Sydney Olympic Games are not very onerous with their transport promises. To use a sporting analogy: the bar has not been set very high. Are the commitments appropriate? Yes, they are, on the supply side of transport, such as achievements in the realm of transport infrastructure provision. Whether travel demand management for the Olympics will amount to a practical demonstration of ESD principles is the key question about transport and the Olympics. By reviewing the 40 recommendations by the Commonwealth Ecologically Sustainable Development Transport Working Group[9] it becomes apparent that the thrust of the Olympic transport strategy is indeed consistent with many of the goals, objectives and values, and the preferred solutions for achieving a more sustainable urban transport sector in Australia. However, careful examination of the other recommendations by the Transport Working Group reveals that there are no explicit commitments on the travel demand side made in the Environmental Guidelines for the Summer Olympic Games. Of course, OCA and ORTA cannot make such commitments. Nor would the International Olympic Committee (IOC) require such behavioural guarantees. It is up to the travelling public to make the appropriate choices.

The second point of note is that a range of diverse social, environmental and community issues were addressed in the design of the athletes' village. Again, we will detect an ESD link. Within easy walking distance of the sporting complex (however, competition athletes travel compulsorily by coach to events), 84 hectares are being developed for residential housing on land surplus to the needs of the Navy on the southern part of the Newington Armament Depot. In 1992, the Olympic Village Design Competition attracted over 100 entries to serve both the short-term needs of some 15 300 competitors and delegation officials for the Olympics (7000 for the Paralympics) and the longer-term needs of a medium-density suburb with affordable housing for some 5000 to 6000 people. Judges selected five innovative designs that were later blended into the Olympic bid documentation. One of these, sponsored by Greenpeace, was at the forefront of applying ESD principles to transport and drew unashamedly on the National Capital Planning Authority's preferred concept for the MFP, by translating its generic design to suit the specifics of the Newington location and topography.

## THE CREATION OF ORTA

Third, great confidence can be placed on delivery of both transport infrastructure and transport services now that there is in place an organisational structure to ensure this. In April 1997, the Olympic

Roads and Transport Authority was established by the NSW government to plan, coordinate and deliver integrated road and transport services for the 2000 Olympic and Paralympic Games, related test events (for example, the 1998 and 1999 Royal Easter Show) and designated major events leading up to the year 2000 Games. As with all other agencies, its Olympic transport strategy is being honed for the year 2000. Public transport is a priority. The 10 000 parking spaces on-site will not be available for private use during the Games. Olympic lanes will be allocated on some major arterial roads such as Victoria Road, and parking restrictions will be put in place and enforced.

The three transport customer groups targeted by the Authority are the Olympic Family (athletes, officials, workers, volunteers, media and others related to the hosting of the event), spectators (ticketed and non-ticketed groups), and the Sydney 'base load', as the city must continue to function, of course, during the Olympics. Transport and the Olympics is not the big issue, because event management will be supported patriotically by compliant travel behaviour. In Atlanta, for example, vigorous public relations campaigns to encourage travel demand management resulted in about a 10 per cent reduction of normal daily traffic within the circumferential beltway. With organisations such as OCA and ORTA developing performance specifications in the delivery of transport to the Olympic family, spectators and the Sydney base load and environmental reporting, there will be greater professional and public awareness of progress towards more sustainability and greater public accountability of the results obtained, providing they are communicated effectively from now on in the lead-up to the Olympic Games.

## TRAFFIC IMPACTS

Given the additional travel during the Olympics and the negative reports from Atlanta, it is time to speculate on the traffic impacts. It can be argued that the transport issue is not the Olympic and Paralympic Games, but how travel behaviour might be changed after the Games. In reviewing the draft transport infrastructure strategy for Homebush Bay,[10] it was clear to the Transport Advisory Group that indicative peak hourly person trips at Homebush Bay could be managed only with public transport (rail, bus and coach) for the Olympics (with a possible 150 000 persons per hour flow rate). But would spectators choose public transport for special sporting events at the weekend (flow rates of about 70 000 per hour), for the Easter Show (50 000 per hour), for those medium (15 000 per hour) to minor sporting events at weekends (7000), and during the week (500 per hour)? Will traveller experiences to the busier events translate positively into leaving the car at home for getting to the smaller events — the kids' swimming carnival, and the like? Could the Green Games be the change agent that persuades society to make better choices on environmental and sustainability criteria (for example, modal energy intensity) and not on strictly economic efficiency grounds (such as travel time and vehicle operating costs)?

## TRANSPORT OPERATIONS DURING THE STADIUM OPENING

Tentative answers can be drawn from the experience of the first sporting events at the stadium and the Royal Easter Show, held for the first time at Homebush in 1998 following its move from the Showgrounds at Moore Park.[11] Public transport and the new rail loop were an outstanding success. Attendance figures at the Royal Easter Show in 1998 were at record levels. Cityrail recorded an hourly peak at Olympic Park Station of 43 645 passengers between 11 am and noon on 13 April. Overall, during the period of the Show, 85 per cent of people travelled by public transport (ORTA's target was 75 per cent), with 79 per cent using rail. Eight special Show bus routes were developed, with the one from Miranda proving the most used with 50 100 passengers on 1727 services. Private transport was constrained by policy so as to encourage the use of public transport. Only 5000 car-parking spaces were available on-site and these needed to be pre-booked at a daily rate of $25. A Special Events Parking Scheme was implemented with the cooperation of local councils to prevent surrounding streets being clogged with parked cars. Transport management was actively supported with an active public relations campaign. Transport for the 1998 Royal Easter Show was strongly endorsed by the IOC Transport Working Group, as shown by Anita DeFrantz's enthusiastic news conference on 11 April. ORTA's public opinion surveys showed 96 per cent of bus travellers and 89 per cent of train travellers to the Show rated their travel experience as 'good' or 'very good'. Road traffic impacts were barely noticeable, according to regular media reports on road conditions.

The Olympic Stadium hosted its first sporting event on the evening of Saturday, 6 March 1999, with the ARL (rugby league) double-header of Newcastle versus Manly and St George–Illawarra versus Parramatta. A close-to-capacity crowd was anticipated. Privately, some of the transport agencies were nervous beforehand, especially since rail track maintenance might compromise the reliability of services. The Premier of New South Wales asked patrons for their patience and understanding with travel on the night. The crowd was a little under 105 000. Once again, the transport was up to the task. The large crowds departing were moved quickly by the trains and buses operated by Sydney Buses and by the private bus operators. Buses were frequent and moved on once all seats were taken. Post-match entertainment encouraged the staggering of departures; a few left early before the final whistle; others lingered to soak up the atmosphere. There were a couple of minor glitches, but no cause for concern in this rehearsal for the Olympics.

## TRANSPORT LEGACY

The implications of the Olympics go beyond 2000. After the Games, there needs to be an ongoing mix of sporting, recreational and commercial events on the Olympic site for patrons that will provide the 'critical mass' of land-use activities to support frequent public transport services over extended hours on both weekdays and the weekend. Experience in event scheduling and timetabling can lead to a growth area in service industries to obtain such critical masses. This long-lasting benefit to Sydney as a major destination will also be a practical example of where land-use and transport are planned and delivered as an integrated whole. However, there is a possible constraint. Commercial activities often demand parking access for motor vehicles, and there may be an ongoing tension as to the appropriate on-site parking provision needed outside of major events.

There are other impacts of the Olympics on Sydney's transport. Experience will be gained both from events in the lead-up to the Games and the Olympic Games proper from an integrated ticketing approach towards public transport and venue entry. Transport is a derived demand that operates to provide access to land-use activities. Integrated ticketing will drive home the concept of transport as a derived demand to consumers. This was a positive feature of the 1998 Royal Easter Show.

Public transport services can be enhanced by information that is provided to travellers. There is an emerging technology of 'intelligent transport systems' and information on routes, on-board, in-trip and pre-trip information, fares, smart tickets, timetables and the time of the next departure or arrival will become essential infrastructure components, especially for those travellers not familiar with Sydney transport. We will see more of this over time and space, possibly as a direct result of the experience gained in the lead-up to and during the Olympic Games.

Transport systems, whether road or rail, are subject to accidents and breakdowns. It was clear from the Atlanta Games that an enormous amount of practical experience was gained in incident management — the detection of incidents and the prompt response by police and emergency service workers. Incident detection and management strategies will be honed before, during and after the Games such that Sydney's transport operations routinely incorporate event security requirements. The legacy for the city will be the overall management of transport incidents on an agreed inter-agency basis that will assist safety and security for all transport users, including pedestrians and cyclists.

Other impacts are of a wider relevance to the transport sector alone. Communications is likely to become one of the crucial areas to provide appropriate and accurate information that allows the travelling public to make informed transport choices. Again, the Royal Easter Show demonstrated this. The public require clear, accurate and readily accessible information on Olympic transport — at a general community level, for business, for adjoining residents and for intending patrons. Communications must target all transport users, including the elderly, disabled, and non-English speakers (local and visitors), and this strategy will remain a legacy for the city. Signposting and markings for the Olympic routes will need to be clear for private vehicles and buses, and such route guidance will extend after the Games in time and in place. Inter-agency communication is crucial to effective cooperation, because during major special events the media need access to accurate information — they serve as the eyes and ears to local, inter-state and international audiences.

The Olympic challenge is encouraging organisations into new ways of business. All of the above policies and procedures — transport operational matters, performance indicators and environmental targets — can, and should, be rolled into an evolving environmental management system (EMS). For example, the NSW Roads and Traffic Authority is well advanced in the implementation of an electronic EMS for city and country regions of New South Wales. Such systems are likely to be developed and extended further to suit the needs of government instrumentalities and public sector transport service providers on compliance-type issues. Marketing overseas of our environmental technologies and environmental management could become a major competency of Australian consultants working in the Asia-Pacific region.

Finally, there is potential to transfer knowledge and mega-project experience gained during the planning and delivering of all aspects of the Olympic Games. There is an increasing need to undertake strategic environmental impact assessment of policies, plans and projects along with life-cycle assessment of transport to provide a bigger picture than is possible through current approaches to project-oriented environmental impact assessment. Experience with the transformation of the foul Homebush Bay site to a jewel in the city with its sporting and recreational activities supported by its multi-modal transport connections demonstrates what can be achieved with an

agreed strategic direction, master plans, accountability and performance measurements. Clear roles and responsibilities are required for
transport organisations within an overall land-use/transport/envi-
ronmental planning framework. Experience from the Olympics will
give further impetus to the role of government to define the strategic directions and performance indicators, and to the private sector
as innovative service deliverers of integrated events and transport.

## CONCLUSIONS

Despite the complexity of the logistics to plan, coordinate and deliver this daunting Olympic transport task, I have every confidence in it
being managed efficiently and effectively with minimal adverse effect
on the Sydney 'base load' of travellers. Environmental commitments
made by the NSW government as part of its winning bid will guide
both transport infrastructure development and traffic management
strategies to deliver a 'Green Games'. Homebush Bay is a tangible
example of governmental policies that aim at the broad evolution of
the land-use and transport complex of Sydney's metropolitan region
in a more sustainable development direction. There appears to be no
constraints in meeting the transport components of the
Environmental Guidelines by the time of the Games. There is also
unlikely to be 'traffic chaos'.

The environmental sustainability of the transport sector is the
important issue for us to consider into the next millennium. To what
extent might transport infrastructure provision, travel demand management and traffic management for the Olympics provide transfer-
able policy and planning processes that will provide a catalyst or
agent of change for a greener metropolitan transport system and
urban development pattern, or for more sustainable transport? Will it
be business as usual? Will there be a greater political, and community, awareness, commitment and action that delivers some marginal
changes? Or will it be a defining moment (a 60-day epoch in the
Spring of the year 2000) which, on reflection, will be a major 'sea-
level change' that assists us to move towards sustainability? The 'wash
up' after the Games is unlikely to give the answers. When our ageless
sports fanatic revisits Sydney again in a couple of decades will be the
time to take stock and address such questions.

## FURTHER READING

Black, J., Burrows, P., Dobinson, K. and Woodhead, B. (1994), 'Homebush Bay
    Corporation Transport Advisory Group Report on a Review of the Draft
    Transport Infrastructure Strategy Direction for Homebush Bay', A Report to
    the Homebush Bay Corporation, August.
Commonwealth of Australia (1991), *Ecologically Sustainable Development Transport*

*Working Group*, Australian Government Publishing Service, Canberra.

Hamilton, W. (1991), *Serendipity City: Australia, Japan and the Multifunction Polis*, ABC Enterprises for the Australian Broadcasting Corporation, Crows Nest.

James, P. (1997), *Environmental Performance Review Report Olympic Co-ordination Authority: Compliance with the Environmental Guidelines for the Summer Olympics*, Green Games Watch 2000 Inc., Bondi Junction.

Property Services Group (1992), *A Transport Strategy for Homebush Bay, Sydney, Property Services Group*, Urban Redevelopment Division, Sydney, Edition 3, July.

Rich, D. C. (1982), 'Structural and spatial change in manufacturing', in R. V. Cardew, J. V. Langdale and D. C. Rich (eds), *Why Cities Change: Urban Development and Economic Change in Sydney*, George Allen & Unwin, Sydney, pp 95–113.

The Earth Council (1997), *Sydney 2000 Olympic Games: Environmental Performance of the Olympic Co-ordination Authority*, Review 1 – December 1996, 23 July.

Ware, C. (1998), 'The Communication Strategies Employed by Olympic Transport Authorities for the Sydney 2000 Olympic and Paralympic Games', unpublished BE (Civil) Thesis, School of Civil and Environmental Engineering, University of New South Wales.

# 9

# SECURITY
## Alan Thompson

The Sydney 2000 Olympics will be the biggest security operation in Australia since the Second World War. It will dwarf by several orders any previous security operation over the previous 55 years. The Olympics will not only be the biggest, it will also be the most complex security operation outside of wartime in Australia's history. It is the complexity, together with the size of the operation, that poses most of the problems for Australia's security planners. Moreover, the nature of the security plan is affected by the stricture, imposed by the International Olympic Committee (IOC), that security must not get in the way of the atmosphere and spirit of the Olympic Games. The IOC has made clear that the Olympics are an international sporting event, not an international security event, and that while Olympic security must be comprehensive it must also be unobtrusive.

## PERSONAL AND PHYSICAL SECURITY

Security of the citizens and visitors relates essentially to crime prevention. The concentration of large numbers of people in hundreds of thousands offers a high potential for crimes against the person and against their possessions. On the other hand, the drawing down of police presence in Greater Sydney and New South Wales to provide security at the Games may provide opportunities for criminal activity away from the Olympic venues.

Protection of the persons and possessions of citizens and visitors consists of protection against designed or specifically targeted acts — that is, murder, rape, mugging, bag-snatching, pocket picking, having your car broken into or stolen, burglary and so forth; protection against non-targeted abuse — for example being hustled by prostitutes, drug peddlers, importuning beggars, con-persons and so forth, or by having your enjoyment spoiled by drunk and disorderly behaviour; and protection against the effects of human error or incompetence — for example, events like a grandstand collapsing because of inadequate quality control in the concrete mix; fires, smoke hazard and toxic chemicals; traffic jams and hazards, and so forth.

None of these may be as stimulating to think about as terrorism, but they are of fundamental importance to the security of the Games. For the security planner, big-time and headline-grabbing events such as made the Munich Olympics the most remembered Olympics in modern history are 'potentials' — events that have a possibility of occurring. Planning for them is contingency planning. Some crimes against persons and property are, however, certain to occur, and planning must address their occurrence in ways somewhat different from planning for a contingency. Moreover, although politically motivated violence affects many arms of government, crimes against the person and property are intrinsically police business, and hence an increase in the frequency of occurrence correlates directly (even if not necessarily proportionately) with a call on police resources. That call, in turn, creates opportunities for some sorts of criminal activities to be displaced into areas in which police numbers have been depleted.

## COMMERCIAL SECURITY

The commercial activities that are attached to the Olympics and will cater for Australians and visitors will create a very large security task. All in all, there will be large amounts of private enterprise cash moving around. In addition, there will be larger volumes of stock to protect, both against diversion by organised crime and against individual appropriators, ranging from the one-off shoplifter to organised, professional thieves.

Commercial security is a shared area, with commercial security firms and the police having spheres of responsibility that overlap to some extent. The private sector servicing the Games will increase its use of private sector security and other security measures. But two points are important. The use of commercial security is referenced to the bottom line. A firm will make its decision in the context of profit. Many firms will look to maximise the profit margin and will deliberately take the risk; for some others, the profit margin will be too slim to allow much of an increase in commercial security. Second, for the efficacy of private enterprise security to work without either grossly increasing prices or greatly cutting into profits, commercial security has to rely on the overall secure environment provided by police forces.

## OLYMPIC-SPECIFIC SECURITY

The bidding country is required under the agreement with the IOC to provide security for the 'Olympic Family', by which is meant the competitors, officials and visiting Olympic dignitaries. Australia is also required under the Vienna Convention to provide security for visiting heads of state, ministers and so forth. The total for these two groups is likely to be cumulative. Dignitary protection is a shared Commonwealth/state responsibility. So, like the other two categories of security outlined above, dignitary protection at the Sydney Olympics will be the responsibility of the NSW Police, with 'liaison officers' provided by the Australian Federal Police. Given the number of dignitaries to be protected, this element of Olympic security is a huge and resource-intensive area.

## THE POLICE ROLE

The core business of the police is the prevention and, if that fails, the detection, apprehension and subsequent prosecution of criminals. Having your wallet stolen in Homebush is not different in kind from having it stolen in Pitt Street or on the Quay. What is different for the NSW Police is that prevention, detection and apprehension will be much more difficult with very large concentrations of people and when it only has finite and limited resources to deal with the peak period in the second half of 2000.

The third category listed, dignitary protection, raises security issues that are to do with basic police functions, but which go much further. At least in theory, the assassination of a visiting president is simply a case of murder, and is no different from the victim of foul play found wherever. But, both under the 2000 Olympic agreement and under the Vienna Convention, all murders are not the same and an assassinated president, prime minister or minister is much more important than the generic victim. In somewhat simple terms, the reason for the difference is that the dead visiting dignitary affects Australia as a nation, whereas the generic victim is a statistic.

## GENERAL SECURITY STRUCTURE

Australia is a Commonwealth of sovereign states, and under its Constitution police powers belong to the states and can only be exercised within the states' borders. The foreign policy power belongs solely to the federal government. The security of dignitaries involves the prevention of crimes against that person — that is, it is a police and state government matter, but there is also a Commonwealth responsibility for the application of international conventions, and for foreign relations generally.

It is not feasible in Australia, as it is in some other countries, for example, to have a central government police security unit that can be deployed into a state, or for the federal government to take over control of the state's security forces. In Australia, except in some rare circumstances, the movement of the Commonwealth's security capabilities into a state's jurisdiction can only be at the request of, or with the agreement of, the state government.

What this unique combination of elements means is that the internal security structure in Australia had to be built on the foundation of the state police forces, and those forces remaining under the control of state governments. What was created after the 1978 Hilton Hotel bombing in Sydney was a state/Commonwealth coordination machinery to cooperatively improve the national capability to prevent or respond to politically motivated violence.

In broad terms, the states contribute to that cooperative endeavour the following capabilities. First, and most importantly, is their police forces. The police capabilities of particular relevance to politically motivated violence include bomb disposal teams where they exist, forensic and crime scene analysis capabilities, police intelligence collection and analysis, police assault groups for dealing with armed criminals, and for the big police forces, high-technology surveillance capabilities. The states also contribute their coordination machinery for decision-making and for pulling in other state capabilities, such as fire services.

Again in broad terms, the Commonwealth contributes the following capabilities: the Australian Federal Police; the Commonwealth's intelligence collection and analysis capabilities; the Protective Services Coordination Centre, which, amongst other things, provides the machinery for the Commonwealth government to draw on the range of its capabilities — for example, specialised aviation security; and various capabilities associated with aviation security and with the protection of diplomatic premises. The Commonwealth also provides the specialist counter-terrorist capabilities in the Australian Defence Force.

To draw this complex of capabilities together, and to coordinate some common training and equipment, the Commonwealth established a joint Commonwealth/state machinery which has the long-winded title of the Standing Advisory Committee on Commonwealth/State Cooperation for Protection Against Violence, referred to for obvious reasons by its initials, SAC-PAV.

Figure 9.1 is a representation of the Commonwealth–state machinery for responding to a terrorist incident. We know that the structure works moderately well in the artificial constructs of exercises. What we do not know is whether it could be made to work expeditiously in a real situation.

Figure 9.1
Counter-terrorism national crisis management response arrangements

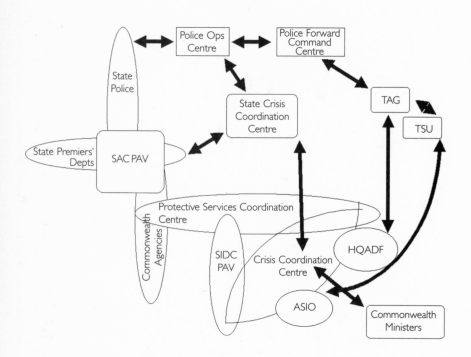

## THE OLYMPIC SECURITY STRUCTURE

The security structure for the 2000 Olympics might be thought of as having four layers. At the centre is the NSW Police Force, which is the NSW government's agent for ensuring the security of the Games. The Sydney Organising Committee for the Olympic Games (SOCOG) is responsible to the NSW government for staging the Games and hence it also has a security planning staff headed by a seconded police officer. Outside, but connected to this core structure, is the IOC's Delegate Security, who is responsible to the IOC for monitoring the security arrangements as they are developed by the host country and in the host city. Then, in another channel, is the Commonwealth government and the national security capability described previously.

## TERRORISM AND THE OLYMPICS

The structure and capabilities described above aim to deal with the whole spectrum of Olympics security planning. At one end of that spectrum is terrorism. It happens that Olympic security as such came into existence as the result of a terrorist incident at the 1972 Munich Olympic Games when the Black September Movement killed two and took hostage nine Israeli athletes in the Munich Olympic Village. They demanded the release of 200 Palestinians held in Israeli gaols. After some considerable confusion, the West German government ordered an assault, but the assault was a disaster during which all of the hostages, as well as five of the eight terrorists and one policeman, died.

Even if Olympic security had not begun as a response to a terrorist incident, judged against the characteristics that international terrorist groups seem to have sought in the past, the Olympic Games are an ideal stage for terrorism. If terrorism is theatre, with the actions of terrorists aiming to gain attention and project a message, then the 2000 Olympics are the biggest theatre of all time with the largest audience. Somewhere between one in every two and one in every three people on the face of the earth will watch some of the Games.

Moreover, history shows that the end of each century attracts individuals and groups who believe that the year signals some fundamental change in the world or its apocalyptic end. Among the extreme are those millennarianists who consider that they have a responsibility to make the fundamental change, or the end, actually occur.

This is not an assertion that the Games are at threat from either international terrorists or from apocalyptic millennarianists. 'Threat' is a combination of the attractiveness of the target, the capability of the potential attackers, and the inhibitors put in the way by the security planners — that is, it is the extent of the attackers' determination and capability to overcome the obstacles. Nevertheless, Olympic Games are by their nature an attractive target, and those who have attempted to suggest otherwise are misleading.

## INTERNATIONAL TERRORISM

The definitions of 'terrorism' that were largely created in the 1970s and 1980s and which described reasonably well the nature and motivation of terrorism then, do not fit well with the trends that have occurred in the 1990s. A useful starting point for an event in Australia might be the definition accepted by governments in Australia. The National Anti-terrorist Plan says that terrorism:

> ... comprises acts or threats of violence of national concern, calculated to evoke extreme fear for the purpose of achieving a political objective in Australia or a foreign country ...

Figure 9.2
Trends in international terrorism

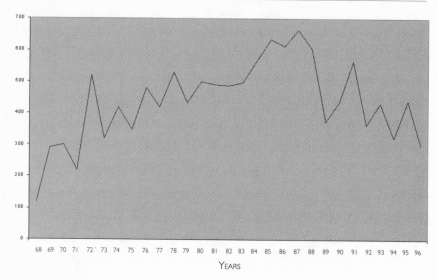

Source: Based on US State Department, *Patterns of Global Terrorism* (1992 and 1996).

Figure 9.3
Casualties from international terrorist incidents, 1991–6

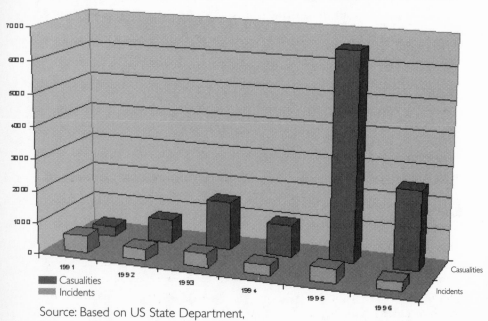

Source: Based on US State Department,
*Patterns of Global Terrorism* (1992 and 1996).

The incidence of international terrorism has been trending downwards since the late 1980s, with a blip or two during the Gulf War (see Figure 9.2). A second macro-trend is that smaller numbers of incidents are producing a larger numbers of casualties (see Figure 9.3).

Contrary to the impression left by selective reporting in the media, most facilities targeted by terrorist groups belong to the private sector, rather than to governments. About 50 per cent of the facilities targeted by international terrorists belong to private enterprise, with attacks against diplomatic premises running at about 14 per cent. About two-thirds of international terrorist incidents continue to be bombings, with most being explosives and the remainder fire bombs. It seems that another trend is that the total of nationalist/separatist groups is falling and the number of religiously motivated groups is increasing (see Figure 9.4).

Figure 9.4
Types of terrorist groups, 1968, 1980 and 1992

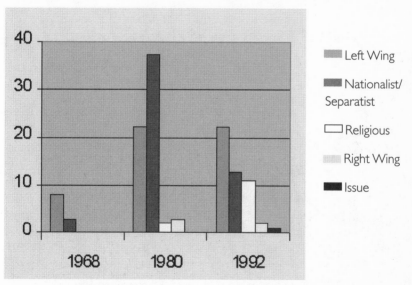

Source: Based on Bruce Hoffman, 'How terrorism is analysed', in Alan Thompson (ed.), *Terrorism and the 2000 Olympic Games*, Australian Defence Studies Centre, Canberra, 1996.

Although the bullet and the bomb continue to be the weapons most preferred by terrorists, there is a sort of fashion-consciousness in the type of incidents preferred. The fashion in terrorism, as well as being to some extent copy-cat, is derived from the relationship between elements such as the relative vulnerability of the targets, and the volume of theatre and audience — and hence the political effect of the incident. The first helps to explain the overall statistical preference for strikes against businesses and the relatively low level of strikes against military targets, and the second helps to explain the early enthusiasm for incidents of siege-hostage — for example, the 1972 Munich Olympic Games — and of aircraft hijacks.

## THE FUTURE OF TERRORISM

There are, however, substantial indications of a change in fashion in terrorism, which is likely to continue into the next millennium. The following examples illustrate the broad trends of change. In February 1993, four people blew up the World Trade Center in New York, killing six, injuring 1000 others and causing about US$550 million worth of damage. Also in 1993, the 20-year-old leader of a small group on the west coast of America calling itself the 'Fourth Reich Skinheads' was arrested and charged with planning a series of bombings against Jewish targets that were intended to culminate in a machine-gun and hand-grenade assault against a Los Angeles Christian church as its members came out from their Sunday worship. On 20 March 1995, sarin nerve gas was released by the Aum Supreme Truth Cult on five trains on three lines of the Tokyo subway system. Twelve commuters died and some 5000 others were affected by the attack. On 19 April 1995, mustard gas was released in the Yokohama railway station, injuring 400. When arrested some months later, the perpetrator said he had done it 'just for fun'. The Yokohama attack hardly featured in world newspapers because, on the same day, Timothy McVeigh bombed the Murrah Federal Building in Oklahoma City, killing 168 persons, the sixth-highest total of fatalities in a single 'terrorist' incident this century. At 1.20 am on 27 July 1996, a bomb exploded in the Centennial Olympic Park in Atlanta during the 1996 Olympics, killing one person and injuring more than 100 others. As a final example, over the last few years, the Armed Islamic Group in Algeria has killed over 50 000 Algerians and some foreign nationals through attacks against villages, buses, indiscriminate car bombs and targeted assassinations.

All the above incidents were defined as terrorism, and yet it is increasingly difficult to fit all of them into the traditional definition of terrorism. The closest is perhaps the Armed Islamic Group in Algeria, which also ran a successful bombing campaign in France in 1995. It obviously has a political objective — in this case, using terrorism as a form of insurgency to change the government.

What may distinguish the Armed Islamic Group from what we tend to categorise as the classic terrorist groups is that that there does not seem to be any upper limit to the killing. This is very different from the classic insurgent, and from the classic terrorist group. Although the IRA, the PLO and its splinters, the Red Brigades, Shining Path, the MRTA et al. cloaked their actions in a cover of apparent indiscriminate killing, in fact their weapons and the volume of destruction were fairly carefully calculated. It could be argued that the difference lies in extreme religious motivation. Bruce Hoffman, who has studied the phenomenon, says:

> The fact that for the religious terrorist violence assumes a transcendent purpose and therefore becomes a sacramental or divine duty arguably results in a significant loosening of the constraints on the commission of mass murder. Religion, moreover, functions as a legitimising force sanctioning if not encouraging wide scale violence against an almost open-ended category of opponents.[1]

The World Trade Center bombing in 1993 might fit loosely within the term 'political' in the sense that at least the leader of the bombers, Ramzi Ahmed Yousef, claimed that his actions were to protest against US support for Israel. Nevertheless, the motivation was not made public at the time of the incident; nor was the cause given publicity at the various trials of the perpetrators.

If the World Trade Center bombing was politically motivated, it was deficient in what had been perceived as the core characteristic of terrorism — that is, the signal that a government must change its policy or suffer further incidents of terrorism. The World Trade Center bombing has more of the appearance of making the United States pay for support of Israel, rather than an attempt to force a change of policy. It has the fingerprints of revenge.

The actions of the 'Fourth Reich Skinheads' may have been political in some sense, but not in the way that we traditionally think of that term. The Skinheads seem to have seen themselves as 'contributing to the armed struggle', but by whom and against what does not seem to be clear to observers, and perhaps not even to the group itself.

The motivation of the Aum Supreme Truth cult for the sarin gas attack on the Tokyo subway remains obscure. The cult attempted to avoid having the attack attributed to it, it made no demands on the government, and it did not seem to have a political aim. And yet we know that it was probably manufacturing, and certainly testing, sarin on a sheep station in Western Australia as early as 1993.

Timothy McVeigh, convicted of the 1995 Oklahoma City bombing, seems to have shared the views of far right-wing militia groups, which considers that the US government is conniving with the United Nations to disarm the population so that the UN can take over. McVeigh, according to the prosecution, considered the 1992 shoot-out at Ruby Ridge, Idaho, between federal agents and white separatist Randy Weaver, and later the siege and subsequent assault against the Dravidian Cult at Waco, Texas, in April 1993, as a 'call to arms', and later commentators talked about McVeigh taking revenge for the Waco massacre. What remains unclear, as in the case of the Skinheads, is a call to arms about what, against what and to what end? These elements, which are essential for the descriptions of terrorism conceived in the 1970s and 1980s, seem missing in some of the terrorism in the 1990s.

A more extreme example that lies outside the boundaries of terrorist action to gain publicity for a political agenda or to force a change in government policy, is perhaps the Atlanta Centennial Olympic Park bombing. Responsibility for two later bombings in Atlanta was claimed by the 'Army of God'. Letters to Reuters and NBC linked together as motives anti-abortion, a war against the 'ungodly communist regime in New York' — that is, the United Nations — the destruction of 'sodomites', and 'Death to the new world order'. The terms of letters and the subsequent police investigation have firmly linked the perpetrator of the Atlanta bombing to the same sort of fundamentalist extremism that motivated McVeigh in the attack in Oklahoma.

Threaded through the examples are reflections of some form of religious fundamentalism. The term is a broad carry-all for individuals and groups whose belief systems include a literal and absolute interpretation of a set of religious tenets. What they have in common is an absolute view that theirs is the only valid interpretation and hence only they can dictate the right way. Of course, most religious fundamentalists are not terrorists, but an increasing number of terrorists are also fundamentalists or are motivated by some form of gnosticism — that is, a belief that they have access to a special and secret knowledge that gives them sole command of the truth and the way. Millennarianist cults tend to be both gnostic and apocalyptic.

Finally, the World Trade Center bombers, the Skinheads, the Supreme Truth cultists and the Centennial Olympic Park bomber had the common characteristic of being 'amateur', not 'professional', terrorists. Classic terrorism — that is, that after about 1970 — has been carried out mainly by defined organisations, using what have become traditional methods, and with a largely definable motivation and purpose. Members tend to be full-time terrorists, to have had some training, and to be underground and covert. Terrorist incidents are a means to an end, and generally the end is well-publicised so that both the government, which is the real target, and the population, whose reaction is the lever on the government, know the aim of the organisation.

The members of the groups carrying out the incidents in the examples just cited do not fit that description. Command and control was largely absent, few if any of the terrorists were trained, and most did not see terrorism as their vocation.

## TWO-TRACK TERRORISM

The two characteristics that are likely to continue into the next millennium are an increase in terrorism by religious fundamentalists and an increase in amateur terrorists. The two can and will continue to overlap. A rather simplified model for terrorism now and into the near future is to think of it as travelling along two tracks (see Figure 9.5). One is a continuation of the professional, essentially full-time terrorist groups, with a defined aim and modus operandi.

The second track might be the 'amateur' terrorist — an individual or small group carrying out essentially idiosyncratic one-offs, not necessarily with the sorts of political agendas that we associate with the formed professional terrorist groups. Overlaid across both tracks is what appears to be the increasing influence of religious extremism, exemplified in the United States by the right-wing Christian fundamentalist militias, and in some other countries by Islamic extremists.

Figure 9.5
Two-track terrorism — the problem for the future?

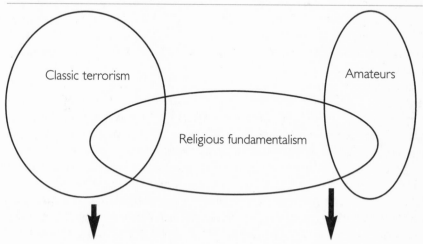

## EXOTIC WEAPONRY

The common practice among 'classic' terrorist groups has been to use fairly simple weapons, mainly the bomb and the bullet, although the forms of these weapons have changed over the decades. But if the two-track model is broadly in the ballpark, then it is a reasonable extension of it to assume that at least the amateur track will involve an increase in the use of exotic weapons. The three categories of most concern are nuclear, chemical/biological and cyber terrorism.

Any rational assessment would have to conclude that the risk of nuclear terrorism has been increased by the end of the Cold War and the break-up of the former Soviet Union. But there are inhibitors that make it doubtful that nuclear terrorism will be the wave of the future for either professional or amateur terrorists. The major inhibitor for the professionals is not the availability of fissile material, or the technology, but in the international reaction. It is one thing for other countries to consider a terrorist bombing campaign to be an internal domestic problem; it would be another international dynamic entirely if a terrorist group had its finger on a nuclear trigger. The obstacles for the 'second-track' terrorist will continue to be getting hold of enough fissile material and technology.

Information technology (IT) terrorism/cyber terrorism is probably also an unlikely contender for the wave of the future. Again, it is not an absence of capability to attack and damage IT systems. Hacking into an IT system is not, however, likely to produce a public theatre on which the terrorist can play out the game. Second, the capability to attack part of a national IT system may be fairly readily available, but the facility to hold large segments of it to ransom is not. Lack of theatre will probably be a deterrent for the professionals. Although the risk from second-track terrorists is higher, particularly as a strike back at society, the effects of destructive hacking or the implanting of viruses is not likely to provide the same buzz as trying to reduce a high-rise building and its inhabitants to rubble.

Two-track terrorism makes incidents of biological terrorism more likely. One hundred thousand out-of-work scientists and technicians from the former Soviet Union's biological weapons program provide a potential pool of expertise. The illegal and covert channels for Iraq to acquire the materials for its biological weapons program are, by and large, still available. The combination of the two provides a possible cocktail for international terrorist groups, but it is doubtful that they are likely to use the opportunity. Classic terrorism is theatre, and Brian Jenkins — one of the world's experts on terrorism — has argued that terrorists want a lot of people watching, not a lot of people dead.

But what the American ABC News has called 'The New Terrorist' doesn't necessarily see it that way. The Institute of Defense Analysis in the United States turned Jenkins's comment on its head. These terrorists want a lot of people dead, not a lot of people watching. They are much less inhibited about mass destruction, and there is no doubt that biological weapons are potentially massively destructive. Anthrax, which is used as some sort of benchmark, is 100 000 times more lethal than the deadliest chemical warfare agent. Unlike a nuclear device, it is relatively easy to produce in large quantities, and it is extremely stable when stored as a dry powder.

The Aum Supreme Truth cult had been stockpiling anthrax and botulus toxin, as well as manufacturing sarin nerve gas. Supposedly, the cult had plans to spray an entire city with biological agents from a helicopter it had acquired.

## DILEMMAS IN SECURITY POLICY AND PRACTICE

It doesn't take much for security agencies and governments to appear to be in the red. Take the 1996 Atlanta Olympics. A passenger aircraft crash off New York that happened coincidentally at the time of the Olympics, and which has now been demonstrated not to have been an act of terrorism or sabotage, is still popularly believed to have been an act of terrorism associated with the Games. The single incident in the fun park in Atlanta is almost universally seen as a failure of the entire Olympic security system.

The first dilemma for Australia's security policy is that it is optimised to deal with siege/hostage incidents. These do not seem to be the way trends are pointing. Many of the capabilities created in the 1980s are not usable against second-track terrorism. The SAS and Police Assault Groups may be highly effective in dealing with an aircraft hijack or a rerun of the Munich siege hostage, but they are next to irrelevant in dealing with a nerve gas attack against the Sydney underground, a bombing campaign along the lines of the Armed Islamic Group in France in 1995, or anthrax pumped through the airconditioning system at a venue.

And yet we cannot abolish the siege hostage response capabilities simply because we might think that the demand curve is falling. One reason is that a government cannot assume, particularly before the Olympics and the millennium, that classic terrorism, siege hostage and playing on the world stage has disappeared. A second reason is that the phenomenon called 'displacement' would make it more likely that siege hostage incidents would occur if a government abolished or degraded its existing capability.

The second element in the policy dilemma is that the second track is so amorphous that it is almost impossible to conceive of a policy framework to deal with it. What sort of tools are available to a democratic government to identify the amateur terrorist, who almost by definition has no past as a terrorist? How do you protect the Australian public from random acts of violence by individuals or small groups who are not motivated by a political agenda, but by revenge against society? How do you sift the large number of religiously motivated groups, sects and cults to finger those that are most likely to go through the tripwire into acts of violence? There are no clear-cut answers.

Finally, there is the problem of applying Australia's security policy in the context of the Olympics. The national counter-terrorism structure is probably the best pastiche possible given the realities of history and decisions made in Westminster almost 100 years ago, and it works amazingly well despite its structure. But because of the elements from which Australia was pieced together at Federation 100 years ago, and the content of its Constitution, a national security system is an organisational designer's nightmare, full of ambiguities and complexity. Moreover, as noted above, it has never actually been tested in a real situation, and the artificiality of exercises can paper over many of the difficulties that are likely when real lives are on the line.

On to this complex national structure has been grafted the peculiar arrangements created by the IOC, and subsequently applied by the NSW government in running the Games.

## FURTHER READING

Thompson, Alan (ed.) (1996), *Terrorism and the 2000 Olympics*, Australian Defence Studies Centre, ADFA, Canberra.

US State Department (1992 and 1996), *Patterns of Global Terrorism.*

# THE MEDIA
## *Reg Gratton*

The broad approach of this chapter is to attempt to look at the importance and significance of the print media in contributing to the continuing success of the Olympic Games as the world's greatest sports festival. In fact, it is more than a huge sporting event; in 2000, like Atlanta in 1996, it will be the world's biggest scheduled news event.

## BROADCAST VERSUS PRINT MEDIA

Before we examine in some detail how media coverage of the Games contributes in large measure to its success, I would like to draw attention to the difference between the broadcast media, television and radio, and the written and photographic press. It seems to have become the fashion to think of the Games as a made-for-television event. Transmitted to living-room screens around the world and watched by billions of people, a spectacle fed by advertising revenue, it appears on the surface that television is now the engine that drives the Winter and Summer Games. And if we look at the sports that are dear to our hearts, not only the Olympic sports, it is easy to draw the conclusion that television holds total sway over the future of sport.

Rugby league, rugby union, soccer, cricket, even swimming — the Skins event at the Homebush Aquatic Centre was a good example of how a sport may be refined for the small screen — all these major sports have undergone significant changes in the last decade as television, particularly pay television, seeks to augment its revenues through sports-loving couch potatoes across the globe.

In Atlanta the television coverage was a stunning success for the Games in terms of the ratings both in the United States and globally.

The success has persuaded the big TV networks like America's NBC to pay record sums for the television rights in 2000 in Sydney. NBC alone has paid more than A$1 billion.

While the television coverage in 1996 was mostly good news, focusing on the sporting excellence, the print media coverage also highlighted the Games as a news event, reporting Atlanta organisational 'stuff-ups', and front-paging the technology glitches and the bus breakdowns as well as Michael Johnson's stunning 200 metres world record. So it is important to be aware of the differences between the two media disciplines. On paper it looks as though the broadcast muscle in sheer numbers should overwhelm the influence of the written media at Games time. The International Broadcast Centre in Sydney, located next to Sydney Olympic Park, will cover 70 000 square metres, housing more than 180 organisations with more than 11 000 rights-holding broadcasters. Our host broadcaster, the Sydney Olympic Broadcasting Organisation (SOBO), will need 3400 personnel in 2000 — that's more people than are at present employed by all the TV networks currently operating in Australia.

But statistics can be misleading. While the accredited photographers and journalists working at the Olympics may number only 5000, almost every one of those accreditations belongs to an opinion-maker — whether in words or pictures. Each writer or photographer will have an impact on what people read or see about the Games. And those images and articles live on, in contrast to the ephemerality of the small screen. And further, while the numbers of accredited broadcasters are significantly greater than the print media, the majority will be working behind the scenes as technicians and camera operators.

Fékrou Kidane, the International Olympic Committee's (IOC) Director of International Cooperation and Public Information, also had some sobering words after Atlanta: 'President Samaranch told Billy Payne [the Atlanta Olympics chief] every time he talked to him that the media are the last judges of the Games.' Samaranch, who is in fact a former chairman of the IOC Press Commission, has always been aware of the importance of the written media. 'The foreign media more than anyone else measure the success of the Games,' he said before Atlanta.

## THE ROLE OF THE PRINT MEDIA

Before leaving the subject of the relative strengths of the broadcast and written media, I would like to point out that reports of the imminent demise of the newspaper industry are premature. Doom-laden warnings that television, and now the Internet, will soon make newspapers obsolete are not borne out by a recent survey carried out by the Newspaper Association of America (NAA). Reuters reported in September 1998 that there are more morning papers in the United States (705) than there were nearly 50 years ago (322) and total daily circulation is up to 56 million versus 53 million in 1950. Even more significantly, the NAA said readership is holding steady, while broadcast TV audiences are slumping.

The NAA, which represents some 1700 newspapers in the United States and Canada, believes that readership, measured by its Competitive Media Index detailed research surveys as opposed to pure circulation, gives a better idea of the health of the industry. Latest figures show an average 58.6 per cent of adults read a daily newspaper and more than two-thirds of adults (68.2 per cent) read a Sunday paper. The daily newspaper figure was down slightly from 1997 when it stood at 58.7 per cent. Reuters quoted a media analyst for Merrill Lynch as saying that people like the way newspapers are edited. 'They are portable and the ability to flip through them and browse is a plus.' I couldn't agree more.

You may ask why the IOC still puts such store by the written word when it has so successfully wooed television and when the Internet is developing as another powerful medium. An angry and frustrated press is a very potent animal indeed.

## WHERE DID ATLANTA MEDIA PLANNING GO WRONG?

I don't think information technology (IT) sponsor IBM in their worst nightmare would have foreseen headlines like the *West Australian*'s of 30 July: 'IBM's Atlanta Games becomes Olympic debacle.' Other local headlines like 'Tin-pot organisation wins Atlanta the wooden spoon' and 'Welcome to the nightmare' also made it hard at breakfast time for the sponsors who had invested scores of millions of dollars to promote their product through the Olympics.

Some of my former colleagues were equally scathing in their responses to questionnaires handed out during the Atlanta Games. Agence France-Presse English-language sports editor Ron Hall wrote: 'We have gone back 20 years. We thought we would be able to have our journalists concentrating on the sports, looking at the events and having time to write.' Roy Eccleston of the *Australian* was just as critical: 'Remember the fact that while the Games is about the athletes and spectators, it is the journalists whose impressions will form world opinion. Atlanta treated journalists down the scale of importance and got universal criticism.'

The Main Press Centre (MPC) location provided the first major headache. Based in downtown Atlanta, it was too far to walk to the competition venues and too far from the hub of the free shuttle bus service. The media usually took a shuttle bus from the MPC to the hub in order to take another bus to a competition venue, time-consuming in the extreme. Atlanta Committee for the Olympic Games (ACOG) volunteer drivers were also, in the main, inflexible. They had orders from above and they had to be obeyed. Journalists told of how they were not allowed to leave buses outside the MPC, even when it was their ultimate destination, because the bus in question had to deliver them to the notorious hub where they then had to get another bus to take them back to the MPC. The more seasoned of the fourth estate found ways around this. I was on a bus where a photographer lit a cigarette when the bus became stuck in a gridlock outside the MPC. 'Sorry, buddy,' said the driver. 'You can't smoke in my bus. I'm going to have to let you off.' That naturally was the cue for a stampede, leaving behind a rather shocked driver. And from another eyewitness: 'If you are gonna be sick, you can just do it outside [the MPC, of course]', which led to another stampede. The shuttle service was close to disastrous — the hub system did not work, out-of-town drivers got lost, and too many buses broke down or got locked in central-city traffic jams. The media were housed in nearly 40 different accommodation venues, which further guaranteed that the shuttle service, an obligation under the IOC's media policy, did not work properly.

The MPC was also too small. It was housed in two interconnected exhibition complexes — the Atlanta Apparel Mart and Inforum buildings. The allocated space was only 27 000 square metres, far less than Barcelona (51 000 square metres) and Seoul (35 000 square metres). The result was that a number of large media organisations that had traditionally rented space within a Games MPC had to be knocked back. Other agencies and newspapers that were given space saw it cut back as the MPC management wrestled with layout constraints.

The housing of the MPC in two separate buildings with two separate lease agreements and landlords made planning and continuity of planning difficult. The fact that ACOG was not the sole tenant of the two buildings when the MPC opened also created problems for security and accredited access. During the MPC operation, there were people inside without proper accreditation and certain areas were not secured.

The fitout itself left much to be desired. The subdivision of space for the 120 or so agencies and newspapers comprised a modular aluminium framework to a height of about three metres, supporting panels of a composite material of only four millimetres thickness. It had little strength or rigidity, offered little enclosure security, and had very poor sound-damping characteristics.

The lease agreement was signed knowing that a jewellery exhibition was going to be in the MPC building until 3 July, giving ACOG only 66 hours to execute the fitout. There was no way that such a complex meshing of offices, communications and equipment could be expected to work perfectly in such a short space of time.

There was at least one instance of equipment being stolen from an office, and there were many cases where journalists or photographers who were locked out of their offices just pushed the wall in to gain entry. It was a standing joke among the media that MPC management had made a big issue of handing everyone a key to their office.

Ask any journalist what his or her priority is for covering a major sporting event like the Olympics or the soccer World Cup and he or she will almost certainly say 'good communications' — phones that work, user-friendly modern connections for lap-top filing, fast and accurate supply of results and flash quotes, and fast delivery of any Games-related information. ACOG's communications fell down during the Games in a number of key areas. The much-touted 96 system failed to provide the promised flow of results and information to computer terminals in the MPC from the competition venues. The IBM results feeds to the agencies were initially non-existent, then slow and in some cases inaccurate. Some boxing matches finished in the sixth or seventh round (even though Olympic boxing consists of just three rounds), a number of athletes had biographies with their date of birth reading 00-00-00. The ill-conceived pigeonhole system in the MPC compounded journalists' problems — they spent fruitless time rechecking to see what was available because no notification of updates had been put in place.

A number of agencies and newspapers had dire problems with cabling, networking and phone installation, due to the rapid fitout and the number of different contractors involved. The TV feed into the MPC main workroom, though it looked impressive, was only half-useful because there was no sound feed. Agencies also complained that the sound feed from the on-site news conferences was of poor quality, a legacy of the fast fitout.

The main workroom or bullpen, the 24-hour working area for the print journalists, looked impressive but fell short of expectations in a number of areas. It was too congested. Space was supposed to be provided for 600 tabled work stations, but in fact there was only enough room for about 500 people and the lines of tables were too close together. The congestion was particularly bad just before the Games began when none of the venues were operating and most of the journalists wanted to work at the MPC. Photographers added to the space problems by setting up camp in the bullpen area, either to make phone contact with their office or to transmit photos via modem. The bullpen also had early problems with phones, some of which were not working because of installation problems.

MPC catering also left a lot to be desired. Journalists can be trapped in the MPC for up to 18 hours a day during the Games. They can also use it as a base and a place to recharge the batteries. In Atlanta, the main cafeteria, Bytes, was well received initially but its lack of variety prompted complaints. Those who delighted in the big sandwiches at the start were repulsed by them at the end. The usage of Bytes before the Games had been underestimated — journalists worked out of the MPC with other venues not operating — and there should have been space for nearly twice the 350 that it accommodated. The food hatches were also too small, and at peak times there was unnecessary congestion at the pay counters.

Small wonder, then, that the print media wrote anti-Atlanta stories. It was a pity because the Games themselves were great and, of course, if you were watching television at home in Sydney and hadn't opened a newspaper you would not have known what a nightmare it was for the journalists and photographers.

This does, of course, underscore the difference in approach to coverage of the Games by the print and broadcast media. Broadcasters in general are not news organisations. Put cynically, they are not paying to be here in Sydney in 2000 to report the Games as a news story. They are paying for many, many hours of television content — that content is the world's largest sporting festival. Any spin-off to their nightly news programs is a bonus.

Broadcasters, with the notable exception of those public, non-commercial networks such as the BBC that can still afford to buy into the Olympics, are doing so because the bottom line is profit. They are spending money to make money. We are dealing with the sale of a sporting program — a very popular sporting program, of course. That is why they paid their rights-holding dollars. The Olympics are no different to any other big sporting event in that broadcasters spend money on the production facilities they need to obtain the coverage.

The written and photographic press, on the other hand, are generally news organisations. They have to come here to cover the Olympics as a news event — specifically, sporting — but also as a global happening. Organisations like Reuters and Associated Press invest a lot of money in sending teams of reporters and photographers to an Olympics, because it is part of the news service they provide to their subscribers.

Let us not forget that the written press has been covering the Olympics day in and day out in the four years following the previous

Games. Samaranch is acutely aware that most Olympic sports do not get widespread coverage on television between Games. It is the press that keeps the sporting public informed about shooting, sailing, rowing and even modern pentathlon.

## SYDNEY MEDIA PREPARATIONS

Let us look at the 1998 sailing regatta in Sydney. We handed out accreditations to about ten TV networks, NHK in Japan, the BBC in Britain, to all our local channels — Seven, Nine, Ten, ABC and SBS. However, apart from a segment here and there about this being SOCOG's first test event and the largest regatta ever sailed on Sydney Harbour, it was the *Daily Telegraph*, through Amanda Lulham, the *Sydney Morning Herald*, through Alan Kennedy, the *Australian*, through Rob Mundle, and the national news agency, the Australian Associated Press, that carried regular daily coverage on the sporting event itself. Because it was the Rugby League Grand Final day, no local TV network turned up for the closing press conference and later medal awards ceremony. Sailing, a spectacular sport for Sydney in 2000, attracted no regular broadcast on an event that featured most of the gold, silver and bronze medal winners from Atlanta and several world champions in Olympic classes.

Our sharp learning curve from Atlanta was an intense realisation that we have to service the written media properly, to ensure that we get the best possible coverage both in the run-up to the Games as well as at Games time.

With this in mind, our head of press operations, Richard Palfreyman, recruited a team of media professionals who have all had Olympic or major event experience. They all know first hand what a journalist or photographer needs to cover the Games. Press operations is within the Media Division, whose general manager is Milton Cockburn, one of Australia's most respected print journalists and a former editor of the *Sydney Morning Herald*.

Richard Palfreyman himself, who will also be the press chief at Games time, had a distinguished career as a foreign correspondent with the ABC. I served my time as a correspondent and bureau chief with Reuters as well as national news editor of AAP in Sydney. Our photos chief, Gary Kemper, had the same role in Atlanta and also worked for Reuters both as a working photographer and photos manager. Our 'info' system and Olympic News Service is being put together by Steve Dettre, who has covered every Games since Seoul in 1988 and had a long career with AAP. Our Venue Press Operations are being managed by Michelle Bartlett, who ran the Press Centre at the Australian Tennis Open in Melbourne for nearly ten years.

## PLANS FOR THE SYDNEY MAIN PRESS CENTRE

At the heart of the media services will be the Main Press Centre, and, unlike Atlanta, we have the advantages of location and size. Again in contrast to Atlanta, we are providing a Media Village, which will have accommodation for 6000 print and broadcast media and is located at Lidcombe, just under five kilometres from Sydney Olympic Park.

The MPC is about 40 000 square metres in size (Atlanta was only 27 000 square metres), and will be housed in six large pavilions built in 1997 for the Royal Easter Show, which was relocated to Homebush in 1998. The MPC will operate for 24 hours a day for a month, before and during the Games, and will provide up to 12 000 square metres of rented private office space for news organisations. The MPC will have a common workroom, with seating for 800 in separate work clusters, each with dedicated video monitors and access to sport-specific information. There is a main press conference facility, also with seating for 800, as well as five smaller conference rooms.

With more than 800 photographers expected in Sydney and the increasing use of digital technology, we will be providing consolidated photo services in one area in the MPC. There will be a dedicated photographers' entrance to the Kodak Imaging Centre, darkrooms, transmitting facilities, Canon and Nikon loans and camera repairs, and a film courier.

The main lobby in the MPC will house the help and information desk, together with services such as a bank, post office, general store, international news stand and pharmacy. The lobby leads on to the main catering area, which will seat more than 600 and offer a wide range of international cuisines as well as an Australian-style barbecue area. There will be a 150-seat restaurant together with bars, cafes and food carts in other parts of the MPC.

We also have to provide press facilities and services across all competition venues that include tribunes, workrooms, mixed zones and press conference rooms. We have already finalised tribune and workroom positions, as well as the key photo positions for all venues.

Why do we have to provide all these facilities? We have to follow fairly stringent IOC guidelines on press facilities, which form part of our host city contract. We are required to provide a Main Press Centre, a press sub-centre at all the competition venues, and a free transport shuttle service from accommodation to the MPC and the sporting venues. The IOC *Written and Photographic Press Guide* is our Bible and details all the services that the Organising Committee must provide: accommodation, transport, the MPC and press sub-centres, Games information and results.

The IOC still puts such store by the written word because the written word survives. People love to savour the great sporting moments; they love to experience vicariously the joy of victory and the tragedy of defeat through the prose of a great sports writer. How many of us, after seeing Kieren Perkins's outstanding 1500 metres swim, salivated over his triumph through the words of the Australian writers in Atlanta?

Whether those words will be on paper or on screen via the Internet may be open to argument, but the written word will survive because, while television has brought the Games to over 200 countries, it still cannot capture the ultimate communication of the ecstasy of winning a gold medal. Sport thrives on the lingering memory of a defining moment — a memory engraved forever by those who can capture that moment in words and pictures.

There is no argument about the power of television in promoting the Olympics during the event itself. Let's look at some fairly mind-boggling statistics on the reach of the Games through television. An analysis released recently on TV coverage not surprisingly showed that the Atlanta Games were the most widely watched sports event in history. The survey showed that nine out of ten television viewers tuned in at least once and estimated that the Games had a cumulative worldwide audience of 19 billion — more than three times the world's population and an increase of 18 per cent over the figure for the Olympic Games in Barcelona in 1992. The increase in the number of countries over 1992 — 21 — was due to the proliferation of satellite broadcasting in Africa and the Middle East and to the assistance provided by the IOC towards wider distribution of the images on the African continent.

As a sidebar to these figures, Australians were the most voracious consumers, with an average of 66 hours watched during the 17 days. In 2000, it is estimated that our host broadcaster, the SOBO, will televise more than 3200 hours of live Olympic Games competition from more than 290 different events. More than 180 different broadcast organisations are expected in Sydney in 2000 — that is, more than 11 000 rights-holding broadcasters.

Will this coverage remain free-to-air or will pay TV companies start snapping up TV rights? I think for the next decade at least the answer is a simple one. The IOC has religiously adhered to the fundamental principle that the broadcast coverage of the Games should be viewed by the widest possible audience. This is why the European Broadcasting Union won the TV rights for Sydney against a much higher offer by Rupert Murdoch's News Corporation.

IOC has entered into long-term partnerships with broadcasters such as the NBC and the EBU, which represents 60 public broadcasters in Europe. Similarly, our own Channel Seven has taken television rights until 2008. These and other deals will guarantee free-to-air coverage of the Olympics until 2008. NBC alone has agreed to pay a staggering US$5 for the rights to five Summer and Winter Olympics starting here in Sydney.

## MEDIA COVERAGE IN 2000

How do we define this coverage, and how do we see it changing for 2000? Will the shape of the coverage be governed on the one hand by the NBC's slick approach which broke all Games prime-time records and pulled in a strong female audience, or will it still be the traditional live coverage delivered by Channel Seven which devoted up to 18 hours of the 24 to the Games. My guess is that you will probably see a merging of the two by 2000.

Let's make no mistake about the success of the NBC's 1996 coverage. It demolished its rivals during the Olympics and boasted a 25 per cent increase in its ratings. Its share of viewers was about four times that of its nearest competitor, CBS. But while it cleaned up the ratings, its over-the-top and jingoistic coverage won it few friends among the non-Americans. Events such as Perkins's great 1500 metres swim and the men's 10 000 metres won by Haile Gebreselassie were not shown at all. NBC also dubbed the mighty Michael Johnson the world's fastest human, ignoring Donovan Bailey who won the 100 metres in a world record time. Bailey, of course, is Canadian.

You only have to look at Atlanta sporting statistics to realise why well over three billion viewers switched on their TV sets. Atlanta boasted more gold medals, more world records and more countries winning medals than ever before. Can Sydney do the same? Despite the fact that the Sydney Games are likely to be less accessible to live audiences in the United States and Europe because of the time difference, we still think the audiences will grow again.

SOBO is estimating a cumulative audience of over 25 billion and an estimated peak of about four billion for the opening and closing ceremonies. While all these numbers are terrifying, I am confident that Australia has the capacity to provide a service to both print and broadcast media that will guarantee great coverage of the competition at a hugely successful Games. The coverage — and the images of Sydney that go with it — will reinforce the strength of the media not only in ensuring the ongoing popularity of the Games themselves, but also in promoting the host country itself.

## CONCLUSIONS

Planning for the local and international media is an important part of staging the Games. The media do more than report on the events and performances of the Games; they also make numerous judgments about the host country and its society and how well the Games have been organised. An 'angry and disgruntled' media is more likely to make negative assessments of a Games.

The international media, more than any group, help to define the reputation of an Olympics in the short term. Atlanta supremo Billy Payne attempted to counter some of the negative assessments of the 1996 Games, but his lone voice has been largely drowned out by the international media. Olympic scholars, working on documents produced by the Games, refine these judgments at a later stage.

## FURTHER READING

Rivenburgh, Nancy K. (1995), 'Images of others: The presentation of nations in the 1992 Barcelona Olympics', *Journal of International Communication*, vol. 2, no. 1, pp 6–26.

Rothenbuhler, W. Eric (1988), 'The living room celebration of the Olympics', *Journal of Communication*, vol. 38, no. 4, Autumn.

Verdier, Michelle and the ITU (1996), 'The Olympic Games and the media', *Olympic Review*, vol. xxv, no. 9, June/July, pp 57–63.

Wenn, Stephen R. (1993), 'Lights! Camera! Little action! Avery Brundage and the 1956 Melbourne Olympics', *Sporting Traditions*, vol. 10, no. 1, November, pp 38–53.

Wenn, Stephen R. (1995), 'The Olympic Movement and television', *Olympika*, vol. 4, pp 1–23.

# MARKETING AND
# SPONSORSHIP
*Amanda Johnston*

The aim of this chapter is to examine the world of Olympic marketing and how it has evolved, particularly since 1984. The chapter will explore why sponsors invest money in the Olympics and the issues relating to sponsorship. It will also introduce some case studies of prominent Olympic sponsors, such as Coca-Cola and IBM.

Promoting and marketing the Olympics is not new. Since the revival of the Games in 1896, there have been various forms of financing the Games and many companies have been associated with them. Marketing and sponsorship have become more prominent since the end of the amateur era under President Samaranch. Athletes are now paid for their endeavours, and many receive endorsements from companies to represent their products.

Figure 11.1 demonstrates that, from 1896, there was significant private funding of the Games, large amounts of revenue coming from individuals with significant private wealth. Tickets, coins and medals constituted important sources of revenue from 1896. This situation hasn't changed. Tickets, coins and medals — along with pins, souvenirs and other forms of Olympic memorabilia — are still highly prized. Although television rights and sponsorship have replaced private donations as an Olympic revenue stream, there is considerable continuity in Olympic fund-raising over the past century.

Tickets also continue to be a large revenue stream for the Olympic Movement, as does licensing. A visit to any of the Olympic stores that have opened in Sydney will illustrate the range of official Olympic-branded apparel and merchandise available in the marketplace.

Figure 11.1
The Games money-go-round

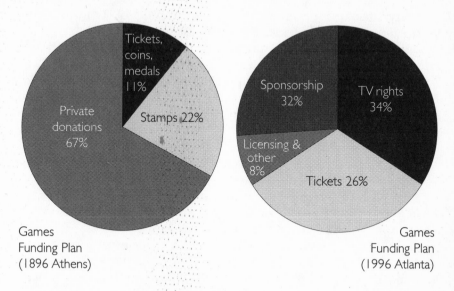

Games
Funding Plan
(1896 Athens)

Games
Funding Plan
(1996 Atlanta)

Source: Mihir Bose, (1996), *Sport Business*, September..

## THE OLYMPIC PARTNER (TOP)

TOP is central to the worldwide Olympic marketing agreement that governs the relationship sponsors have with the IOC and the Olympic Games. TOP, which now stands for 'The Olympic Partner', but was formerly 'The Olympic Program', was a product launched following the Los Angeles Olympic Games of 1984. It came about as a result of the increasing cost of staging the Games and the desperate financial status of the Olympic Movement.

Financially the Montreal Games of 1976 left the citizens of that city with a substantial Olympic debt, which took decades to pay off. As a result, Los Angeles was the only serious bidder for the 1984 Games. Peter Ueberroth, head of the 1984 Games organisation, was determined that the citizens of Los Angeles should not have to underwrite the Games. He determined that the Games should be marketed aggressively so that they would return a profit to the organisers.

Ueberroth chased sponsorship wherever he could find it, and there are reports that he enlisted the support of hundreds of sponsors for the 1984 Games. The sponsors who lined up included the big names such as Coca-Cola and American Express. The result at Los Angeles was a clutter of sponsorships and an out-of-control mayhem of signs. Ueberroth's prime concern was to run a successful and profitable Games — which he achieved.

The IOC was faced with several dilemmas after 1984. If Olympic property and signage were spread around an army of sponsors, their worth and value would be diminished. Another problem raised by the Los Angeles Games was that the bulk of the sponsorship revenue and television rights were US-based. If Olympic revenue was concentrated almost exclusively in US companies, this would be detrimental to the long-term growth of the Olympics as a global movement. A third area of concern was that IOC marketing structures were fragmented. There was also a danger that the IOC would become too dependent on television money and the media would become too influential in Olympic decision-making. However, at the same time, the IOC recognised that the successful Los Angeles Games offered a solution to the problem of the escalating costs of staging the Games. Ueberroth demonstrated that the Olympic Movement could develop revenue streams that would advance its interests.

The TOP program was the IOC's response to the issues raised by the Los Angeles Games. It was a carefully planned worldwide sponsorship agreement to secure the long-term financial needs of the Olympic Movement and diversify its revenue base so that the IOC did not solely rely on television income. The concept of exclusivity was crucial. Rather than having a proliferation of sponsors, the IOC settled for a small number of elite international sponsors — 11 in all, with each covering a particular category of sponsorship. The Coca-Cola Company became the official beverage; Visa, consumer payment systems; Fuji, document processing; IBM, information technology; and so forth. Each TOP contract generation lasts for four years before the agreement is renegotiated. TOP is in its fourth generation with contracts finishing on 31 December 2000. TOP provides the Olympic Movement with continuity in funding, enabling the IOC to develop longer-term planning.

TOP members pay very large sums of money for the right to be the chosen Olympic sponsor in a particular category. In return, companies such as Coca-Cola enjoy a breadth of Olympic exposure in over 200 member countries and an IOC 'delivery system'. Because the IOC channels some of the sponsorship money to the various National Olympic Committees (NOCs), TOP members gain leverage in many countries. Sponsors can then represent themselves as the official 'X' of the IOC and each member country — for example, of the Australian Olympic Committee (AOC).

## LONG-TERM FINANCIAL SECURITY

TOP has provided the IOC with long-term financial security. Initially, TOP contracts were for four years, but some sponsors have signed up for eight and even 16 years. Coca-Cola and Channel 7 established relationships with the Olympic Movement in 1996 to cover the period until 2008. Long-term investment in the Olympics represents a form of partnership. This was one reason why there was a change in the TOP acronym, to 'The Olympic Partner'.

What are the returns for individual companies? How are Olympic ideals and values enhanced by such partnerships? TOP represents a convenient package; it brings together the rights of the IOC, all NOCs, all national Olympic teams, and the Summer and Winter Games organising committees. One benefit of this worldwide program is that companies can identify their logo both with the five rings and the emblems of the NOCs. The AOC, for instance, has an emblem that combines the rings with the Australian coat of arms. Sponsors also have rights of association with the national Olympic team, which is assembled three months before a Games, and with the Summer and Winter organising committees. A worldwide TOP sponsor, such as Coca-Cola, has an assured sponsorship relationship with SOCOG.

The TOP program is one of the most prestigious and exclusive worldwide sponsorship programs. It has become the prototype of desirable marketing initiatives in the realm of sports, culture and the arts. It is a 'one-stop shop' for global corporations that deal directly with the IOC, which then develops those wider connections. It is a proven program and is growing in stature.

## MANAGEMENT OF TOP

Before 1995 the IOC used agencies that went into the marketplace to broker individual 'deals' with sponsors. Since that time, the IOC has developed its own company, Meridian, to undertake its marketing initiatives. Meridian, which has offices in Lausanne, Atlanta, Sydney and a number of other cities, is the exclusive marketing agency for the IOC and the TOP program. A sponsor such as Coca-Cola will negotiate their TOP contract with Meridian. Meridian has the authority to construct and broker programs to suit the particular needs of each worldwide partner. While Meridian services these programs, it is not responsible for the end result of the partnership.

There has been spectacular growth in TOP revenue from TOP I to TOP IV, as demonstrated in Table 11.1. At the time of TOP I, when there were 157 NOCs, nine sponsors contributed US$97 million. From 1988 to 1994, TOP II brought in US$175 million; and by 1996, TOP III contributed over US$300 million. The expected revenue from TOP IV for the period up to 2000 will be over US$400 million contributed by 11 worldwide sponsors. The dramatic increase in the program reflects both the success of the TOP program and the spread of the Olympic Movement, which will involve more than 200 countries in the year 2000. The association of a brand with the Olympic symbol has become highly valued in the global market.

Table 11.1
Growth of TOP, 1988 to 2000

| | COMPLETION DATE | No. OF SPONSORS | No. OF NOCs | REVENUE (US$ MILLION) |
|---|---|---|---|---|
| TOP I | 1988 | 9 | 157 | 97 |
| TOP II | 1992 | 12 | 172 | 175 |
| TOP III | 1996 | 10 | 197 | >300 |
| TOP IV | 2000 | 11 | >200 | >400 |

Seven of the nine original worldwide partners are still involved in the TOP program. Samsung is the most recent addition to the program, having taken the position from Motorola for 'Wireless Communication Partner'. Coca-Cola and Kodak can trace their Olympic connection back to 1896. IBM is currently a partner but will cease to be after the 2000 Games. The implications of this decision and who will be IBM's likely replacement partner are still under consideration. Other partners include McDonald's, Fuji-Xerox, John Hancock, Visa, Panasonic, Sports Illustrated-Time Inc. and United Postal Service (UPS).

## OTHER TIERS OF SPONSORSHIP

Below the 11 worldwide partners are other tiers of sponsorship. Team Millennium Olympic Partners are corporations that only have regional access in the local or Australian market, in the case of those signed up for the Sydney Games. So while there is a worldwide category for sponsors, there is another set of local categories enabling companies like Ansett to become the local Olympic partner for air travel, Westpac to have the local Olympic rights for banking, and so forth. Team Millennium Olympic Partners have rights relating to the sponsorship of a particular Games. The marketing rights of Australian Team Olympic Partners are restricted to Australia, and the emblems or logos that they can use are those developed by the AOC and SOCOG. These partners do not have access to the five rings.

The Team Millennium Olympic Partners include AMP, Westpac, Telstra, BHP, Westfield, Ansett, Energy Australia, Holden, Channel 7, Swatch, News Limited, Pacific Dunlop and Fairfax. These companies have all made large financial contributions to the Olympics and hope that associative marketing and Olympic branding will enhance the image of the respective companies and materially add to their profits.

There have been some interesting marketing initiatives in regard to the Sydney Games. For the first time the media partnership has been shared between the Fairfax Group and the News Limited Group. While radio will be the primary responsibility of Radio 2UE, the ABC will also have some Olympic role. The involvement of Westfield, a retail chain, is another innovation that will present an Olympic face to the community. Westfield operates over 30 shopping centres Australia-wide and also has some operations in the United States. Westfield will set up Olympic kiosks in its shopping centres, which will become Olympic information distribution points. Given that over five million people visit Westfield nationally every week, this is a fascinating marketing innovation.

## THE EXTENT OF SPONSORSHIP

The size and scope of an Olympic sponsorship is tremendous. When an Olympic Partner signs on as a worldwide sponsor, the amount negotiated is in the vicinity of US$40–50 million. But that is only the entry fee. There are many other levels of costs involved to shore up the value of this investment in the Olympic property.

Further costs can include establishing arrangements with television broadcasters, such as NBC and Channel 7, to communicate the message of the firm's Olympic partnership. Investment also tends to develop within the arena of relationships with the United States Olympic Committee, International Sports Federations, National Sports Federations, hospitality and ticket packages, athlete appearances, on-site presence and product showcasing initiatives, public relations campaigns, athlete endorsements and local-market promotions. Consequently, it becomes evident that the real cost of an effective Olympic Games sponsorship is far greater than the initial entry amount.

## PROMOTION AT OLYMPIC VENUES

You will not see signage at Sydney's Olympic Stadium during the 2000 Games because Olympic venues are 'clean'. The IOC is working with its TOP sponsors to create a clean and very professional Games environment, and to avoid the exploitation of the venues as sites of crass commercialisation. The IOC does not allow signage at a venue, and there are strict rules about the size and display of any logo at a venue. It is permissible, for instance, for Samsung to have their logo on their product, a phone, and for the Coco-Cola logo to appear on cups. There are, however, restrictions and guidelines about any display on athletic shorts and tops. (Logos must be no larger than ten centimetres, for example.)

There are ongoing debates between sponsors and the Olympic Movement concerning the acceptable level of sponsorship display. Should the Swatch name — of the Swiss company which produces timing mechanisms — be displayed at an Olympic venue because the company name is already installed on the timer installed at the venue before the Games? And should there be any control of logos that appear on beverage containers carried on to the field by athletes?

Interestingly, the Paralympic Games are treated slightly differently, and signage is permitted at Paralympic venues.

## MARKETING ISSUES

Although the IOC has attempted to develop a global sponsorship market, nine of the 11 sponsors are US-based corporations. The other two are Samsung and Panasonic. For a company like Samsung, becoming a worldwide Olympic sponsor provides an opportunity to launch the company as a truly global leader in its field. The investment in Olympic sponsorship, and the consequent enhancement of its product, are thus designed to help the company achieve its long-term goals.

There are certain ethical issues raised by sponsorship in sport that have generated considerable debate. For example, should alcohol and tobacco be associated with sports sponsorship? Now that the IOC has adopted the environment as the third strand of Olympism, should it look more for clean and 'green' sponsors?

There is also the question of whether the established 11 sponsorship categories should be extended. Pacific-Dunlop and Reebok have recently signed as Team Millennium sponsors, giving them access only to the Australian marketplace. Their sponsorship category, apparel, is not yet classified as a worldwide category. Extending the range of categories may attract more sponsors, but it could diminish exclusivity and detract from TOP branding.

When considering a potential TOP sponsor, the IOC looks at both the calibre of the corporation and its brand. Because the Olympic brand is the most powerful brand in the world, it is important to maintain its image and status. Olympic property is currently restricted to multinational companies.

Category definition, and the avoidance of ambush marketing, are other current issues of concern. The IOC is keen that SOCOG and the city of Sydney deliver a 'clean city', uncluttered with ambush marketers, for the Olympic Games. The IOC wishes to avoid what happened in Atlanta, where there was much ambushing and 'commercial clutter' throughout the city, both in the Olympic precinct and around the venues.

## COSTS AND BENEFITS

What return does Coca-Cola or IBM get for its investment? How does the company measure the benefit of associative marketing? Why does TOP sponsorship continue to grow?

TOP partners are sophisticated. They would not invest so much in Olympic sponsorship if it wasn't working for them. Olympic property and branding have become highly prized. Although drug allegations and the bribery scandals of 1998 and 1999 have tarnished some of the Olympic 'gold', the Olympic Games still retain their credibility as a peak event for sport, and its logos and emblems, such as the five rings, have worldwide status and value.

Some companies, such as Coca-Cola, spend more money on sponsorship than advertising. While advertising sends a one-way message, sponsorship is part of a two-way communication. While the reception of a one-way message is uncertain, a two-way dialogue through Olympic sponsorship enables a company to develop partnerships that are deemed beneficial. Through associative marketing, consumers develop a rapport, or affinity, with the product. This finding has been confirmed through research.

Companies such as Coca-Cola have particular global needs that can be addressed by Olympic sponsorship. They are keen to construct strategic business-to-business relationships with key corporate players around the globe. Their Olympic partnership also helps them to develop business opportunities in new markets in places such as China and Thailand. Through their Olympic networks, companies such as Coca-Cola already have relationships with the NOCs in these countries and links to powerful business interests and key government figures. This may help them to gain access to these new markets.

The Olympic bribery scandal was a matter of great concern to TOP and Team Millennium partners. Because the scandal threatened to tarnish the Olympic brand, many sponsors were vocal in their call for the IOC to set its house in order.

## FURTHER READING

Huey, John (1996), 'The Atlanta Games: How Atlanta stole the Olympics', *Fortune Magazine*, 22 June, pp 24–40.

IOC, *Olympic Marketing Matters: The Olympic Marketing Newsletter*, Issue 1, Summer 1993–Issue 13, Summer 1998.

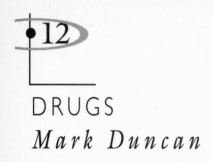

# DRUGS
## *Mark Duncan*

The public want and expect a drug-free Olympics. It is their belief that most athletes do not abuse performance-enhancing agents, but that if they do, the drug testing programs integral to the Games will catch all the offenders. Certainly the official view of the International Olympic Committee (IOC) is consistent with this philosophy, as described by Juan Antonio Samaranch, IOC president:

> Doping is cheating. Doping is akin to death. Death physiologically, by profoundly altering, sometimes irreversibly, normal processes through unjustified manipulations. Death physically, as certain tragic cases in recent years have shown. But also death spiritually and intellectually, by agreeing to cheat and conceal one's capabilities, by recognising one's incapacity or unwillingness to accept oneself, or to transcend one's limits. And finally, death morally, by excluding oneself de facto from the rules of conduct required by all human society.[1]

Drug testing began in 1972 at the Munich Olympics, and has continued ever since. The IOC Medical Commission, founded in 1967, has established a long list of prohibited agents, a Medical Code detailing the procedures for drug testing, and has accredited specific laboratories worldwide to monitor drug abuse by athletes. All this has been undertaken at considerable cost. The IOC justifies this effort, claiming two objectives: to ensure fair competition (that is, by establishing a level playing field), and to protect the health of the athletes.

Some, however, are cynical of the whole exercise, the motives of the IOC and the effectiveness of the program:

Since his accession in 1980, Juan Antonio Samaranc's campaign to minimise the extent of doping in sport has become an art form. He dissembles and makes preposterous claims believed by few in sport, and gets away with it. He must do this to preserve the IOC's luxury lifestyle. If the public ever catches on to how dirty elite sport has become, the sponsors and TV networks will pull the plug on the billions they pay the IOC for a clean, moral sport.[2]

This view has been echoed by Geoffrey Crowley and Martha Brent in *Newsweek* in 1996:

No-one knows just how many athletes use banned substances, but experts use words like epidemic to describe the problem. Says Olympics chronicler Gary Allison: 'Drugs are the single biggest threat to the Games'.[3]

Dr Robert Voy, director of drug testing for the US Olympic Committee, added in 1997 that 'athletes are a walking laboratory, and the Olympics have become a proving ground for scientists, chemists and unethical doctors'.[4]

It is reasonable, if not critical, to question just how effective this initiative has been. Are the Olympics drug-free and, if not, are the policies and procedures that are in place effective in catching the cheats? Here I examine the history of performance-enhancing drug abuse, the policies and approaches in place to prevent drug abuse, and, just as importantly, I assess the effectiveness of these programs.

## HISTORY OF DRUG ABUSE IN COMPETITIVE SPORTS

Drugs have been used (or abused) by athletes for as long as there has been competitive sport. Early drug use included agents such as strychnine, caffeine, ephedrine and cocaine (from coca leaf). In 1865, during the canal races in Amsterdam, it is alleged that some competitors were taking performance-enhancing agents. By 1886, there were claims that coaches were administering their cyclists a mixture of heroin and cocaine — commonly known as a speedball — to enhance their performance. The first reported death associated with drug abuse came in 1886 when an English cyclist died during the Bordeaux to Paris race. By the end of the 19th century, drug-taking in sport was rife, and a plethora of agents was being abused including caffeine, alcohol, nitroglycerine, digitalis, cocaine, ether, heroin, opium and strychnine.

The skilful application of performance-enhancing drugs — now both an art and science — continued unabated into the 20th century. Amphetamines became popular agents, and there were several reported deaths associated with their use, notably among cyclists. By the 1950s, anabolic steroids began to appear on the scene. These agents had a pronounced impact in the power sports, particularly weight-lifting. In the 1952 Helsinki Olympics, the USSR weight-lifting team, competing for their first time, won a swag of medals, and it was widely believed that their remarkable performances were a consequence of steroid abuse.[5] As soon as new drugs were developed, either for veterinary or human use, they made their way into sports, regardless of the associated dangers. Even today, competitive athletes appear to be prepared to risk their health — even their lives — to increase their chance of winning.[6] Today's athletes have a wide range of agents available to them that may enhance their performance, as illustrated in Table 12.1. Presently, of particular importance is the class of peptide hormones and glycoproteins, including human growth hormone (hGH) and erythropoietin (EPO), as discussed later in this chapter.

## THE IOC AND ATTEMPTS TO ELIMINATE DRUG ABUSE

To counter the problems introduced by these agents, the Medical Commission has defined, in detail, what is prohibited, how samples should be collected and the procedures for testing. The IOC declares that doping contravenes the ethics of sport and medicine and specifies banned agents under five pharmacological classes: stimulants, narcotics, anabolic agents, diuretics, and peptide hormones and their analogues. In addition, the use of various procedures (blood doping, and pharmacological, chemical and physical manipulation) is prohibited. There is also a subset of agents that are subject to restriction under specified conditions.[7] Other agents that have been employed to enhance performance include bicarbonate (increased anaerobic performance in track events in the 200–800 metres range), and caffeine (increased aerobic performance in distance running, swimming and cycling events).

To assist in enforcing this policy, the IOC reserves the right to collect urine from competing athletes, under carefully controlled conditions, and to test this for the presence of banned agents.[8] Any competitor who refuses to submit to testing, or is found guilty of doping, can be excluded from the current and future Olympic Games.[9]

This elaborate exercise is generally regarded as successful, and the several million-dollar price tag as appropriate. To attest to the success of the program, the IOC points to the fact that over 50 athletes have been found guilty of doping since the program began in 1972.[10] Of special significance is the fact that four medallists were stripped of their awards at the Seoul Olympics.[11] However, the IOC drug testing initiative has its detractors. Some have even gone so far as to suggest that over the 25 years since its introduction of testing, the abuse of performance-enhancing drugs has become more widespread than ever (see Table 12.2).

Table 12.1
Some performance-enhancing drugs and their actions

| AGENT | ACTION | SPORTS WHERE DRUG IS USED |
| --- | --- | --- |
| Diuretics | Promote the flow of urine and hence result in short-term weight loss. Can also be used to mask the presence of other drugs by diluting the urine. | Sports with strict body weight classifications including weight-lifting, rowing and boxing. |
| Steroid hormones | Increase muscle size and strength, aid in repair and enhance aggression. | All strength-related events. |
| Stimulants | Agents such as amphetamines, ephedrine and cocaine can enhance performance on the day by sharpening reflexes and increasing alertness. These agents also mask fatigue. A wide array of events, including individual and team events. Blockers reduce tremor and slow the heartbeat. | Archery and shooting. |
| Agonists | Agents such as clenbuterol and salbutamol can be administered orally. They improve muscular strength and muscle mass. | Sports involving strength. |
| Growth hormone hGH | Encourages the growth of muscle and aids in the reduction of body fat. Increases metabolic rate. | Sprinting, jumping and strength-related events. |
| Erythropoietin (EPO) | Stimulates the formation of red blood cells. | Endurance events, particularly cycling. |
| IGF-1 | Promotes muscle growth. | Sprinting, jumping and strength-related events. |
| Blood doping | Blood, or packed red blood cells, are collected earlier and then returned to the athlete immediately prior to competition. This enhances the oxygen-carrying capacity of the blood. | Cycling and other endurance events. |
| Growth inhibitors (brake drugs) | Employed to inhibit the growth of an individual at the time of puberty. | Women's gymnastics. |

Table 12.2
Positive tests reported at the Summer Olympics* since testing began

| VENUE | YEAR | POSITIVES |
|---|---|---|
| Munich | 1972 | 7 |
| Montreal | 1976 | 11 |
| Moscow | 1980 | 0 |
| Los Angeles | 1984 | 12 |
| Seoul | 1988 | 10 |
| Barcelona | 1992 | 5 |
| Atlanta | 1996 | 2 |
| Total | | 47 |

*Testing is also undertaken for the Winter Olympics, but the number of positives reported has traditionally been very low.

## IS TESTING EFFECTIVE?

While some argue that the positive results are a clear indication of the success of the program, it may simply be that what we catch is only a small proportion of all those athletes who actively abuse agents. In a less than perfect environment there is, of course, no relationship between the number of athletes testing positive and the extent of drug abuse. We are left to question whether there is a way around the system. Can athletes abuse banned agents without getting caught?

The simple answer is 'yes'. For many reasons the system is less than foolproof — in fact, it might be more appropriate to suggest that only the foolish get caught. Many athletes and officials believe that 'To be caught is not easy; it only happens when an athlete is either incredibly sloppy, incredibly stupid, or both.'[12]

While some athletes have gone to enormous lengths to avoid submission of their urine for testing,[13] others have challenged test results and sampling protocols in the courts.[14] However, avoiding detection need not be so complicated. These instances relate to only a small proportion of athletes; the majority of those employing performance-enhancing agents are unlikely to be detected.

Abused agents can be divided into two categories: those that occur endogenously in humans, and those that don't. For example, testosterone is a normal constituent of human plasma (and urine). To detect testosterone in urine is hardly surprising; it is always there, both in males and females. By contrast, stanazolol, a synthetic veterinary steroid, is a product of laboratory synthesis; it is not present in humans unless administered exogenously.[15] Only markedly elevated testosterone levels in urine raise suspicion;[16] by contrast, even a trace of stanazolol is an issue. Athletes would therefore be well-advised to avoid exogenous agents, and wherever possible, elect to use compounds that are always present, albeit at lower levels. By doing so, it becomes very difficult to establish unambiguously that drug doping has occurred.

Even if synthetic steroids are employed for one reason or another, they do not remain in the circulation indefinitely. Agents with a short biological half-life may only be detectable in urine for a day or so. Furthermore, if the administered dose is given at a low dose — as is the case for a potent agent — then the 'time window' during which the drug is detectable is reduced even further. Athletes can therefore abuse some synthetic steroids outside of competition as long as they are not subjected to random testing during that narrow time window. A well-advised athlete, mindful of issues such as half-life, dose and detection limits for the analytical methods, can eliminate the risk of testing positive in almost all instances.

Testing is even more difficult for what is likely to be the most widely abused class of performance-enhancing drugs: the peptide hormones. Both human growth hormone (hGH) and erthyropoietin are present in all humans, all of the time. At normal circulating levels, these compounds have important biological functions; at increased levels, they become pharmacological agents (that is, they act as drugs). In recognition of this, the IOC has banned the exogenous administration of these agents; however, policing that ban is difficult, if not impossible.

Growth hormone has a short half-life — it disappears from the circulation within hours — so only immediately after administration are blood levels elevated. Those that abuse hGH for its metabolic actions — including decreased body fat storage and increased muscle mass — reap the benefits following long-term use and without any fear of detection. At present, there is no way to distinguish between the hGH produced by the pituitary gland and that administered by injection.[17] The issue is further complicated because hGH disappears rapidly regardless of its source, and our own hGH supply is secreted in a pulsatile manner, with 10–15 spurts of hGH released throughout a 24-hour period. Consequently, our own circulating hGH levels are subject to pronounced fluctuations, making it difficult to assign significance to a single elevated level. To add further to the problem, only urine samples can be collected according to the IOC guidelines, but only a fraction of circulating hGH is ever excreted in the urine. Together, these factors conspire to make it almost impossible to detect hGH abuse by the athlete.

The extent of hGH abuse among competitive athletes is

unknown: the agent is banned, so athletes or coaches are unlikely to admit to its use. However, there is evidence that the problem is widespread, and as long as it offers benefits and cannot be detected, there is the likelihood it will continue to be abused. For example, on 8 January 1998, when the Chinese swimming team arrived in Sydney en route to Perth to compete in the World Swimming Championships, one team member was found to possess 13 vials of hGH in a Thermos flask.[18] Under Schedule 8 of the Customs (Prohibited Imports) Regulation, importation of hGH is prohibited unless prior permission is granted by the Department of Human Services and Health (that is, under Regulation 5H). Consequently, the supply was seized. There is no evidence or finding as to why hGH was imported by the Chinese swimmer in this case, so it is not possible to say why it was imported. However, if an individual was deputed to import hGH on behalf of team members, some Chinese swimmers could have used hGH right up to competition. Because a urine test for hGH is not performed — it is ineffectual — possession of hGH by the athlete(s), as was the case in this instance, rather than detection in their urine, is probably the only indication we have of the extent of hGH abuse.

## CONSEQUENCES AND OUTCOMES

Bans are only effective when tests are available to detect the prohibited agent(s), but present drug testing methods are hopelessly behind the play. Few dispute that it would be better if potentially harmful agents were not employed in competitive sports, but the rewards for winning — financial and otherwise — serve as powerful incentives to all involved to win at all costs. Potentially dangerous agents are employed if there is any possibility that they offer the athlete a competitive advantage in their chosen sport; the only disincentive to their use is the risk of being caught. Consequently, Olympic sport is not drug-free and is unlikely to be so in the foreseeable future.[19] And when considering drug use, we should appreciate that the problem is not restricted to just a few unscrupulous individuals or countries, contrary to popular belief. While we point the finger accusingly at China, Russia and, in the past, East Germany, the reality is that the problem is more widespread. The late Manfred Donike, a major player in the IOC drug testing initiative right up to his untimely death a few years ago, saw it this way: 'The Russians know a few drugs, the Eastern Germans are much more sophisticated, but the Americans are the world champions of doping.'[20]

# CONCLUSIONS

Finally, some question the commitment of the IOC itself in this endeavour. There is solid evidence to suggest that the officials have not laid bare the true extent of the problem. Positive test results were not disclosed from the Los Angeles Games, and documents detailing these finding were shredded. Similarly, scandals taint the testing and reporting efforts for the Games in Moscow, Seoul, Barcelona and Atlanta. Throughout all this, however, the IOC persists with the claim that all is well and that their testing has led to dope-free sport. Those close to the IOC must ensure it is determined and consistent in its approach to eliminating drug use, but their determination is sometimes questionable at best. As long as we continue to reward sporting achievement so handsomely, athletes, in conjunction with skilled trainers, pharmacologists and clinicians, will be tempted to employ agents that may make the difference between winning and losing.

Doping and manipulating youth is a barely disguised wish of some sports officials around the world. The only solutions to this culture are enhanced laws and the opposition of parents and athletes. Laboratory-based testing can play a part in detecting some instances of drug abuse, but skilful selection of the agent, the dose and the dosing regimen, will make it impossible to catch the adroit user.

# FURTHER READING

Aamo, T. O. and Guldberg, H. C. (1995), 'The doping rules: A set of rules in good Olympic spirit?' (see comments), *Tidsskr Nor Laegeforen*, vol. 115, pp 2120–5.

Bowers, L. D. (1998), 'Athletic drug testing', *Clinical Sports Medicine*, vol. 17, pp 299–318.

Catlin, D. H. and Murray, T. H. (1996), 'Performance-enhancing drugs, fair competition, and Olympic sport' (see comments), JAMA, vol. 276, pp 231–7.

Clarkson, P. M. and Thompson, H. S. (1997), 'Drugs and sport: Research findings and limitations', *Sports Medicine*, vol. 24, pp 366 -84.

Fuller, J. R. and LaFountain, M. J. (1987), 'Performance-enhancing drugs in sport: A different form of drug abuse', *Adolescence*, vol. 22, pp 969-76.

Hardy, K. J., McNeil, J. J. and Capes, A. G. (1997), 'Drug doping in senior Australian Rules football: A survey for frequency', *British Journal of Sports Medicine*, vol. 31, pp 126-8.

Kleiner, S. M. (1991), 'Performance-enhancing aids in sport: Health consequences and nutritional alternatives', *Journal of American College Nutrition*, vol. 10, pp 163–76.

Nocelli, L., Kamber, M., Francois, Y., Gmel, G. and Marti, B. (1998), 'Discordant public perception of doping in elite versus recreational sport in Switzerland', *Clinical Journal of Sport Medicine*, vol. 8, pp 195–200.

Radford, P. F. (1990), 'Recent developments in drug abuse and doping control in sport', *Journal of the Royal College of Surgeons Edinburgh*, vol. 35, pp S2–6.

# TOURISM
*Ray Spurr*

This chapter raises some basic but important questions about the impact of the 2000 Olympic Games on the Australian tourism industry and, through this, on the economy as a whole. Will the Olympics lead to an increase in tourism? If so, will it be before, during or after the Games? What will be the extent of any tourist increase? How significant is this Olympic effect for the tourism industry? Will Olympic tourism have any real effect on the Australian economy? How significant are the tourism impacts relative to the overall impact of the Olympics?

## ECONOMIC IMPACT OF THE OLYMPICS

The NSW Treasury released a new report on the 'Economic Impact of the Sydney Olympic Games' (the NSW Report) in November 1997.[1] The paper, produced in collaboration with the Centre for Regional Economic Analysis of the University of Tasmania, is the first major attempt to analyse the likely economic impact of the Sydney Olympics since the so-called KPMG Report,[2] which was prepared for the Sydney Olympics 2000 Bid Limited in 1993. The new report provided an opportunity to revisit the questions of the likely impact of the Olympics on tourism and of tourism on the economics of the Olympics.

These questions are of particular interest in the light of arguments put forward by Leiper and Hall, Leiper, and Bailey[3] which question the conventional wisdom that the Olympics will provide a strong boost for inbound tourism to Australia. The contrary view — encapsulated in Bailey's phrase 'Big Event Blues' — is that while significant events such as the Olympics may bring in new travellers, much of the existing travel business, including holiday-makers and business travellers, will be diverted elsewhere. This loss of visitors occurs because people assume that there will be disruption to normal travel activity and prices.

Major events are also seen as encouraging outbound travel by residents who are disinterested in, or who wish to avoid disruption caused by, the event and by those attracted by cheaper air fares on the return legs of heavily booked inbound flights. Dangers of post-event tourism downturns are also identified. Sometimes the loss of visitor expenditure may be carried, at least in part, by neighbouring regions or other parts of the country as much as the host city itself. The experience from previous Summer Olympics, including Los Angeles, Barcelona and Atlanta, has provided evidence that major events are likely to have these negative impacts on tourism. Other events, such as the America's Cup in Fremantle in 1987 and the Brisbane Expo in 1988, have also been cited to support this argument.

The NSW Report is disappointing because it throws little light on this debate about the likely tourism effects of the Games. The concerns expressed by Leiper, Hall and Bailey appear to have not been properly considered; they were discarded by the authors without comment in the final version of the report. In justifying the use of a 20 per cent adjustment to the central international tourism estimates for its sensitivity analysis, the report states that, while this was 'much less than the degree of variability between some previous forecasts', it 'would seem appropriate in light of a much higher degree of conformity among recent forecasts'.[4] The more 'recent forecasts' were not identified.

Essentially the NSW Report finds fairly similar overall economic impacts for the 2000 Olympics to those identified in the KPMG Report, although the methodology adopted differs significantly. The NSW Report uses a CGE-type modelling approach rather than the simpler input–output modelling used in the KPMG study. The NSW Report's 'Central Scenario' generates total additions to NSW and national GDP of some $6 billion over the period 1994/95 to 2005/06 (as against $6.3 to $8.2 billion for the KPMG scenarios).

For those interested in the tourism impacts of the Games, this raises a number of obvious questions. How robust are the tourism estimates adopted to underpin the report? How important are they to the overall outcome of the report and its estimated $6 to $6.5 billion addition to GDP? Further, in view of the KPMG claim that 'winning the Olympics offers Australia a major marketing vehicle to significantly increase international tourism',[5] it is worth asking how significant will the impact of hosting the Olympics be for Australia's tourism industry.

## METHODOLOGY

Because of the integrated nature of the analysis in both the NSW and KPMG reports, it is difficult to separate out what precise proportion of the estimated overall economic impact is attributable to tourism, as distinct from other causes. However, we do get a reasonably clear picture from this assessment. The KPMG Report, for example, concludes that: 'By far the most important impact associated with the Olympics is the "induced visitor" effect.'[6] It appears that tourism probably accounts for around 50–60 per cent of their total projected economic benefit to Australia from hosting the Olympics (that is, in the range of $3.2 to $5 billion over the period 1991 to 2004).

The report looked at two broad types of tourist impacts: additional visitors coming specifically to attend the Olympics (including officials, athletes, media and spectators), and visitors 'induced' to visit Australia as a result of increased publicity associated with the hosting of the Olympics. Visitors induced to come to Australia were assumed to be spread throughout the period from 1994 to 2004. Only visitors from outside Australia were included in this estimate. Visitors who, it was presumed, would come to Australia anyway, but who might alter the timing of their visit to coincide with Olympic-related activities, were excluded. Over the full 11-year period from 1994 to 2004 the report's 'Most Likely' estimate for induced tourism, using Bureau of Tourism Research Forecasts (BTR) as the base estimate plus Olympic-related visits, was 1.2 million.

The NSW Report has direct expenditure by an estimated additional 2.3 million international tourists induced to visit Australia as a result of hosting the Olympics (using Australian Tourism Commission [ATC] Targets as the base estimate) at $4.3 billion. It seems likely that the NSW methodology gives a lower estimate of the total economic impact of this spending than does the KPMG study — given the different methodologies employed; but clearly, spending by induced international tourists remains one of the key direct contributors to the NSW Report's outcomes. If it were to account for between 40 and 50 per cent of the overall outcome, then tourism would be driving $2.5 to $3 billion of the estimated economic impact from the Olympics.

The NSW Report also included a sensitivity analysis to examine what the main causes are of the differences between its 'Central' and 'Constrained Supply' scenarios. For this purpose, a 20 per cent change in the forecast for induced international tourism was adopted. The change in induced tourism accounted for only one-quarter of the difference in overall economic impact of the Games between the two scenarios. From this, the NSW Report concluded that the induced tourism impacts, while important, are less important than macroeconomic considerations (which drove most of the remainder of the difference).

However, the macroeconomic influences referred to in the NSW Report only begin to take effect in response to direct effects. And probably at least 40 per cent of the direct effects come from the estimated expenditure from induced tourism. (Other important sources of impact include construction in the pre-Games period, sale of TV rights, and assumed productivity gains in the post-Games period.)

The conclusions of the sensitivity analysis thus become questionable, if the potential forecast error in estimating likely induced tourism flows has been set too low at plus or minus 0.2 per cent. Is this likely? There are good reasons why we might be sceptical of the reliability of the tourism estimates and of whether a 0.2 per cent margin of forecast error, as adopted for the sensitivity analysis, is sufficient.

## HOW RELIABLE ARE THESE ESTIMATES?

The NSW Report uses the same basic methodology for estimating induced tourism as that used in the previous KPMG Report. This begins with base forecasts for each year of the period for what international tourism inflow would occur in the absence of the Olympics being held in Sydney. These figures are then adjusted upward by a percentage that is assumed to reflect the Olympic influence.

Where KPMG used BTR forecasts from 1991 for its 'Most Likely' scenario and the ATC Targets of the time for its 'Optimistic' scenario, the NSW Report uses the ATC Targets only (on the grounds that these had performed more reliably for the 1994 and 1995 years). It is not clear why the now more widely accepted Tourism Forecasting Council (TFC) projections were not adopted.

While the base forecast methodology can be said to have some degree of 'science' (econometric forecasting techniques in the case of the BTR base used by KPMG and 'marketing' projections or 'targets' for the ATC ones used in the NSW Report) on its side, it is not at all clear that this can be said of the more important element, the percentage adjustment used to derive the Olympics-induced tourism effect.

The methodology which KPMG used for estimating how many tourists would be 'induced' to come to Australia on top of these pre-Olympics base forecasts appears to have simply replicated earlier work for Melbourne's 1996 bid which was itself based on estimates of the impact of the Seoul Olympics on tourism to Korea. There is nothing in either report to indicate that the basis of the Melbourne bid figures was put to any serious re-examination.

Yet the parallels between the Sydney and Seoul Olympics must be regarded as at best tenuous, and there is little evidence of anything more than a temporary 'blip' on the longer-term trend of Korean tourist arrivals.[7] This raises fairly fundamental questions about the basis of the KPMG and NSW report tourism estimates.

If the basis for the estimates used in these reports to forecast likely induced tourism numbers, and hence expenditures, is in doubt, then, given the very significant role that induced tourism plays in the calculation of the economic impacts of the Sydney Olympics, these estimates are themselves open to considerable question. And even the sensitivity analysis used in the NSW Report becomes questionable if there is an inadequate underlying framework for their tourism estimates and hence for the adoption of a 20 per cent variation from the central tourism estimate.

These apparent deficiencies highlight the absence of any discussion in the official reports of why concerns about the impact on tourism flows of displacement effects, such as those expressed by Hall, Leiper and Bailey, have not been considered valid. Yet the implications of this judgment are substantial, given that these writers cite evidence from various past hallmark events to suggest that displacement effects might be sufficient to make the net effect of the Olympics on tourism to Sydney (and Australia) negative.

## ARE THE PROJECTED TOURISM IMPACTS SIGNIFICANT?

Putting this issue to one side for a moment, it is worth also looking at another related issue, the claim made in the KPMG Report that the Games will 'significantly increase international tourism'.[8]

The NSW Report separates travellers whose visit occurs specifically in relation to the Olympic Games from tourists induced to visit Australia as a result of having their awareness of Australia raised through media and other attention. It identifies 84 000 Games-related visitors in the year 2000 (of which 36 000 are Olympic Family, media, sponsors, and athletes and officials) plus a further 20 400 pre-Games 'Olympics-related visitors' per annum spread over the period 1994/95 to 2000. Total expenditure for all of these 245 000 specifically 'Games-related' visitors is estimated at just under $150 million. Clearly, these figures for estimated net additional arrivals coming specifically in relation to the Games themselves is of little consequence in the context of long-term forecasts of six million tourist arrivals for the year 2000.

We need to look at the estimates for 'induced' tourism to test the assertion of 'significant' impacts. The KPMG Report's 'Most Likely' estimate was for 1.2 million international arrivals during 1994 to 2004 (see above). The NSW Report had 2.3 million arrivals, with an estimated $4 billion in additional tourist expenditure over the 11-year period as flowing from this.

At first glance this appears a very significant figure and, clearly, some parts of the tourism industry will benefit substantially if the estimates prove justified. The Meetings and Conventions sector, already prospering, is an obvious case in point. But put in context, the $4 billion in additional tourism expenditure amounts to less than 2 per cent of total projected tourism export earnings over the period. With TFC's projections, at the time the NSW Report was prepared, of some 9 per cent annual growth in tourist arrivals, this level of impact looks marginal at best and well within the range of forecasting error. A minimal, but sustained, change in the overall growth rate of, say, 0.2 per cent in either direction would, over the 11-year period, have had a greater impact than the KPMG estimate for the total induced tourism effect of the Olympics!

The TFC has already revised down its forecasts as a result of the Asian currency crisis and is likely to reduce them again shortly. The effect of these adjustments, however, would be to revise the base for the NSW and KPMG estimates downwards, and hence their tourism impact estimates generally, assuming that they continue to use the same methodology as previously.

## LONGER-TERM IMPACTS

This example of how sensitive international tourist expenditure is to a relatively small change in the underlying growth trend makes it interesting to explore the potential for the Olympics to influence longer-term tourism revenues.

As noted earlier, there appears to be little evidence that hallmark events have lasting effects on tourist arrivals. Some of the precedents have shown negative growth in even the Olympic year itself (Los Angeles) or little discernible change from existing growth trends (Seoul). Post-event years have often suffered significant tourism declines and a severe and financially debilitating oversupply of newly constructed infrastructure. This was the case in Fremantle after the America's Cup in 1987 and in Australian hotels following the Bicentennial and the Brisbane Expo year in 1988. That the 'promotion' impact of an event should be short-lived is what we might expect given that marketing generally has time limited effects unless repeatedly reinforced.

## BARCELONA — AN EXCEPTION?

However, Barcelona may be an exception. While there is little statistical evidence of a positive impact from the Barcelona Olympics on tourism to Spain as a whole, there is evidence that the tourism industry of Barcelona itself has benefited greatly. While the post-Games year of 1993 was mixed, with visitor arrivals up but commercial nights and airport arrivals down, it is difficult to separate this from the effects of 1993 being a recession year in Europe. Certainly, since 1993, all tourism indicators have steadily improved.[9]

Barcelona's tourism success is attributed to a combination of factors: media coverage during the Olympics; Olympics-related investment in Barcelona's waterfront precinct, which has made the city more attractive to visitors; improved accommodation infrastructure; and a major boost to the confidence and entrepreneurship of Barcelona's tourist industry. Some or all of these factors contributed to putting Barcelona, for the first time, on the list of city short-break destinations for European holiday-makers.

## WILL AUSTRALIA BE A SPECIAL CASE?

Sydney is unlikely to become a 'city break' destination for international tourists in the way that Barcelona has. The long-haul nature of travel to Australia, and the geographic spread of its attractions, means that Sydney will probably remain a gateway for visits to Australia as a whole. Very probably, then, the Barcelona precedent will work for Australia as a whole or not at all.

The sale of television rights for the 2000 Olympics incorporated arrangements for tourism-related promotion of Sydney not only during the Games but also in the years leading up to them. Television coverage by NBC in the United States promoted Sydney during the recently completed US Super Bowl. This kind of advertising at the high end of advertising cost, and penetration in the United States would be far beyond the budget of normal Australian tourism promotion.

In the year 2000 itself, media coverage is expected to reach a worldwide viewing audience of some four billion people. Following the pattern of recent major sporting event television coverage, it will include promotion of Sydney and Australia at frequent intervals within the coverage. Events such as the yachting on Sydney Harbour, the marathon, which will cross the Sydney Harbour Bridge, the triathlon, which will begin at the harbour, and a wide range of other outdoor events, will showcase an exceptionally beautiful city to an unprecedented international television audience.

In contrast to major tourism countries like Spain (which receives over 40 million tourists annually) or very well known cities like Los Angeles and Rome, Sydney and Australia are relatively little known to much of this media audience. This suggests the possibility of a disproportionately large impact on Australia's international profile. Cities like Atlanta and Seoul, on the other hand, may have lacked the intrinsic visual and tourist attractiveness of Sydney. It could just be that Sydney has what it takes to be, like Barcelona, another exception.

## CONCLUSIONS

If the methodology and the data used in the KPMG and the NSW Treasury reports to estimate the tourism impacts of the Olympics is unsatisfactory, then is there a better approach to the problem? The answer may well be no. There is probably scope to improve those projections by addressing some of what appear to be significant flaws in the approach referred to above. But it is difficult to see how the television coverage impacts on longer-term awareness of Australia might be effectively modelled.

The closest parallel on which we do have some information is probably the ATC's international marketing programs, which largely target generic promotion of Australia through image and awareness advertising. Even here there remains considerable uncertainty about the impact of promotion on tourist arrivals and expenditure, certainly in terms of quantifiable measurement. A 1991 Evaluation Report on the ATC's marketing and promotion included an attempt to measure returns from international expenditure through a multi-variable regression analysis-based approach.[10] The 1991 study found a return on each dollar of promotion spending of $30. A report by Access Economics duplicated some aspects of that work in 1997 and produced a 10:1 result.

These studies indicate gross expenditure increases rather than net economic returns and therefore do not tell us the return on public sector investment in tourism promotion. There is also no consensus on their reliability. But it would be surprising in the extreme if generic advertising of the kind carried out by the ATC did not play a significant role in promoting awareness and subsequent travel to Australia by international tourists. The promotional reach of the television coverage that Australia is likely to experience over the Olympics-related period would seem to involve a quantum leap over anything we have experienced before.

If it is possible to use the Olympics to achieve any degree of upward shift in the base for our longer-term rate of growth in international tourist arrivals, or in the growth rate itself, that could be sustained into the years following the 2000 Olympics, then the economic benefits from this would seem likely to be substantially greater than those being measured in studies such as the KPMG and NSW Treasury reports as flowing more directly from the Olympics.

The above implies a very different outcome from that perceived by Hall, Leiper and Bailey and the 'Big Event Blues' scenarios. However, it does accord more closely with the instincts of most tourism marketing practitioners in Australia. Having said that, the precedents provided by past Olympics and hallmark events suggest that excessive optimism among tourism marketing professionals may not be an uncommon phenomenon.

However, the above discussion does attempt to identify an alternative scenario for further research on prospective tourism impacts of the Olympics — and one that is of some importance. If massive worldwide television coverage of Australia of the kind that has already begun, and that will peak in September 2000, does not have a very significant impact on travel to Australia, then we would need to substantially re-evaluate the expenditure of close to $200 million per annum by the federal and state governments, along with financial support by industry, on this kind of generic destination advertising. If, on the other hand, the promotional value of the Olympics could be to shift the growth curve upward for Australia, then thought should be given now to how such a result can be sustained into the post-Olympic period.

This chapter has suggested that there has been insufficient research on the impact of tourism before, during and after the 2000 Games. Consequently, views on the likely tourist benefits of staging the Games vary remarkably from the extremely optimistic to the decidedly pessimistic. Any plans for Olympic tourism will have limited benefit if they are not based on accurate tourist forecasting.

## FURTHER READING

Bailey, M, Travel and Business Analyst, Hong Kong; see, for example, N. Cockerell (1997), 'Big Event Blues', *Issues & Trends*, Pacific Asia Travel Association, San Francisco, March.

Carmody, G. (1993), *Comparison of Sydney with Seoul 1988*, Access Economics, Canberra.

KPMG Peat Marwick in association with the Centre for South Australian Olympic Studies (1993), *Sydney Olympics 2000: Economic Impact Studies*.

Leiper, N. (1997), 'A Town Like Elis? The Olympics: Impact on tourism in Sydney', *Proceedings of the Australian Tourism & Hospitality Research Conference*, Sydney, 6–9 July.

Leiper, N. and Hall, M. (1993), 'The 2000 Olympics and Australia's tourism industries', Paper for House of Representatives Committee.

New South Wales Treasury (1997), *Research and Information Paper: The Economic Impact of the Sydney Olympic Games?*, produced in collaboration with the Centre for Regional Economic Analysis the University of Tasmania, November.

Rowe, D. and Lawrence, G. (eds) (1998), *Tourism, Leisure, Sport: Critical Perspectives*, Hodder Education, Sydney.

# PART 4

## THE OTHER GAMES

# 14

# THE CULTURAL OLYMPIAD

*Debra Good*

Art and sport may seem an odd mix, but their combination is an essential component of Baron Pierre de Coubertin's original vision of Olympism, which to this day is etched in the International Olympic Committee's charter of 'fundamental principles': 'Olympism is a philosophy of life, exalting and combining in a balanced whole the qualities of body, will and mind.' The *Olympic Charter* states: 'Blending sport with culture and education, Olympism seeks to create a way of life based on the joy found in effort, the educational value of good example and respect for universal fundamental ethical principles.'

From 1912 in Stockholm to 1948 in London, artists competed at Olympic Games in much the same way as sporting Games held during this period. One hundred and forty-five medals were awarded to the winners and placegetters in Olympic arts competitions. At the 1912 Games, Coubertin himself won a gold medal in poetry for his poem *Ode to Sport,* written under the pseudonym of George Hohrod and M. Eschbach.

After an extensive debate these competitions were replaced with exhibitions, beginning informally in Helsinki in 1952 and officially in Melbourne in 1956. In 1960, Rome's art program focused on the historical relationship between sport and art; in 1964, Tokyo presented traditional Japanese art; Los Angeles hosted the first international festival in 1984; and the opulent 1992 Barcelona Olympics celebrated the city's rich cultural heritage. This history has either been ignored or misrepresented in the multitude of Olympic fact books and media reports. Even *Time* magazine — a sponsor of the 1984 Cultural Olympiad at Los Angeles — claimed that, although he was 'the greatest champion in Olympic history', Coubertin 'won no medals'.

When Los Angeles' Cultural Olympiad director, Robert Fitzpatrick, was approached for the job, his first thought was: 'If a culturally aware person such as myself did not know that the Olympic Games had a cultural component, how aware would other people be? And how receptive? Wouldn't the artistic program still be overshadowed by the sports?'

In 1986, British Olympic scholar Donald Masterson argued that 'the media have ignored them [the Olympic arts programs] and the general public — even the competing athletes — have been unaware of them'. Ten years later at the Atlanta Olympics, Malcolm Jones wrote in *Newsweek*: 'Every host city whips up a cultural sideshow to accompany the Games and then, well, do you remember those remarkable arts offerings in Seoul, in Los Angeles, Barcelona? Neither does anyone else, but on they roll.'

Since the first of the arts competitions held in 1912, the structure of local and international arts communities has changed enormously. With the growth in arts competitions, public and private funding, festivals and management, there has been an accompanying growth in the number of arts companies internationally. At the same time, changes to the rules and structure of the International Olympic Committee (IOC) have further alienated the arts component of the Games from the host arts communities.

The Olympic Arts have been excluded from the IOC's marketing and sponsorship developments and, in combination with the lack of commitment of the National Organising Committees (NOCs), they have been completely overlooked. This is also due in part to the lack of a representative group, equivalent to the International Federations which advance the interests of individual sports. All of which leads to the inevitable question: Is there a continued role for the arts in the Olympic Games?

## HISTORY

The late 19th century, like today, was a time of rapid economic globalisation, driven by falling transport and communications costs due to the spread of industrial age inventions such as the railroad. This sparked an internationalisation of commerce and culture, which was reflected in multilateral postal and copyright agreements and a fad for world fairs.

At the same time, there was a revival of interest in classical Greek civilisation — including its notion of a sound mind and body — from which Coubertin derived his ideas of physical exercise, spiritual elevation and international cooperation. After launching the modern sporting Olympics in Athens in 1896, Coubertin convened a Consultative Conference on Art, Letters and Sport in Paris in the spring of 1906 with the express aim of officially adding fine arts competitions in architecture, sculpture, music, painting and literature to the Games. Entries had to be original works 'directly inspired by sport' with 'such contests henceforth to become an integral part of the celebration of each Olympiad'.

Coubertin ranked the results of this 1906 conference as second in importance only to the original 1894 conference which led to the start of the modern Olympics two years later. The first fine arts competitions were to be held at the 1908 London Games, but organisers argued that there was insufficient time to include them. Then the IOC itself was forced to organise the competitions for the 1912 Stockholm Games after Swedish arts groups argued that they were too difficult to stage. Of the arts competitions at the seven Olympic Games held between 1912 and 1948, contestants won 45 gold, 52 silver and 48 bronze medals.

Although it was the managerial and logistical problems experienced while staging and promoting the fine arts competitions that were repeatedly recognised in the official reports of the successive Olympic Organising Committees, it was the question of amateurism that led the IOC to decide in 1949 to replace the arts competitions with 'exhibitions'. This produced a backlash among the IOC's ideological Coubertinites, led by the outspoken Greek IOC member, Angelo Bolanki, forcing the IOC to reinstate the art competitions.

However, the organisers of the 1952 Helsinki Games were not interested in staging competitions. The then IOC president, Sweden's Sigfrid Edstrom, replied that 'it concerns a historical problem which Coubertin valued enormously' — and set up yet another committee to examine the issue. But, before the committee's conclusions could be presented, the IOC had a new and very different president.

American Avery Brundage's long and dominating IOC presidency was characterised by his uncompromising commitment to amateurism. In 1953, he strong-armed the IOC executive by claiming, 'One can be practically sure that under present conditions the winners of Olympic Fine Art medals will do everything possible to capitalise on their victories professionally. This is not beneficial to the Olympic Movement.' At the same time, Brundage dismissed the quality of previous arts competitions, incorrectly claiming that 'half the time the entries have been so mediocre that medals have not been awarded'. Brundage instead advocated a shift to 'special exhibitions' which 'would ensure higher standards, eliminate any possible commercialisation, and probably attract more general interest'.

Amateurism had been a birthmark of the modern Olympics; a particularly British upper-class ideal which Coubertin had enlisted to bring his grand plan to fruition. Coubertin wrote:

> Today I can admit it; the question [of amateurism] never really bothered me. It had served as a screen to convene the Congress designed to revive the Olympic Games. To me, sport was a religion with its church, dogmas, service, but above all a religious feeling, and it seemed to me as childish to make all this depend on whether an athlete had received a five franc coin as automatically to consider the parish verger an unbeliever because he received a salary for looking after the church.[1]

The great irony of Brundage's amateur attack on the arts competitions is that, under President Juan Antonio Samaranch, the IOC's embrace of professionalism has helped rescue the Olympics from its near demise after the traumas of the terrorist attack in Munich in 1972, the financial disaster of Montreal in 1976 and the Cold War political boycott of Moscow in 1980. Today, 'Dream Team' American basketballers with multi-million dollar sneaker contracts are as much a feature of the Olympics as are bare-footed African distance runners. An even greater irony is that, at the ancient Greek Olympics, valuable prizes were awarded for both sporting and artistic achievement.

Brundage's focus on amateurism perpetuated the marginalisation of the arts at the Olympics. This focus ignored the more deep-seated management problems raised by successive Olympic Organising Committees — in particular, the difficulty in integrating the artistic events with the sporting events and the low attendance and awareness of the art competitions. In 1966, Brundage stated: 'For too long the world has failed to recognise that the Olympic Games and the Olympic Movement are about fine athletics and about fine art.'

## SYDNEY

The fine arts competitions and subsequent Cultural Olympiad came to life in a complex socioeconomic environment, influenced by ancient myths and ideals and the realities of turn-of-the-century Europe. In the late 20th century, Coubertin's vision has been transformed by the complexities of our current socioeconomic environment. Globalisation, the commercialisation of both sport and culture, and the communications revolution have played essential roles in determining how the profile of the Olympic Games has soared. President Samaranch will be remembered for bringing the Olympic Movement into the late 20th century world of high commercialism. But the impact of this change has landed squarely in the

Main Stadium, with the sporting world gaining the most from increased international exposure and expenditure. With the controversial amateur code finally scrapped, athletes are now free to pursue lucrative professional careers. But for the remainder of the Olympic Movement, not much has changed.

IOC rule 44 says that the organising committee of each Olympic Games must hold a program of cultural events which 'serve to promote harmonious relations, mutual understanding and friendship among the participants and others attending the Olympic Games'. The *Charter* states that the cultural program 'must focus on the culture and traditions of the host country but also involve international artists from the world of entertainment, dance, music, theatre and the arts'.

Surely, though, the Olympics are overwhelmingly about pure and simple sporting contests? Surely art and culture can only be a minor sideshow? Yet of all the events at each Olympic Games, the biggest demand, the highest ticket prices and the largest global television audiences are drawn to events where virtually no sporting contest takes place — the opening and closing ceremonies.

'Where does the abstract conception of Olympic ideology as a movement for peace and international understanding take on human flesh and blood?' asks University of Chicago Olympic scholar Professor John MacAloon. He adds: 'Where does it most materialise into living representations for the vast majority of people outside the Olympic family who encounter the Olympic phenomenon from their living rooms or corner-bars every two years?' The answer is in the ceremonies, and Olympic sports events only in-so-far as they are contextualised, encased within and punctuated by the flame relay, and the opening, victory and closing ceremonies. Otherwise, as wonderful as they are, these sports contests would be 'mere world championships'.

These ceremonies, however, have evolved outside the formal Cultural Olympiad. Sydney's opening and closing extravaganzas are being devised by Ric Birch, who has suggested that Sydney's opening ceremony could include Paul Hogan to represent Australia's 'likeable larrikinism'. But, over at the Olympic Arts Festivals, Craig Hassall stated that 'Crocodile Dundee and the outback' is 'not what and who we are'.

In the search for an identity that works, each successive Organising Committee tends to pinpoint an apparent reason why the previous one didn't work. Barcelona's organisers suggested that neither Los Angeles in 1984 nor Seoul in 1988 were culturally rich enough to put on a substantial cultural festival. Atlanta's Jeffrey Babcock argued that Barcelona was geographically too spread out, so

Atlanta's solution was to keep the arts festivities within a five-kilometre inner-city Olympic ring.

SOCOG suggests that the success of Sydney's bid for the 2000 Games owed much to the ambitious four-year calendar for its cultural program which began with the *Festival of the Dreaming* in 1997, *A Sea Change* in 1998, and *Reaching the World* in 1999 and ends with the *Harbour of Life* in 2000. Craig Hassall has said: 'For the first time in a modern Olympic Games, Sydney is mounting a four-year cultural program.' For Hassall, this is the distinguishing feature that will save Sydney's Olympic arts program from being swamped by the sporting Games, which, he says, occurred in Atlanta and Barcelona.

But both Barcelona and Atlanta ran cultural programs over the four years of their Olympiads. Barcelona's program involved a major urban renewal effort that included the renovation and construction of museums and theatres throughout the city and was launched in 1988 with *Gateway to the Olympiad*. Although having to scramble for funds, Atlanta's cultural organisers put on what they described as 'a four-year, multi-disciplinary arts, culture and entertainment program that culminates in the Olympic Arts Festival in the summer of 1996'. 'The Cultural Olympiad honours in arts and culture what the Olympic Games honours in sport: the highest achievements of mankind', claimed the Atlanta organisers.

Sydney's *Festival of the Dreaming* was Australia's first international arts festival to be directed by a woman — Rhoda Roberts — and was a critical and popular success in Sydney. Here, at least, the Cultural Olympiad has provided the resources for an overdue showcasing of traditional and modern indigenous art. 'I suggest that perhaps *The Festival of the Dreaming* is the arts extravaganza this country should have had back in 1988', says Roberts, referring to the troubled memories of the Bicentennial. But, amid the positive publicity for *The Festival of the Dreaming*, there was little acknowledged connection to the Olympics or Olympism. The SOCOG press releases provided a perfunctory linkage, merely describing *The Festival of the Dreaming* as 'the first of four arts festivals in the lead up to the Olympic Games', a form of words dutifully repeated in media coverage.

*A Sea Change* examined the 'historic global movements of exploration and settlement, men and women as immigrants, explorers, adventurers or fugitives' and celebrated 'Australia's evolution as a multicultural society'. Yet, because of its tiny $1.3 million budget, its director, Andrea Stretton, was forced to put the Olympic stamp on many events that have happened before, will happen again or were going to happen anyway. Hassall argued that SOCOG's $1.3 million investment can lever a much greater cultural output by using the selling power of the five-ringed Olympic brand, but the thinly spread result lacked cohesion and any obvious link to the Olympics.

*Reaching the World* is envisaged as a 'touring program' of Australian artists and performers to the 'five continents of the world'. But its $1 million budget won't buy many plane tickets. As with *A Sea Change* Festival director Andrea Stretton has been forced to buy into events already scheduled. The opening of *Reaching the World* in New York passed without any obvious link to the Olympics.

## BUDGET

From an arts management perspective, the Cultural Olympiad is a unique phenomenon. Unlike other international art festivals, it is held in a different city and organised by a different managerial team each time. And, until 1992, when Barcelona held the first series of four annual arts festivals covering the period of the Olympiad, its format has continually varied. Unlike other art festivals, its survival does not depend on box office receipts. And, for now, the IOC *Charter* assures that the Olympiad will be part of the Summer and Winter Olympics every two years. However, despite the Cultural Olympiad's substantial financial backing and association with the most recognised symbol in the world, it has not raised its international public profile.

The IOC rules require each bid city to include an outlined cultural program and proposed budget in the bid documents but do not insist that the host city adhere to the budget. The budget of each Cultural Olympiad, determined by the host's National Organising Committee, has varied significantly over the years, peaking at the 1992 Barcelona Games at US$59 million. Montreal's one-month program in 1976 was budgeted at C$12.875 million. In comparison, the 1984 Los Angeles Games, which ran over ten weeks, listed direct festival expenses in its official report at US$11.5 million. Fitzpatrick has said that his total budget was more likely around US$20 million (equal to about A$60 million today) and that US$7 million of that came from foreign governments.[2] Atlanta's initial budget was a reported US$40 million. By the end of the Games this figure was cut back to a reported US$25 million. Sydney's budget has been cut from the original A$51.5 million listed in the bid documents to a widely quoted A$21 million. Craig Hassall reports that the budget is now A$30 million for the entire four-year period. The bid documents also listed US$14 million for the 2000 Olympic Arts Festival, *The Harbour of Life* this has now been reportedly cut to A$4 million.[3] Sydney's first Cultural Olympiad director, Jonah Jones, identified the budget as the core reason for deciding to quit the position in October 1996. Jones argued that, 'if SOCOG needed to buy a

stop watch for the track and field, the money would more than likely come from the cultural budget'.

## SPONSORSHIP

The arts have missed out entirely on any benefit gained by the sporting Games from the introduction of the IOC's global marketing program, TOP (The Olympic Partner): 'The Olympic Games remains,
together with the Wimbledon Tennis Championships, the only major
sporting event in the world that does not have advertising in the stadium.' Millar points out that to change this would lead to 'an immediate drop in revenue from both television and TOP sponsors due to
the loss of exclusivity'.[4]

Even so, participating arts groups must fall into line over the bare
or clean venue policy of the IOC. At the expense of its own sponsor
deals, arts companies are promised little more than 'legacies'.

The most obvious legacy the Australian arts community could
hope for after hosting the 2000 Olympic Games would be a more
sophisticated international profile and increased demand for our
cultural product. As well, it could hope to cultivate a more sophisticated and dedicated group of cultural sponsors. The first will
depend on the vision of Festival directors and deft marketers. The
second relies on the vision of Olympic and other corporate
sponsors, the individual arts companies and the vagaries of our
globalised economy.

The SOCOG Team Millennium Olympic Partners have promised
to invest more than A$500 million in the Sydney 2000 Games.
According to SOCOG figures, this represents almost 60 per cent of
the total sponsorship income to be raised. But how much of this will
go to the arts community? The current bribery crises will undoubtedly impact on the level of sponsorship finally negotiated for 2000 —
how much, remains to be seen.

To date, corporate sponsorship of the Olympic Arts Festivals has
been fleeting. In 1996, Equifax sponsored the blockbuster *Five Rings
of Passion* exhibition at Atlanta's High Museum for US$1 million.
*Time* magazine sponsored LA's 1984 Olympic Arts Festival for an all-
up figure of around US$10 million, and John Fairfax is backing
Sydney's Olympic Arts Festivals as part of its overall 2000 Games
sponsorship.

A large part of Australia's arts community has complained that
Olympic sponsorship has diverted sponsor funds and locked out the
cultural industry. But for many of the Olympic sponsors the initial
cost of buying into the greatest marketing opportunity on earth is
just the beginning. As one of the sponsors at the 1996 Olympics, US
Giant AT&T spent an extra US$50 million on an advertising

campaign that promoted the cultural diversity of the Olympic Games — and AT&T, of course.

Craig Hassall argues that Australia is experiencing new levels of corporate support and sponsorship. For Hassall, the flow-on benefit of the Olympics will be increased corporate sponsorship for the arts. He says the very fact that Qantas is not an official Olympic sponsor means that it 'is spending more on sponsorship now than ever before'. Hassall also claims that there is no evidence to support the argument that the Olympics has caused a drain on arts sponsorship dollars.

As general manager of the Australia Council, Michael Lynch argued that 'there are no stars in the eyes from the point of view of cultural organisations — the Cultural Olympiad was going to change the history of life as we know it'. Lynch continued: 'But in essence the Olympics has made life much harder for cultural organisations. It has taken out huge amounts of sponsorship money that could have been competed for and that was spread in different ways.' Even so, Lynch said, 'there are opportunities there for companies that may not have had involvement with the Olympics'.

The fundamental question facing the arts community in Sydney, Lynch argues, is the amount of money that is going to be spent on the Cultural Olympiad. The issue for Australia, he says, is that to 'really make an impact on the world it is going to require money; it doesn't matter whether it's Australian Government money, SOCOG's, private or state'.

TOP Olympic sponsor, John Hancock Mutual Life Insurance claimed that: 'Sponsorship attracts customers and inspires agents. Contests offering trips to the Lillehammer Games helped generate about $50 million in revenue.' At the same time, Visa estimated 'incremental profit increases of 7 per cent globally because of the Olympics'.

President of John Hancock, David D'Allessandro, said in Sydney in late 1998 that while the Olympic brand is 'absolutely unique' in being consistently inspiring to consumers, the first rule of sponsors is to make the multi-million dollar sponsorships work by 'finding a direct and emotional way to bring the Olympics home to consumers year after year'.

## CONCLUSIONS

Despite the number, quality, range, and national and international cultural significance of the programs at recent festivals, the modern Cultural Olympiad has remained one of the least known of international arts festivals among art world professionals and the general public.

Despite being overshadowed by the sporting events and the surrounding ceremonies, the Cultural Olympiad plays an important role as the launching pad for host city cultural events that otherwise would not happen. One of its least recognised bonuses is the opportunity it presents for cultural festivals that would otherwise be scrambling for funding had the Olympics not come along. This was the case with *The Festival of the Dreaming*, which should have been staged in 1988 in the opinion of Rhoda Roberts. LA's 1984 Olympic arts festival put 'countries without diplomatic relations with one another on the same stage'.[5]

But in today's international cultural environment, 'festivals' have become the by-word for tourism — the foundation for public funding, the basis of marketing and a tool for arts education. If the event is not a 'festival', it is not an 'event'. As well, the emphasis placed on festivals as a method of building arts audiences and international interest has grown to fever pitch in recent years. Is Barrie Kosky right — does Australia have 'too many festivals'?

Certainly, both here and in Atlanta, the arts companies would have willingly jumped at the chance to put on their best shows for the influx of tourists expected for the duration of the Games — without IOC regulations. One problem for these increasingly sophisticated arts companies is dealing with, as one Sydney arts administrator put it, 'yet another round of red tape and bureaucracy'. Atlanta's Dr Koehler asked, 'Why do we need them to come in here and tell us what to do? We have plenty of world-class local artists, companies and managers who would do all this without their [ACOG] having to come in and tell us what to do!'

The IOC Cultural Committee has briefly considered re-establishing art competitions on a number of occasions. Arguments against such a move still focus on the reasons given in the past (in particular, the standard of the works and lack of interest in the Cultural Games) and ignore the development of an international cultural environment which supports an increasing range of arts scholarships, awards and competitions. The disposal of the amateur ruling could ensure a higher standard of entries today and could attract a new kind of Olympic sponsor. So far, little mention has been made of developing, in conjunction with National Organising Committees and sponsors, a more sophisticated marketing plan incorporating the cultural.

With few exceptions, Olympic sponsors focus their marketing on the sporting Games and ignore the potential increased exposure that could be gained from simultaneously associating with the Olympic arts festivals. Instead, with the lack of a long-term and active Olympic arts sponsor, the IOC clearly favours an expanded four-year cultural program. Apart from Barcelona, these programs drain the overall

Games budget and at the same time experience a continual squeeze on its own budget. Local arts communities in Atlanta and Sydney have quickly been disillusioned by their own expectations and the realities of dealing with NOCs.

If the IOC is to continue with a cultural program, it needs to seriously consider at least either: assisting the NOCs with the search for funds and, in this age of global capitalism, finally establish its role in the Olympics through its own version of how Coca-Cola has branded that other sacred symbol of ancient Greek Olympism revived by Coubertin — the Olympic torch; or, assume that the local arts communities will put their own shows on and re-establish the art competitions.

## FURTHER READING

Burnosky, R. L. (1994), 'The history of the arts in the Olympic Games', unpub. MA thesis, American University, Washington, DC.

De Coubertin, P. (1997), *Olympic Memoirs*, IOC, Lausanne.

Good, D. (1998), 'The Olympic Games' Cultural Olympiad: Identity and management', unpub. MA thesis, American University, Washington, DC.

Hanna, Michelle (1997), 'Reconciliation in Olympism: The Sydney 2000 Olympic Games and Australia's indigenous people', BA Theory Hons thesis, UNSW.

Levitt, S. H. (1990), 'The 1984 Olympics Arts Festival: Theatre', unpub. PhD thesis, University of California, Davis.

# THE PARALYMPICS
## *Anthony Hughes*

The Paralympics, as the name suggests, are the parallel Olympic Games. The Paralympics are an elite sporting event catering for supremely fit and skilled elite athletes who, through accident or birth, have some physical limitation.

While centuries-old stigma attached to notions about the disabled are being steadily eroded, especially in the developed world, there remain fears, discomfort and misunderstanding about people who have physical handicaps and about their involvement in sport. In the popular mind the Paralympics are the Games of the disabled — an inferior sporting festival.

The Paralympics are primarily about elite athletic performance. However, these Games can serve other objectives: they can play a broader role in assisting in the integration of sports-minded disabled people into society; break down stereotypes of the disabled; improve public utilities so they become 'disabled friendly'; and bridge the gap between the world of the 'able' and 'disabled'.

The staging of the Paralympics in 2000 will raise important issues both about Paralympic sport and about the status of the disabled in Australian society. These parallel Games will raise many other issues. How can the profile of the Paralympics be raised? How can elite Paralympians gain greater support from the government and the sponsors?

There are a range of more general questions that can be posed. What are the Paralympics and how are they organised? What is the relationship between the Olympics and the Paralympics? Will the Paralympics lead to a better understanding of the disabled generally and of elite disabled athletes?

## PUBLIC ACCEPTANCE

The public acceptance of the Paralympics remains a qualified one. While the Australian public support the Games in a general sense — they rejoice in the success of Paralympic athletes in international competition — this does not necessarily translate into a commitment to the Paralympics, as Paralympic basketballer Donna Ritchie noted.[1] Paralympic sport doesn't rate very highly in the media, and there is no certainty that large numbers of the sporting public will pay money to attend the Paralympics in 2000. While the Paralympics may benefit from its link with the Olympics, there is also the danger that the overpowering presence and symbolic importance of the Olympics might marginalise the Paralympics.

The organisers of the Paralympics have to overcome a number of barriers to achieve public acceptance of Paralympic sport. The public has only a vague idea of what constitutes Paralympic sport and the various categories of Paralympic sport. They do not fully understand that Paralympians are elite athletes who have to train as hard and as long as Olympic athletes. It would come as a surprise to many Australians that champion wheelchair athlete Louise Sauvage trains hard six days a week, covering 130 to 190 kilometres in her chair every day. Australian wheelchair basketballer Troy Sachs shot a record 42 points in the final of this event at the Atlanta Olympics — beating the Olympic basketball record. Nigerian amputee Ajibola Adoeye ran a world-class time of 10.72 seconds in the 100 metres that was within a second of Donovan Bailey's Olympic record of 9.84 seconds. There is also all too little appreciation of the obstacles that have to be overcome and the benefits of Paralympic sport to individual athletes.

Perhaps there is some awkwardness and discomfort in watching athletes with some obvious disability perform. They pose the issue of otherness, reminding the sporting public that not all elite athletes have ideal physiques and attractive body shapes.

In some quarters the Paralympics may be seen as a necessary evil, an inferior sports event that has to be tolerated because they are part of the Olympic package. Although Australian Prime Minister John Howard is supportive of the Paralympics, his government's contribution of $1 million was seen as a funding cut by the Australian Paralympic Committee.[2] Because the media often ignore elite disabled sport, the public is unfamiliar with it. In this respect, the Paralympic struggle for column inches, television time and wider recognition is similar to the long battle of women's and minority sports to gain public attention.

There are some grounds for cautious optimism that the Sydney

Paralympics will be successful. Barcelona proved that when the Games are exposed to public view, they are seen to be spectacular and exciting events in their own right. Some Paralympians, such as Louise Sauvage in wheelchair track, and Donna Ritchie and Troy Sachs in wheelchair basketball, have a high public and media profile, providing the Paralympics with a human face and personalities. The response to the World Wheelchair Basketball Championships in 1998 was outstanding and it received good coverage in the Sydney media. The sporting public was able to observe for itself that players such as Sachs had highly developed skills that could be admired. However, this growing interest in Paralympians has not yet translated into public commitment to the Games. A Paralympic fund-raising concert held at Parramatta Park, in Sydney, in October 1997 attracted only 250 people instead of the anticipated 30 000. In 1998 the funding of the Australian Paralympic team was far from secure and there was the possibility of a reduced team in 2000.

## HISTORY

Sir Ludwig Guttmann, an English neurosurgeon who worked with disabled ex-servicemen in post-Second World War Britain, devised the concept of sport for the disabled. Guttmann was convinced that sport could be a catalyst for rehabilitation therapy and a means of reducing boredom. He organised a wheelchair archery event for his paraplegic patients at the Stoke-Mandeville Hospital near Aylesbury in 1948, and 14 men and two women took part.[3] This event was held on the very same day, 28 July 1948, as the opening ceremony of the London Olympic Games. By 1952 the Stoke-Mandeville event had become sufficiently popular to attract athletes from Holland.

Sport for the disabled gained wider acceptance during the 1950s, and in 1960 the first Paralympics were held in Rome, also the Olympic city. The first official Paralympics represented a quantum leap for the Movement. The Games attracted 400 wheelchair athletes from 23 countries. An even more important development was that the Paralympics became an official adjunct to the Olympic festival. By becoming associated with the Olympic Movement, the Paralympics gained a unique and privileged status in world sport.

Hosting 400 wheelchair athletes presented many difficulties for the organisers. There was a lack of appropriate and accessible accommodation for Paralympic athletes, so that 'the organisers arranged for soldiers to carry every wheelchair user up and down from the upper floor of the substitute buildings whenever required: this prevailed throughout the games'.[4]

Since 1960, the categories of athletes represented at the Paralympics has been expanded: vision-impaired athletes competed for the first time in 1972 and amputee athletes made their debut in 1976. Athletes with intellectual disabilities were added to the program in 1992. By the 1990s there were six categories of athletes that competed in the Paralympics — the other categories being cerebral palsy and *les autres* (the others). Similarly, the range of Paralympic sports was expanded to 18 by 2000 (see Table 15.1).

Table 15.1
The Paralympics since 1960

| YEAR | VENUE | COUNTRY | ATHLETES | NO. OF SPORTS | NATIONS |
|------|-------|---------|----------|---------------|---------|
| 1960 | Rome | Italy | 400 | 6 | 23 |
| 1964 | Tokyo | Japan | 370 | 7 | 22 |
| 1968 | Tel Aviv | Israel | 750 | 7 | 29 |
| 1972 | Heidelberg | West Germany | 1000 | 7 | 44 |
| 1976 | Toronto | Canada | 600 | 8 | 42 |
| 1980 | Arnhem | Holland | 2000 | 9 | 42 |
| 1984 | New York | USA | 1700 | 10 | 41 |
| | Stoke-Mandeville | England | 2300 | | 45 |
| 1988 | Seoul | South Korea | 3053 | 13910+ | 62 |
| 1992 | Barcelona | Spain | 3020 | 15 | 82 |
| 1996 | Atlanta | USA | 3310 | 179(2)* | 103 |
| 2000 | Sydney | Australia | 4000 | 18 | 127 |
| 2004 | Athens | Greece | | | |

Notes:
+ One demonstration sport — tennis.
*Two demonstration sports — sailing and wheelchair rugby.

Although the Paralympics had some standing within the Olympic Movement, they were mostly held in different cities and venues from the Olympics in the years between 1964 and 1988. The Seoul Games of 1988 were a watershed for the Paralympics when their athletes competed at the Olympic venues, the Paralympics being held after the Olympics had been completed. There was also significant international media coverage of the Paralympic Games for the first time when the Games were broadcast by a public company. The advances made at Seoul were consolidated at Barcelona in 1992 when the Games were covered by a commercial television station for the first time.[5] The Barcelona Paralympics attracted an impressive 1.5 million spectators. However, it should be noted that spectators were not charged to attend these events.

Although the Paralympics now have status within the Olympic Movement, the relationship has not been without its problems. At the Atlanta Games in 1996, the Olympics and the Paralympics were organised by separate committees and the changeover from one to another was far from smooth:

> Atlanta was not ready for the Paralympic Games: the village was not ready; the venues were not ready; so we learnt from that experience we extended the time between the Games — to get enough time to keep that momentum alive for the Paralympic Athletes. That is very important and it was highlighted in Atlanta. We got off the plane in Atlanta, there were no decorations. We went to Centennial Park, which I was so looking forward to seeing. It was rubble; they had knocked it down.[6]

Sydney hopes to avoid these problems in 2000. The two organising committees, the Sydney Organising Committee for the Olympic Games (SOCOG) and the Sydney Paralympics Organising Committee (SPOC), are working closely together to coordinate and integrate the two festivals. SPOC and SOCOG operate out of the same offices and share many of the same staff and board members. Sydney authorities have also decided there will be 18 days between the Olympic closing ceremony and the opening of the Paralympics on 18 October. The Paralympic Village will open on 11 October to allow athletes time to settle into their environment and to allow staggered arrivals.

There is an element of danger in having such a large gap between the two Games in 2000. It may be hard to restore public enthusiasm after the 'loss' of the Olympics. Commercially, it makes sense to have an integrated festival

It is clear from Table 15.1 that the Paralympics have evolved into a mega-sporting event in their own right, a 'hallmark' event as described earlier by Kevin Dunn. In Sydney, 4000 athletes from 125 countries will compete in 18 sports, compared to the 10 000 in the 43-event Olympic Games. Sydney's Paralympic Games will be larger, in terms of athletes and countries represented, than the 1956 Melbourne Olympics and the 1998 Kuala Lumpur Commonwealth Games.[7]

## WHAT IS PARALYMPIC SPORT?

Table 15.2 sets out the current list of Paralympic sports and disability categories. In some ways the Paralympics replicate Olympic sports, with events such as athletics, swimming, cycling, equestrian and team sports. However, many sports have different rules to cater for the particular abilities of athletes. For example, cycling is open to athletes with cerebral palsy and to the vision-impaired — where a sighted person partners the rider. Swimming is open to all disability categories, but vision-impaired swimmers may be assisted by a coach, who uses a tapper to warn the swimmers of the approaching wall. Football (soccer) was introduced to the Paralympics in 1984 and is open to athletes with cerebral palsy. The rules are the same as laid down by FIFA for Olympic and international football, with a few modifications — there are seven players per side rather than 11, the playing pitch is smaller, there is no off-side law, and matches are 30 minutes each half as opposed to 45 minutes. Tennis was introduced in 1988 and as a full-medal sport in 1992. It is open to wheelchair athletes, and the only difference from traditional tennis is that the ball may be allowed to bounce twice before being returned. In volleyball there are sitting and standing events, with the sitting events players using a modified court with a lower net. Powerlifting involves the bench press only, but is no different from the traditional bench press. Judo is considered an ideal sport for vision-impaired athletes due to their highly honed senses of touch and balance and is little different from Olympic judo. Archery, athletics, basketball and fencing, while catering for many different categories and many wheelchair events, nevertheless feature the same rules and aims as traditional forms of these sports. The equestrian event, which is open to four categories including wheelchair athletes, is limited to dressage and complies with the same rules as the Olympic event.

The only sports that are unique to the Paralympics are goalball and boccia. Goalball is for vision-impaired athletes and men and women compete together. The game is played on a wooden-floored court, and teams are made up of three players who defend a goal. The object is to roll a ball that contains a bell past the opposing players into their goal. The game is played over two seven-minute halves. Boccia is played by cerebral palsy athletes in wheelchairs. It is similar to the Italian form of bowls, known as bocce. In this version of a bowling game, leather balls are thrown as close as possible to a white target ball on a long, narrow alley of play.

## WHY STAGE THE PARALYMPIC GAMES?

Since 1988, it has become customary for the Olympic city also to bid for the Paralympic Games. While there is no obligation for an Olympic city to host the Paralympics — the Paralympics do not feature in the *Olympic Charter* — the Games have become part of an associated package of festivals that includes the Cultural Olympiad. The Olympics and the Paralympics will extend Sydney's Olympic celebration to 60 days.

Table 15.2
Paralympic sports

| Sport | Open to | Wheel-chair | Standing | Introduced | Ind. | Team |
|---|---|---|---|---|---|---|
| Archery | All disabilities | Yes | Yes | 1960 | Yes | Yes |
| Athletics | All disabilities | Yes | Yes | 1960 | Yes | Yes |
| Basketball | Wheelchair Intellecual disability | Yes | Yes (2000) | 1960 | No | Yes |
| Boccia | Wheelchair Cerebral palsy | Yes | No | 1992 | Yes | Yes |
| Cycling | Amputees Vision-impaired Cerebral palsy | No | No | 1988 | Yes | Yes |
| Equestrian | All disabilities | No | No | 1996 | Yes | Yes |
| Fencing | Wheelchair | Yes | No | 1960 | Yes | Yes |
| Football | Cerebral palsy | No | Yes | 1984 | No | Yes |
| Goalball | Vision-impaired | No | Yes | 1988 | No | Yes |
| Judo | Vision-impaired | No | Yes | 1988 | Yes | Yes |
| Power lifting | A physical disability | No | Bench press | 1964 | Yes | Yes |
| Rugby | Quadriplegics | Yes | No | (1996)# 2000 | No | Yes |
| Sailing | Amputees Cerebral palsy Vision-impaired Wheelchair Les autres* | Yes | Yes 2000 | (1996)# 2000 | Yes | Yes |
| Shooting | A physical disability | Yes | Yes | 1980 | Yes | Yes |
| Swimming | All categories with 3 classes: Vision-impaired Functional with a physical disability Intellectual disability | Yes | Yes | 1960 | | |
| Table tennis | A physical disability | Yes | Yes | (1988)# 1992 | Yes | Yes |
| Tennis | Wheelchair | Yes | No | (1988)# 1992 | Yes | Yes |
| Volleyball | A physical disability | Yes | Yes | 1976 | Yes | Yes |

Note: # Demonstration sport.

International Paralympic Committee (IPC) president Robert Steadwood describes the Olympics and the Paralympics as 'one festival, two distinct games'.[8] The Paralympics has a bidding system similar but smaller than that of the Olympics. It makes sense for the Paralympics to be held in the same city as, and in conjunction with, the Olympics. Locating the Paralympics in an Olympic city also accords with the Paralympic philosophy and with the ideal of Olympism laid out in the *Olympic Charter*. This Paralympic philosophy was summarised at the opening ceremony of the 1992 Paralympic Games by Jose Maria Arroya: 'I am sure that the social integration of the disabled, which we wish for in all fields, will spread naturally and inevitably to top level sports competitions.'[9] We can read into this a desire for the Paralympics of the future to be totally integrated into the Olympic Games. Landry has argued that the sports movement for the disabled was bound from the start to converge on the sports movement for the able-bodied.

The Paralympic Games demonstrate that the sports movement for the disabled has focused its energies vigorously, has expanded and diversified its programs and services internationally, and has penetrated public consciousness. It is now accepted fact that sports, including high-level performance sports, are no longer the exclusive monopoly of able-bodied and 'normal' individuals.[10]

## FUNDING

Despite a tough economic environment and with the Olympics attracting so much sponsorship, SPOC has had some success in attracting sponsors (see Table 15.3). There are probably a number of reasons for this: first, the integration of SPOC with SOCOG and the professionalism of both organisations; secondly, the high profile of some Australian Paralympic athletes such as Louise Sauvage; and, finally, the staging of events such as the 1998 World Wheelchair Basketball Championships at the State Sports Centre at Homebush Bay from 23 to 31 October 1998. Sponsorship for the Paralympics ranges from direct financial contributions to support 'in kind'. In 1998, the SPOC chief executive officer reported that the original budget of $136 million had blown out to $150 million. However, SPOC had secured 75 per cent of the funding it required and was well on track to achieve this. It expects $14 million from ticket sales, with $7 million of that coming from the opening and closing ceremonies.

The NSW and federal governments have contributed $25 million towards the funding for the Paralympics. However, funding for the Australian Paralympic team, which is not the responsibility of SPOC, has been more difficult to come by. The Australian Paralympic Committee (APC) was allocated $1 million from the Australian

Table 15.3
Sydney Paralympic sponsors

| WORLDWIDE PARTNERS | TELSTRA, IBM |
|---|---|
| Partners | Motor Accidents Authority of New South Wales, Franklins, Westpac, AMP, Bonds, Fuji Xerox, Energy Australia, Ansett Australia |
| Providers | Woolcott Research, Rogen Australia, Gerflor Taraflex |

Sports Comission (ASC) towards the team. The ASC claims it does not discriminate against the Paralympics but that funding will be determined by medal prospects. The Paralympic Committee has the difficulty of having to fund its national Paralympic sporting organisations, while the AOC can rely on its national federations for support.

It was reported in 1998 that there was a significant shortfall in Paralympic funding for the Australian team, which was a matter of concern. While the Paralympic Committee had $5 million in its coffers, it claimed this was not enough to adequately fund the team. Australian Paralympic officials lobbied for a greater federal government commitment so that Australia could maintain its level of representation at the Paralympics. Without such support, there was the possibility that Australia would name a much smaller team than at Atlanta in 1996, where Australia finished second to the United States on the medal tally with 42 gold, 37 silver and 24 bronze medals. Given that Australia will field a full team in the Olympics, it would be a travesty if the Australian Paralympic team was substantially cut in this first home festival. After a protracted battle, the federal government granted two further increase in 1998, bringing the total funding for the team to $1.8 million. Currently the ASC is reviewing the criteria under which sports bodies, including the Paralympics, are granted funding. When these guidelines are established, Paralympic funding may increase or decrease in the future. In the long run, as with able-bodied sport, international athletic success can only be achieved by the commitment of public money and sporting infrastructure.

## DESIGN

Staging the Paralympics places a heavy responsibility on the host city to plan venues, accommodations and other infrastructure that are 'user friendly' and accessible for people with a range of disabilities. This means that the design of facilities should integrate the needs of the able and disabled alike. This, in turn, would advance one of the philosophical goals of the Paralympic Movement, the integration of disabled athletes into the Olympic Movement and society itself. Beasley has stated that 'Paralympic Athletes have dispelled commonly-held attitudes concerning persons with disabilities. Their achievements have also caused architects and planners to reconsider many fundamental assumptions concerning accessibility in sports facility design.'[11] Despite well-documented problems in Atlanta with management and the treatment of Paralympians, Beasley considers the village there as the most integrated in design in Paralympic history, 'with a barrier-free environment and a planning process that addressed key operational issues'.[12]

The Atlanta Village was constructed on the campus of Georgia Tech, leaving a legacy for the university which now boasts accommodation for prospective students of any disability group. Sainsbury speculates that one day the term 'Paralympic' will disappear and that the Olympic Games will be one festival integrating all elite athletes.

In Sydney, all athletes will be housed in the Athletes Village adjacent to Sydney Olympic Park. Low-rise, medium-density housing will ensure adequate ground-level bedrooms for up to 1500 wheelchair athletes.

## CONCLUSIONS

Paralympic archer Antonio Rebollo will forever be a part of Olympic visual history. It was he who shot the flame-bearing arrow into the cauldron high in the Estadi Olympic, igniting the Olympic flame at the opening ceremony of the Barcelona Games in 1992. He performed the same feat at the opening of the Paralympic Games a few weeks later.

Unfortunately, the achievements of most Paralympians are not properly recognised. Landry argues persuasively that the notion of Paralympism is one and the same as Olympism. The ultimate aim must be to integrate the two events fully:

> If Olympism is a philosophy of life, exalting and combining in balanced whole the qualities of body, will and mind, then there is little basis or need to use a different expression, Paralympism, to allude to an ideology which in every way also speaks of the same principle.[13]

Can Sydney advance this notion? Can Sydney stage a good Paralympics as well as an Olympics? The close cooperation between SOCOG and SPOC, and the efforts to create an integrated infrastructure in Sydney, promise that the Paralympic cause may be advanced in 2000. However, ultimately the success of the Paralympics depends on public commitment, and an acceptance of disabled athletes as part of the 'main show'. Public interest in the other Games may encourage TV networks, sponsors, International Federations and National Olympic Committees to give greater support to disabled sport. However, at the time of writing, a host broadcaster had not been procured.

The Paralympics, like the Cultural Olympiad, are the poor relations of Sydney's 2000 Olympic festival. The immediate aims of SPOC are to ensure that the Games are a success and that they generate significant public interest.

It remains to be seen if the profile of disabled athletes can be raised and whether there will be continuing support for Australian Paralympians beyond 2000. Will the Australian public accept that the Paralympics are a serious athletic endeavour? If they can, then Sydney will have contributed more than design innovation and efficient event organisation.

The Paralympics will only be successful in the long run if it has some impact on government policy and public attitudes towards disabled athletes and disabled people in general. This will be a key indicator of the social, cultural and political success of Sydney's 60-day festival.

## FURTHER READING

Bariga, J. (1998), 'The role of the media in the promotion of sport for the disabled', ONCE Foundation, Madrid, www.ibsa.es/rules/doc/imesa2.txt, 10 February, p 1.

Beasley, K. A. (1997), 'The Paralympic Village: A barrier-free city', *Olympic Villages: One Hundred Years of Urban Planning and Shared Experiences*, IOC, Lausanne, pp 105–9.

Landry, F. (1995), 'The Paralympic Games of Barcelona '92', in Moragas and Botella (eds), *The Keys to Success*, Centre for Olympic Studies, Barcelona, pp 124–38.

Ritchie, D. (1998), 'The Paralympics', in R. Cashman and A. Hughes (eds), *Mosman Council: Forum on the Impacts of the Olympics*, Centre for Olympic Studies, Sydney, p 11.

Sainsbury, T. (1997), 'Paralympic Villages', *One Hundred Years of Urban Planning and Shared Experiences*, IOC, Lausanne, p 173.

Steadwood, R. (1998), 'The Olympic/Paralympic Movement — Normalisation through sport', ONCE Foundation, Madrid, 10 February, www.ibsa.es/rules/doc/imesa1.txt, p 2.

# PART 5

## BEYOND THE GAMES

# LEGACY
## *Richard Cashman*

Almost every Olympic city, since the Games were revived in 1896, has some form of legacy, whether it be in the form of buildings, monuments, art galleries and museums, repositories, archives, stamps, souvenirs, memorabilia, plaques or even street names. Then there are the local Olympic champions, who are living reminders of a city's and country's Olympic experience. There are also oral memories and stories of the Games that are treasured by individual citizens. More mundane legacy includes debts (and occasional profits) for a city and its taxpayers. Most cities have some post-Games ceremonies, to mark anniversaries of the Games, which are, in part, attempts to recapture some of the magic of the Olympic moment and to place the Olympics in the history of the city.

All the above forms of legacy demonstrate that a particular city has a unique status — that of an Olympic city. It is one of only 21 cities on four continents that have earned the right to stage the Summer Games and another 16 cities that have staged the Winter Games. There is also an elite group, which have earned the right to stage the Games twice: Athens, London, Los Angeles and Paris (Summer Games); and Innsbruck, Lake Placid and St Moritz (Winter Games).

## VARIETY OF LEGACY

The legacy of the Games varies enormously from city to city. The organisers of the 1896 Games, for instance, restored the ancient Panathenian Stadium, using pure marble from Mount Pentilicous that had been used in the original construction in 330 BC. The stadium marble, which glistened brilliantly in the sun, added to the sense of occasion when the Games began. The major event at preliminary ceremonies, the day before the Games, was the unveiling of a life-size statue of Georgios Averoff in front of the stadium. Averoff's donation of approximately one million drachmas enabled 'Athenians to restore one of its most historic sites'[1] and to create a grand monument for the modern Olympics. Money from the generous benefactor also enabled Athens to build a shooting gallery, a velodrome and a pier for spectators.

The 'legacy' of the 1900 Paris Olympics, by contrast, was one of 'confusion and controversy' because its organisation was so chaotic.[2] Initially, it was de Coubertin's dream to 'reconstruct the ancient site of Olympia at the exposition — its temples, stadia, gymnasia, and statues',[3] but the organisers decided to scrap these plans, preferring instead to showcase French culture and civilisation. Because the Olympic Games had such a low profile, there were no special athletic facilities: swimming and diving took place in the polluted River Seine, and track and field was performed in the Bois de Boulogne, the private property of the Racing Club of France. The Olympics occupied this site on a temporary basis and the organisers were allowed few liberties with this attractive property. There was a line of trees between spectators, who sat in a hastily erected and temporary grandstand, and it was disconcerting for discus and javelin athletes when their throws ended up in wooded areas. The 1900 Games, which were lost in the World Fair of that year, left no footprints on Paris; there were no monuments, medals or memorabilia. Not even the memory of the Paris Olympics has been treasured: one Australian athlete, Stan Rowley, described the Games as a 'HUGE JOKE': '[T]o treat these events as world's championships would be really an insult to the important events they are supposed to be.'[4] Although the St Louis Games of 1904 also suffered, because they were an adjunct of an exposition, the city has attempted to take some pride in its Olympic legacy. In this regard, an Olympic Museum has been created to commemorate the city's Olympic involvement.

Reflecting the growing status of the Olympic Movement, legacy was built to last by the time of the Stockholm Games in 1912. A stadium, which was specifically erected for the Games in the Royal Zoological Garden, was a 'fine edifice ... with mighty arches, vaults, and towers' and could accommodate 22 000 spectators. The Swedish architect Torben Grutpreferred to create 'a new style that reflected practicality and the Northern European tradition' rather than imitating Greek art.[5] The stadium had an ongoing purpose in that it was constructed both for sport and festivals of all kinds and, in winter, could be converted into a skating rink.

The emergence of the Cultural Olympics was yet another facet of an interest in legacy. It was a Movement which was dear to de Coubertin's heart: he sent a circular to International Olympic Committee (IOC) members in 1906 convening an advisory conference 'to come and study the way in which art and literature could be included in the celebration of the modern Olympiads'. It was an attempt to 'reestablish the original beauty of the Olympic Games ... [when] ... the fine arts were combined harmoniously with the Olympic Games to create their glory'.[6] Although culture has struggled to compete with sport in the Olympics, the conscious development of a cultural tradition is an important part of the Olympic legacy.

## THE TREND TOWARDS PARAMOUNT STRUCTURES

There is also great variation in terms of legacy as to whether an Olympic stadium was built simply to serve the immediate pragmatic purpose of staging the Games, or whether it was built to last beyond the Games so as to convey a longer-term Olympic vision. Held just after the First World War, the Antwerp Games of 1920 were hastily organised and suffered from a shortage of money and materials. Athletes were housed in primitive accommodation in local schools. The rebuilt Beerschot Stadium had some impressive-looking 'Greek decoration, including a grandiose arch and columns', but it was not made to last because the decorations were made of plaster.[7] They had disappeared within a year of the Games.

In recent decades there have been more extravagant attempts to create permanent Olympic monuments and precincts. The ambition of Montreal Mayor Jean Drapeau was 'to create a lasting symbol of *la survivance*, the will of French Canada to survive two centuries of English Canadian attempts at assimilation'.[8] Some of the extravagant monuments included an Olympic Stadium which included a 'retractable roof and a fifty-storey tower' and a spectacular and innovative velodrome which consisted of a 'giant arc of roof sweeping over glass walls'. The main legacy of Montreal, however, was a massive debt incurred due to the large capital costs, a debt which was not paid off until 1993. It is ironic that while the Montreal organisers have been criticised for their extravagance, and many of the new facilities proved too costly to maintain for sports, the Olympic precinct has proved successful as a tourist attraction.

Barcelona, by contrast, planned a permanent Olympic precinct, which included a reconstructed main stadium, a magnificent indoor facility and an Olympic gallery, run by a foundation. Although it was created in 1988, four years before the Games, the Centre for Olympic Studies at the Autonomous University of Barcelona is part of the city's legacy in two senses: it is part of Barcelona's Olympic heritage; and it is one of a number of bodies that oversees and maintains the city's Olympic legacy. Barcelona attempted to use the Games to enhance the profile of the city: US$8.1 million was spent on new roads, an airport, hotels, telecommunications and a new seafront resort.

## THE AFTERMATH

There is an interesting history yet to be written of what happens to Olympic facilities (such as stadia), artefacts and material used in opening ceremonies, after the Games. Atlanta's main stadium has been converted back to a ball park, and the cauldron, home of the Olympic flame during the Games, 'was dismantled and moved up the street so it wouldn't mar the sightlines of the Olympic stadium turned baseball park'.[9] Some Olympic facilities, such as Montreal's velodrome, have been given a new non-sporting use. The velodrome is now a biodome and botanic gardens.

The vision that inspired developments at other Olympic sites has not always been sustained, resulting in decline and degradation in some instances. Melbourne's Olympic Village was built on 24 hectares at Heidelberg, about 13 kilometres from the main stadium. The Olympic program described how the 840 brick-and-concrete houses were painted in 'gay modernistic colours'. The desired effect was that of an English village, and £60 000 was spent on landscaping the site.

However, by the 1990s the model village had degenerated into a suburban slum. One writer commented in 1993:

> If the Olympic spirit flickers there still, it is for the endurance events — endurance of poverty, crummy housing and, above all, of being consistently marked down as a failure, For even the staunchest supporters of this blight-ed public housing estate ... concede that while it was constructed as a model village for winners, the reputation that has lingered longer is that of a dumping ground for losers.[10]

Melbourne represents one of those mid-20th century hosts which has few visible reminders of the Olympics. The Melbourne Cricket Ground (MCG) is better known as a home for cricket and Australian football. It was converted to an Olympic stadium for 1956, the out-field was dug up and cinder tracks were laid, but after the Games it reverted to its original use. Ironically, the issue of Olympic legacy was not really addressed until 1986 when the Australian Gallery of Sport was opened at a site attached to the MCG. While this museum has a good Olympic collection, it also covers all the major Australian sports. It is intriguing to note that, for over two decades, the cauldron, the receptacle for the Olympic flame, was misplaced. When it was rediscovered in the 1980s, it was restored and erected in the vicinity of the Australian Gallery of Sport.

Legacy is an important issue, because much of the power of the Olympic Movement derives from its sites and symbols and its ancient heritage. It is one of the strengths of the IOC that it has carefully nurtured and guarded Olympic legacy at its two central sites, Olympia and Lausanne. Olympic sites, whether it be the sacred grove at Olympia or the Olympic Museum at Lausanne, document both the history and ideals of the Olympic Movement.

Because it has a permanent home and a more than adequate funding base, the IOC can address the question of legacy in a sustained and systematic fashion. The IOC also rightly recognises that its rich array of sites and symbols add to its legitimacy and appeal and are the core way in which Olympic values are spread. The sites and symbols of the Olympic Movement are powerful and compelling. The Olympic hymn, oath, flag, five rings, torch and torch relay, and the opening and closing ceremonies, add to the legitimacy and transcendence of the Olympics, which draws on ancient traditions and religious symbols. In an era where sport has become more profane and even over-exposed, or where sporting officials attempt to enhance a particular event by razzle-dazzle and razzamatazz, the Olympics has credible symbols which add to the solemnity and dignity of its events.

It is a different story for Olympic organisers in cities nominated to host the Olympics. Because the time frame is so short and the demands are overwhelming, all the core efforts of the Games authorities are directed towards the short-term goal of hosting a successful Games. The pressing nature of immediate funding and planning issues make it difficult for any of the city organisers to think beyond the Games in any systematic fashion.

Sydney is no exception to this experience. While many members of the local Olympic Family have expressed keen interest in legacy issues, such as the creation of an Olympic Museum — a museum dedicated to the Sydney Olympics — it is a low-priority issue. A common response is that the idea is a good one, but all the funds available are committed to staging the Games.

## ISSUES RELATING TO OLYMPIC LEGACY

Time in an Olympic city can be divided into three periods. First is the pre-Games period, which can last for a decade or even two: developing a successful bid plan and then organising the Games themselves. Then there is the actual duration of the Games of three weekends and two weeks — a mere 16 or 17 days — which pass for most in a twinkling of an eye. Finally, the post-Games period is by far the longest; it stretches for decades after the Games and is clearly the least-planned period.

One year after the Atlanta Games there was a revealing headline in the *Atlanta Journal and Constitution*: 'Remains of the Games: One year later, we're still looking for a legacy'. The article suggested that Atlanta lacked a focal point for post-Games celebrations:

> We don't even have a centerpiece for the one-year anniversary celebration. At Centennial Olympic Park, the heart and soul of the Games even after the bombing, we're still laying pipe and pushing dirt. Few of us have ventured back, and most of the park remains cordoned off by the chain-link fence. 'Had the park been finished I would have been a very strong advocate of a one-year celebration that tried to bring back the magic we all experienced,' commented Billy Payne.[11]

Consequently, there were just a sprinkling of events to mark Atlanta's first anniversary. They included an exhibition of Olympic memorabilia opened at the Atlanta History Centre, a five-kilometre fun run, a parade, a round-the-clock showing of Bud Greenspan's official Olympic film and a rededication of the Olympic cauldron.

Atlanta, more than many recent Olympic cities, seems to have been keen to dispose of its Olympic history and its legacy, almost to the point of denying that the Games took place there. There are no plans for a more substantial legacy, such as an Olympic Museum or a Centre for Olympic Studies.

Another issue to consider is: what is an Olympic city? Should it be marked by some special common elements? If the IOC has its sites at Olympia and Lausanne, should an Olympic city have some form of legacy to commemorate the event? And, if so, what? Or, should a city, having invested so much in the Olympics, pack up its Games kit bag and get on with 'normal' life?

Helen Wilson provides an initial starting point for a consideration of the issue:

> What, then, is an Olympic city? It must, of course, have the sporting infrastructure to be able to accommodate the events, providing the technical conditions to induce personal best performances from the athletes, provide a sufficient crowd to give the sense of a mega-event, and to make good television. The main stadium should particularly signify newness and monumentality in itself. The city must have the transport and tourism infrastructure to be able to accommodate the esteemed visitors and participants. It must have the communications facilities to be able to shoot, package and distribute footage and commentary instantly to the media of over 200 nations.[12]

The stadium as a central monument is an interesting idea, because it suggests that the main stadium should not merely be functional; it should also enhance the Olympic vision. Is a city obliged to create a core monument that will proclaim the Olympic message for the long term? The Games, Wilson adds, are about a 'city as spectacle', in which television 'manipulates' and 'theatricalizes' urban sites. The organisers in Sydney, like the organisers of most recent Games, have paid a 'great deal of attention to the physical form of the city, to building and rebuilding, salvaging, cleaning up and detoxifying for the year 2000'. Planners are well aware that the Olympic site is a special, even a sacred, site. One purpose of a tree-lined boulevard at Sydney's Olympic Park is to replicate the notion of a sacred grove, which was part of the site at Olympia.

However, landscape architect James Weirick has been critical of Olympic Park, largely on legacy grounds. He has pointed out that a 'disappointing aspect' of the masterplan developed by the urban design team is that it:

> ... has retreated from a poetic ambition to invoke the gods of Olympia. The reconstructed hillock at the western terminus of the main axis has been named the Hill of Kronos and the masterplan report ends with an appropriate quotation from Pindar. This appears to be all that is left of a set of classical references which sought to structure the site along the lines of the sanctuary and stadium at Olympia.[13]

The escalating costs of staging the Games have often led to more pragmatic rather than poetic decisions. Why, then, should a city incur more costs in planning for its post-Olympic period? Or, if the purpose is to place the city on the stage for 16 days — to advertise a city's claim to be a global city — won't this be achieved at the time of the Games?

There are a number of important reasons why the issue of legacy should be approached in a more serious and systematic fashion. Some of these are discussed below.

## COMMEMORATING A PEAK EXPERIENCE

One important public issue is how to best commemorate an event that will loom large in the public imagination. For many people in a city or other parts of the country, a home Olympics will be a peak experience in their life. There is a need for the public to re-connect with that experience after the event; many will want to re-live the magic of the Olympic moment. 'Touching' the Games is even more important for those who watched the Games on television; they will want to assure themselves that their Olympic experience was real. Post-Olympic tourists will want to visit the site where a particular local athlete performed heroically.

## MOURNING THE GAMES

After the Games are over, many residents will feel a great sense of loss that the Games have come and gone and that they can no longer look forward to them. One year after the Games in Atlanta, volunteer

Peggy Mayer felt unsatisfied and even a little depressed. 'It was all over so quickly, like being in fifth gear and trying to come to a screeching halt.'[14] Part of this represents a post-Olympics depression, coming back to the humdrum routine of life after the all-too-brief 'high' of the Olympics. The post-Olympics depression is a short-term but very real problem, which should be addressed by the Games' planners.

However, a sense of loss, mourning the Games, can be a longer-term problem. Once the Games are over, the city loses part of its identity, as the attention of the world media shifts to another city. Legacy is a constructive and positive way of dealing with mourning. A city has to deal with its 'death' — when the Games have gone — in the same way that an individual may have to deal with the loss of a close family friend. Symbols, rituals and memory are all part of the healing process. One constructive way of approaching this issue is to suggest that, while Sydney or some other city has 'lost' the Games — and they are unlikely to return in anyone's lifetime — the memory of the Games is still alive and Sydney will forever be an Olympic city. Legacy is one way that 'memory' can be reconstructed in a positive way.

## THE MEMORY OF THE GAMES

The dedication of Olympic sites and the establishment of Olympic museums are ways in which the public can 'touch' the Games after the event and recapture some of the magic of the event and deal with a sense of loss. The trend to establish Olympic museums is a relatively recent phenomenon, but there is considerable evidence that Olympic museums at Calgary and Barcelona have been successful both from a point of view of attracting Olympic tourists and in enhancing Olympic education. At Calgary there is an ongoing and attractive educational program which utilises the Games site effectively.

There is a need, then, to develop a strategic plan for the establishment of Olympic sites in the city after the Games. Ideally, each city should have an integrated plan for the location of Olympic papers, memorabilia and displays. No city has yet integrated research, documentation and display into a 'one-stop shop'. Barcelona's Olympic legacy is spread over three sites: the Olympic Galleria (at the main Olympic precinct), the city library (which holds most of the Olympic papers), and the Centre for Olympic Studies, which is involved in research and documentation of the Games. If it were located at a central point in the Olympic precinct, it would be a very attractive meeting-place for a great variety of Olympic visitors and researchers.

Galleries, museums, archives and Centres for Olympic Studies, set up during or even after the Olympic event, can also enhance the

Olympic precinct and provide it with a continuing life and liveliness. They all in various ways represent ways of coming to terms with the past, questioning it and even profiting from it.

## CORE LEGACY

An important issue to consider is: what constitutes the core legacy? No one would suggest that all the city's many Olympic venues should be recognised as part of legacy. So there is the practical issue to decide what should be retained in its original form, what should be modified or have a change of use, and what should be discarded, demolished or sold off. In the case of Sydney, venues within the main precinct at Olympic Park will have greater long-term significance than those on the periphery. However, even sites that will have a complete change of use — the Olympic Village will become a suburb — may be enhanced with appropriate 'marking', whether this be in terms of plaques, street names or public art.

## GUARDIANS OF LEGACY

Legacy beyond the Games is a daunting task, because it involves a post-Olympics vision that flows out of the Olympic experience. It also requires some form of coordinated strategy and some 'guardians' of legacy who will maintain the best traditions of the city's Olympics.

## COSTS

While some may look at legacy as a costly extravagance and a distraction from the main game, investments in legacy may provide a way of recouping some of the costs of the Games. There is an enduring interest in the Games after the event which re-emerges gradually — after a dramatic fall in interest at the end of the Games — over the following weeks and years. Barcelona has proved that a city that plans its legacy well can reap the benefits over a number of years.

# PROBLEMS OF OLYMPIC LEGACY

There are a number of reasons why it is difficult for most cities to plan for life beyond the Games. During the rush to organise the Games, there is all too little time to consider the post-Games plan. At the time when legacy comes under serious consideration, after the Games, many of the important local Olympic institutions, including the local organising committee, are winding up. There is a great danger that key decisions will be made 'on the run' or on an ad hoc basis.

Legacy is frequently shelved, because it seems to represent a range of additional costs for budgets that are already stretched in the pre-Games period. Unfortunately, many planners fail to see that while legacy will require some additional outlay, it is a way of recouping some Olympic costs (through tourism). It is also a way of recouping some of the costs that have already been spent on facilities.

Legacy is often looked upon as a side issue, something that will be tackled after the Games. Because it is not seen as a central issue, few cities have well-developed post-Games plans.

The concept of an Olympic city, so far as it exists, is an implicit rather than an explicit one and is left to each city to interpret in its own way. Barcelona has made a point of preserving its Olympic precinct, whereas Atlanta's has been largely dismantled.

Legacy also provides valuable information about how best to stage the Games. It has been customary for the organisers of the next Olympics to 'look over the shoulders' of those staging a current Games. However, the bulk of Games 'knowledge' is not passed on in any systematic way to the next Olympic city, which tends to be left with the immense task of 'reinventing the Olympic wheel'.

## THE CASE FOR OLYMPIC LEGACY

Far from being a side issue, legacy is a vital issue to the staging of the Games. Every city has a core set of objectives (which are usually unstated and mostly unarticulated) as to why the city should want to host the Games. For the city of Melbourne, the 1956 Games:

> ... may be seen as a curtain-raiser to modernist Melbourne. Between 1950 and 1970, Melbourne became ... the fastest growing capital in Australia. Perhaps more than any other Australian city it exemplified the Fordist paradigm of urban growth — high investment in manufacturing, especially of protected consumer products such as cars and electrical goods, high levels of immigration, high levels of car and home ownership and high levels of government intervention in the provision of infrastructure ... The Games were pivotal to the process of self-definition through which the city, and especially its business and political elite, adjusted to the new paradigm.[15]

The general director for sport for the Generalitat de Catalunya commented that Barcelona's plan to use the Olympics for the benefit of the city was far more explicit:

> The Olympic Games permitted the transformation of the city, providing it with those services it so much needed, and the heavy investment that would otherwise have taken so many years to have come. Barcelona once again turning its face to the sea, the Olympic village, the airport, the roadways and communications, the hotel network, all of which were essential to its becoming a competitive city in the scenario of to-day's Europe.[16]

Implicit in the bid to win the right to stage the Games are many untested and even vague statements about how the staging of the Games might bring long-term benefit to a city and a country. Given that the local community invests so much in the Games, it is important that the wider benefits of legacy should be canvassed and articulated. Too often, costs and benefits narrowly focus solely on economics. However, legacy involves casting the gaze wider to poetry and art, architecture, the environment, information and many other non-tangible factors.

## A MODEL FOR AN OLYMPIC CITY

At the very least, every city should deal with the issue of legacy in a systematic fashion. Plans should be developed for the post-Games period, which will deal not only with monuments and museums but the issue of memory as well. Legacy should be integrated into the city's master plan. Other issues that could profitably be addressed might include a definition of core legacy. What objects and facilities are so central to the Olympic experience that they should be retained? Is there an appropriate model for housing of archives, memorabilia and items of display? Is a 'one-stop shop' feasible? Can it cater for the varied needs of scholars, students and tourists? Is it an appropriate venue for Olympic education?

What are the ways in which Olympic cities (and centres) can develop stronger links with each other, to pass on in a more organised way the store of knowledge that has been gained from the Olympic experience? How can knowledge about staging the Games best be communicated from one city to another? Is there a case for a more global definition of an Olympic city? If so, what should this consist of?

## CONCLUSIONS

Olympic cities, in a sense, are as important as the legacy developed at the Olympic headquarters of the IOC. Few citizens will have the chance to visit the IOC Museum at Lausanne or to travel to Olympia. They are more likely to connect with Olympic legacy in their own country by visiting sites and museums. Although there has been much discussion of legacy from the time of de Coubertin, it remains a neglected area and one that can profit from more systematic and sustained analysis.

While I have argued that Olympic legacy should be taken seriously and has much to offer both to a local city and the Olympic Movement as a whole, not everyone might agree with this perspective. Emory University sociologist Alvin Boskoff suggested:

> The Olympics is a temporary thing. It's like a rocket that shoots up in the sky, a big expensive rocket, and then it's gone … Maybe the best thing is to forget about the Olympics and go about the business of becoming a first-class city.[17]

I think not. There are many parallels between Sydney's Olympic Park and its Opera House. Both have endured plenty of controversy and stretched budgets on both occasions. But both were 'vision' things. The big task of Sydney 2000 is to make the 'vision thing' work after 2000.

## FURTHER READING

Bagnall, Diane (1993), 'Hell of a village', *Bulletin*, 9 November.

Wilson, Helen (1996), 'What is an Olympic city? Visions of Sydney 2000', *Media Culture and Society*, vol. 18, pp 603–18.

# COSTS AND BENEFITS
*Richard Cashman and*
*Anthony Hughes*

M uch of the debate concerning the staging of the Games focuses on issues of costs and benefits. What are the real costs, both direct and indirect, of staging the Games? Will the taxpayers have to foot a much larger bill than was at first anticipated? Who will benefit from the Games? Will the Games be assessed in the long term to be a worthwhile investment for Sydney and Australia?

'The cost of the Olympics,' noted Bob Walker, Professor of Accountancy, 'cannot be easily answered ... because accountants can calculate "costs" in many different ways.' Walker asked, by way of an example, whether the following indirect costs should be attributed to the Olympic budget: the cost of the rail loop to Homebush Bay; the erection of a bus interchange at Strathfield (to provide a bus link to Olympic Park); the placing of powerlines underground at Homebush; and the dredging of the Parramatta River to enable ferries to travel conveniently to Homebush Bay.[1] Similar questions can also be asked about the completion of major city projects by the year 2000, such as the airport-to-Central rail link, the modernising of Sydney airport, the building of the Eastern Distributor and the beautification of George Street.

John O'Neill, of the *Independent Monthly*, claimed that the original budget of the Sydney Olympic bid company, which predicted a surplus of US$15 million, 'was misleading because there was always a second budget for the public works needed to host the Games'. The remediation of the contaminated Homebush Bay site was the biggest 'hidden' cost: reclaiming the site and building on it was estimated to cost $807 million (in 1992 dollars).[2]

It is difficult to secure a clear picture of the costs of staging the

Games because such issues are highly sensitive, contentious and political. Organisers of the Games develop their own balance sheet, but it is one that puts the best spin on the Games. As in an election campaign, official estimates are frequently challenged at various points by the media and even by other channels of government. The Auditor-General of New South Wales, Tony Harris, took issue in December 1998 with the official balance sheet for the Games. Harris stated that SOCOG's 1998 projected budget surplus of A$30 000 was 'largely symbolic' because it did not include all costs, such as security and transport.[3] This view of the Auditor-General was contested by SOCOG.

Another problem that inhibits analysis is that Sydney's host city contract is a confidential document and has been exempted from the *Freedom of Information Act*. Auditor-General Harris was particularly concerned that information about tenders was withheld from public scrutiny. Harris warned that 'State taxpayers may have been misled about the potential cost of the Olympic Games because of secret undertakings contained in confidential documents'.[4]

There is also limited agreement among scholars about whether the Games will provide a long-term boost to the economy of an Olympic city and country and will stimulate tourism. While it seems clear that, in the lead-up years to the Sydney Games, there has been a boost to the local (and particularly the New South Wales) economy, it is uncertain whether these benefits will flow on after the Olympics. Ray Spurr (see Chapter 13) has suggested that while some authors forecast a sizeable Olympic-related tourism boost, others are less optimistic because tourism will be affected by 'Big Event Blues'.

Assessing the worth of the Games is also difficult because the reason for bidding for the Games included both stated and unstated aims. While it is feasible to measure the explicit costs — such as building the Main Stadium and core costs — it is more difficult to assess the implicit costs. James Weirick (Chapter 6) contends that 'the main impulse behind the Games' was to promote Sydney as a 'global' city and to challenge the financial leadership of Asian cities in the region. It will not be possible to judge the role of the Games in achieving this until well after the Games, and even then there are many other factors involved in Sydney's drive to achieve this status.

Some potential benefits to Sydney and Australia cannot be measured or costed. How can the 'value' of the Games be weighed in terms of 'morale' and a possible related improvement in business confidence? What is the worth of Olympic legacy? Will Sydney benefit after 2000 from the tag 'Olympic city'?

A final problem is that too many commentators look at the costs of the Games in isolation. The true worth of the Games can only be gauged if the costs are weighed against potential benefits. If the tax-payer has to foot the bill for additional costs of the Olympics, what will they get in return? Will the expenditure be worth it? One of the underlying themes of this book is that the balance sheet for assessing the Games should be much broader than hitherto attempted.

Costs can be divided into a number of compartments. First, there are the immediate costs of staging the Games. Leaving aside the cost of staging the bid (estimated at A$25.2 million), the original budget prepared by the bid company projected an income of US$975 million and expenditure of US$960 million, leaving a modest surplus of US$15 million. Since that time, the budget has been revised upwards: in 1996, revenue was projected to be A$2331.5 million, expenditure, A$2288.8 million, leaving a surplus of A$42.7 million; and again in 1998, when there was a reported rise in expenditure of A$128 million, which was matched by a sharp increase in revenue of A$142 million.

Since the original bid budget, there have been significant changes both in income and expenditure. SOCOG benefited from a larger than anticipated television rights fee of US$705 million, a dramatic increase over the figure of US$456 for the Atlanta Games, from the lucrative US market (see Chapter 1). However, in other areas, it is still not certain whether budget projections will be met. The Olympic bribery scandal has not helped SOCOG to meet its sponsorship budget of A$464 million; in early 1999, there remained a shortfall of A$116 million. Income generated from the projected sale of 9.6 million tickets will not be known until closer to the Games.

SOCOG's budget only covers costs (and returns) for staging the Games; it is the state government, through the Olympic Co-ordination Authority, that is remediating the site of the Olympics, building the facilities and providing the infrastructure, such as rail transport. The government has argued that the Games have provided the climate in which some large-ticket public works, which will be of wider benefit, can be undertaken. This reorientation in state spending on capital works raises a number of issues. Does the increased Olympic-related spending mean that there will be less spending on health, education and welfare? Is the claim of some country politicians valid that the Olympics mean more spending on the city and less on the country? Some commentators have argued precisely this: that increased spending on capital works for the Games can only be at the expense of new schools and hospitals.[5]

There are also hidden costs to the state taxpayers. There is no information about what non-Olympic agencies are spending on the Olympics. To what extent are agencies such as the State Rail Authority and the Roads and State Transit Authority indirectly subsidising the Olympics? There are also costs contributed by the federal government to increased airport services and customs surveillance.

There are various categories of benefits that may offset costs, but they are even more difficult to assess. Undoubtedly, Sydney will benefit from improved sporting facilities in western Sydney, where they are most needed. It seems evident in 1999 that venues such as the Main Stadium, the Aquatic Centre and the Showground will be well used after 2000 and enhance the provision of sport and culture in Sydney. However, there is also the challenge to make the best and most cost-effective use of other facilities, such as the rowing venue at Penrith, the equestrian centre at Horsley Park and the velodrome at Bankstown. Who will maintain and pay for these state-of-the-art facilities after 2000?

It is also clear that Sydney, New South Wales and Australia will reap some short-term economic benefits. The federal government will collect more taxes from income on new jobs and the sale of goods and services. Given that Olympic Park has become the largest building site in the country, there has been a boost in jobs in the building and related sectors in New South Wales, where the employment rate is higher than the national average. Local planners hope that this confidence will flow on after 2000 and will be boosted by post-Games tourism and greater interest in Sydney as a global destination.

There is considerable debate as to whether the Games will improve the quality of life for those who live in Sydney and nearby regions. The 'Green Games' have already helped to educate the public about the environment, but it remains to be seen whether the Games will advance Australia's green technology and whether advanced energy features of the village will inspire emulation in the wider community (see Chapter 7). While the 1998 and 1999 Royal Easter Shows proved a boost for public transport, it is uncertain whether transport innovations for the Games may lead to a change in commuter behaviour. And will transport innovations developed for the Games, including the railway station at Olympic Park, be of long-term benefit to the city (see Chapter 8)?

There is also the issue of the 'other Games', whether Sydney's celebrations can advance the link between sport and culture (see Chapter 14) and enhance the ongoing relationship between the Olympics and the Paralympics (see Chapter 15). While there are some hopeful signs in the organisation of the Paralympic Games, it remains to be seen whether the public will fully support the elite athletes that perform there and whether the Paralympics can enhance public understanding and acceptance of Paralympic athletes.

The debate on costs and benefits of staging the Olympics is an ongoing one. While some costs and benefits are now known, others will not be evident until the Games or even well after the Games.

## AN OLYMPIC PARADOX

It is ironic that while the cost of staging a hallmark event inevitably seems to escalate along the way and involves many unstated and implicit costs, many cities continue to chase hallmark events (see Chapter 2). No less than five Australian cities — Adelaide, Brisbane, Darwin, Melbourne and Perth — expressed an interest in staging the 2006 Commonwealth Games. This suggests that politicians perceive considerable benefits, whether real or imagined, in staging a hallmark event.

Only one recent Games has clearly produced a positive balance sheet. The Los Angeles Games of 1984 produced a sizeable profit for its organisers. The citizens of Los Angeles did not have to foot any bill for the Games. The Montreal Games of 1976, by contrast, left its citizens with a huge debt that took decades to pay off. If one looks narrowly at profit and loss, no other Games since 1976 has produced a sizeable profit.

The Barcelona Games of 1992 are perhaps the model most applicable to Sydney in terms of assessing costs and benefits, as Chapter 13 suggested. The cost of staging the Games in Barcelona was high, because Barcelona used the Olympics to create a magnificent Olympic precinct and to undertake extensive urban renewal. There is considerable evidence to suggest that Barcelona has benefited from the Games: enhancing its status as a global city and attracting more international finance and tourists.[6]

However, it is instructive to note that benefits to a city do not flow as a matter of course, simply because a city hosts this peak event. The Olympics have to be made to work for Sydney and Australia: the Games have to be well run; advertising to attract tourists has to be sharp; and the city (and regions) have to deliver services. The plans for the post-Games legacy have to be put in place.

Since the taxpayer is footing a large part of the Olympic bill, the Olympics should benefit the whole community and not simply the transnational companies and corporate leaders who may reap the dividends if Sydney attracts a greater amount of global capital or tourists. The argument that the wealth created by a hallmark event will 'trickle down' to everyone, may not appeal to those members of society — such as people living close to event sites, or the homeless who may have to move because of the event — who have had to pay a larger cost than others.

The Games should not improve the wealth of one section of society at the expense of others, or people in the bush, those on welfare or on the margins. To run the Game properly, the organisers and the various governments will have to look carefully at the social implications of the Games and to take appropriate measures to deal with any Games-related inequities and injustices.

The Olympic Games, like the Opera House, are a costly exercise and have generated their share of debate and controversy. The true test of the Games will not be known until long after the event: whether the public judge the exercise to be worthwhile. The other test is whether the Olympic facilities, and Olympic Park in general, provide inspiration and lively public activity in the same way as the Opera House does.

# NOTES

CHAPTER 1

1   Guttmann, *Games and Empires*, pp 120–38.
2   Paddick, 'Amateurism', pp 1–15.
3   MacAloon, *This Great Symbol*, p. 5
4   Guttmann, *The Games Must Go On*, p x.
5   Hanna, 'Reconciliation in Olympism', pp 72–82.
6   Müller, *Coubertin and Olympism*, p 10.
7   Brohm, 'The Olympic opiate', p 110.
8   Simson and Jennings, *Lords of the Rings*.
9   Gillen, 'The Olympics and global society', p 14.
10  Paddick, 'Amateurism', p 13.
11  Lawrence and Rowe, 'The Olympics as popular culture', pp 26–9.
12  Kidd, 'The Myth of the Ancient Games', pp 71–83.
13  Hoberman, 'Towards a theory of Olympic internationalism', pp 1–37.
14  Gillen, 'The Olympics and global society', p 11.
15  Reproduced from Slater, 'Changing partners', p 56.
16  Cahill, *Running Towards Sydney 2000*.
17  Blue, *Grace Under Pressure*.
18  Krüger and Riordan, *The Story of Worker Sport*, p vii.

CHAPTER 2

1   Whitson and Macintosh, 'Becoming a world-class city'; Ley and Olds, 'World's fairs'.
2   Hirst and Thompson, *Globalization in Question*; Cox, *Space of Globalization*.
3   Dicken, *Global Shift*, p 1.
4   Gertler, 'Between the global and the local'.
5   Hirst and Thompson, *Globalization in Question*; Le Heron and Pawson, *Changing Places*; Allen, 'Crossing border'.
6   Stimson, 'Processes of globalisation'.
7   McKenzie and Lee, *Quicksilver Capital*.
8   Ohmae, *The Borderless World*.
9   Hoogvelt, *Globalisation and the Postcolonial World*.
10  For Australia's case see Pusey, *Economic Rationalism*.
11  Cox, *Space of Globalization*.
12  Hall and Markusen, *Silicon Landscapes*; Daniels and Moulaert, *Changing Geography*.

13  M<sup>c</sup>Guirk et al., 'Entrepreneurial approaches to urban decline'.
14  Rydin, 'The enabling local state'.
15  Anderson, 'The "new right" enterprise zones'; Leitner, 'Cities in pursuit of economic growth'.
16  Hall and Hubbard, *The Entrepreneurial City*; Winter and Brooke, 'Urban planning and the entrepreneurial state'.
17  Pearson, *Place Reidentification*; M<sup>c</sup>Guirk et al., 'Entrepreneurial approaches to urban decline'.
18  Harvey, 'From managerialism to entrepreneurialism', p 11.
19  Wilks-Heeg, 'Urban experiments limited revisited'.
20  Winter and Brooke, 'Urban planning and the entrepreneurial state'.
21  Imrie and Thomas, 'Urban policy processes'.
22  Charlesworth and Cochrane, 'Tales of the suburbs'.
23  See M<sup>c</sup>Guirk et al., 'On losing the local'.
24  Hunt, 'Providing and financing urban infrastructure'.
25  Cochrane et al., 'Manchester plays games'.
26  Ward, 'Coalitions in urban regeneration'.
27  Leitner and Garner, 'The limits of local initiatives'.
28  Huxley, 'Making cities fun'.
29  Allison and Keane, 'Position in the new economic landscape'; Moon, 'Reforming the Queensland land-use planning legislation'.
30  Albany Consulting, *Social Capital*, p 65.
31  Kerkin, 'Towards democratic planning?'.
32  Bell, 'Public participation'.
33  Costello and Dunn, 'Resident action groups'.
34  Turner and Hodges, *Global Shakeout*.
35  Ward, 'Coalitions in urban regeneration'.
36  Charlesworth and Cochrane, 'Tales of the suburbs'; Herod, 'Local political practice'.
37  M<sup>c</sup>Guirk et al., 'On losing the local'.
38  French and Disher, 'Atlanta and the Olympics'.
39  Boyle, 'Civic boosterism'; Ritchie and Lyons, 1990; Hillier, 'Impact and image'.
40  Cochrane et al., 'Manchester plays games', pp 1328–9.
41  French and Disher, 'Atlanta and the Olympics'.
42  Simson and Jennings, *Lords of the Rings*.
43  'Games Chief defends buying votes', *Sun-Herald*, 24 January 1999, pp 1, 6.
44  *Sydney Morning Herald*, 24 March 1998, p 6.
45  French and Disher, 'Atlanta and the Olympics'.
46  Whitson and Macintosh, 'Becoming a world-class city'.
47  Audit Office of NSW, Table 5.3.
48  French and Disher, 'Atlanta and the Olympics'.
49  French and Disher, 'Atlanta and the Olympics'.
50  Albany Consulting, *Social Capital*, p 64.
51  Freestone, 'Urban impacts', p 1.
52  Albany Consulting, *Social Capital*, p 64.
53  Quoted in Sproats, 'Local government', p 38.
54  Letter to SHOROC, 21 January 1997, p 2.
55  *Green Games Watch Newsletter*, Issue 6, 1997, p 8.
56  SHOROC, Attachment No. 4.
57  Albany Consulting, *Social Capital*.
58  Knight quoted in SOCOG, p 1.
59  Albany Consulting, *Social Capital*.
60  Furrier and Waitt, 'Sharing the spirit?'
61  Ritchie and Lyons, 'Olympulse V'.
62  French and Disher, 'Atlanta and the Olympics'.
CHAPTER 3

1   *Australian,* 15 December 1998.
2   *Australian,* 14 December 1998.
3   *Australian,* 11 January 1999.
4   *Sydney Morning Herald,* 21 January 1999.
5   *Sydney Morning Herald,* 21 January 1999.
6   *Australian,* 16–17 January 1999, p 6; *Sydney Morning Herald,* 22 January 1999.
7   *Sydney Morning Herald,* 21 January 1999.
8   *Sydney Morning Herald,* 15 January 1999.
9   Members appointed prior to 1965 are elected for life. Members appointed after 1965 must retire at the age of 80.
10  Hargreaves, *Sporting Females,* p 209.
11  Simson and Jennings, *Lords of the Rings.*
12  Lenskyj, 'The case against Toronto's bid', pp 16–18.
13  Booth and Tatz, 'Swimming with the big boys', p 8.
14  Gordon, *Australia and the Olympic Games.*
15  Booth and Tatz, 'Swimming with the big boys', pp 14–15.
16  See Chapter 5.
17  *Australian,* 14 December 1998.
18  Simson and Jennings, *Lords of the Rings.*
19  Table reproduced from Booth and Tatz, 'Swimming with the big boys', p 20.
20  Booth and Tatz, 'Swimming with the big boys', p 9.
21  Coakley, *Sport in Society,* p 424.
22  *Australian,* 20 January 1999.

CHAPTER 4
1   Neuhart et al., *Eames Design.*
2   De Pree, *Business as Usual.*
3   Gorb, *Design Management Papers,* p 745.
4   Gorb, *Design Management Papers,* p 745.
5   Marzano, 'Flying over Las Vegas'.
6   Gabra-Liddell, *Alessi.*
7   Gabra-Liddell, *Alessi.*
8   McGeoch with Korporaal, *The Bid,* pp 67–8
9   McGeoch with Korporaal, *The Bid,* p 68
10  Susskind, *Sydney Morning Herald,*

CHAPTER 5
1   The 'identity' or 'character' involved emphasises not so much what Australians actually are but what they think they are. For some discussion see Ward, *The Australian Legend,* and J. Bradley, 'Inventing Australians and constructing Englishness' and *The Oxford Companion to Australian Sport [OCAS].*
2   Blainey, 'The rise of the sporting hero', pp 9–12; Gordon, 'Olympic legends', pp 14–16; Hartz, *The Founding of New Societies; Australians: A Historical Dictionary;* Farrell, *Themes in Australian History;* Clarke, *Australia;* Luck, *This Fabulous Century; When Was That?*
3   *Australians: A Historical Library;* Gordon, 'Olympic legends'.
4   Clark, *A Short History of Australia;* Jaensch and Teichman, *The Macmillan Dictionary;* Vamplew and Stoddart, *Sport in Australia;* Molony, *Eureka.*
5   *When Was That;* Karskens, *The Rocks;* Henniker and Jobling, 'Richard Coombes and the Olympic Movement'.
6   Blainey, 'The rise of the sporting hero'.
7   Broome, 'Theatres of power', pp 1–23; *When Was That?*
8   Nicholas, *Charles Darwin in Australia.*
9   Davidson, 'Welcoming the world', pp 64–76; Burkhardt et al., *The Olympic Games; The Olympic Movement; OCAS;* Cashman, *Paradise of Sport;* Atkinson,

*Australian and New Zealand Olympians*; Jobling, 'The making of a nation'.
10   Wells, *Boxing Day*.
11   Phillips, *Australian Women at the Olympics*.
12   Phillips, *Australian Women at the Olympics*.
13   *Daily Telegraph*, 3 October and 7 November 1997; Stanner, 'The history of indifference', pp 3–26.
14   Yates, *Theatre of the World*; Rowley, *The Destruction of Aboriginal Society*; Proudfoot, *Seaport Sydney*.
15   Vamplew and Stoddart, *Sport in Australia*. The Fig Tree Baths were near to the present-day Andrew 'Boy' Charlton Pool in the Sydney Domain.
16   Davison, 'Welcoming the World', notes that the issue of amateurism resurfaced to blight Beaurepaire's later Melbourne career, 'Wowser' was a term used to describe the religious advocates of social restraints and restrictions, particularly in relation to drinking and gambling.
17   McLuhan, 'The medium is the message', pp 6–21.

CHAPTER 6
1   Searle, *Sydney as a Global City*.

CHAPTER 7
1   Beder, 'Discussion', *Green Games*, p 108.
2   Kiernan, 'Opportunities for education', pp 71–6.

CHAPTER 8
1   Rich, 'Structural and spatial change in manufacturing'.
2   Hamilton, *Serendipity City*.
3   Hamilton, *Serendipity City*, p 104.
4   The Earth Council, *Sydney 2000 Olympic Games*, p 5.
5   The Earth Council, *Sydney 2000 Olympic Games*.
6   The Earth Council, *Sydney 2000 Olympic Games*, p 15.
7   James, *Environmental Performance Review Report*.
8   James, *Environmental Performance Review Report*, p 7.
9   Black et al., 'Homebush Bay Corporation Transport Advisory Group Report'.
10   Property Services Group, *A Transport Strategy for Homebush Bay*.
11   Ware, 'The communication strategies'.

CHAPTER 9
Most references are taken from two sources: Thompson, *Terrorism and the 2000 Olympics* and US State Department, *Patterns of Global Terrorism*.

1   Paper delivered at the 1995 Australian Defence Studies Centre Conference, 'Terrorism and the 2000 Olympics'.

CHAPTER 12
1   IOC website: www.olympic.org
2   Jennings, *New Lords of the Rings*.
3   *Newsweek*, 22 July 1996.
4   Cited in *Sports Illustrated*, 14 April 1997.
5   The abuse of these agents was not restricted to men. Women also took anabolic steroids and showed pronounced physical change, notably increased body hair, deepening of the voice, and a loss of breast tissue. By the 1970 Olympic Games there were women athletes competing from the Eastern bloc countries who looked like men.
6   In a poll undertaken by a leading US sports magazine, 50 per cent of a sampling of 198 US Olympians, or aspiring Olympians, admitted that they would take a banned substance, given the assurance that they would not be caught, if it

allowed them to win every event that they entered over the next five years, even if it then killed them. (M. Bamber and D. Yaeger, *Sports Illustrated*, 14 April 1997.)

7   As one example, beta-blockers are only banned in some sports. These agents reduce tremor and slow the heartbeat. Consequently, they may offer a significant advantage in sports such as shooting and archery. Alcohol, marijuana and local anaesthetics are also covered under Article III: Classes of Drugs Subject to Certain Restrictions.

8   Typically, about 2500 samples are tested over the 15 days of competition.

9   If the competitor is a member of a team, the competitor, event or match during which the infringement took place may be considered as forfeited by that team.

10  This number includes positive tests from both the Summer and Winter Olympic Games. The majority of these (c. 90 per cent) were associated with the Summer Games.

11  Three gold medallists and one bronze medallist were involved: Ben Johnson (Canada, 100 metres), Mitko Grubler and Angel Guenchev (Bolivia, weight-lifting) and Kerrith Brown (GBR, judo).

12  Quoted in *Inside Sport*, January 1998, p 10.

13  There are reports of female athletes inserting a urine-filled balloon (or artificial bladder) inside their vagina, then, at the time of collection, using their fingernail to pierce the balloon and allow the urine to flow into the collection vessel.

14  Most challenges to the test results relate to the sample collection, storage and record-keeping process. There are specific requirements involving: authority to collect, collection protocol, sample shipment and chain-of-custody of the sample. In addition, queries are sometimes raised as to whether the agent in question arose from the diet, or whether the compound actually belongs to a banned category or not. The validity of the analytical findings is rarely, if ever, an issue.

15  It has been argued that a synthetic steroid, such as stanazolol, in urine, may arise from the consumption of meat (e.g. beef) contaminated with the agent. After all, this is a veterinary product. While this defence has been employed, diet is unlikely to provide detectable levels of stanazolol in human urine under anything but the most exceptional circumstances.

16  The situation is a little more complicated in practice. It is not testosterone itself, but the testosterone to epitestosterone ratio that determines a positive result. This example is used to simply introduce the concept of endogenous versus exogenously administered agents.

17  Growth hormone is a protein and, if taken by mouth, would be rapidly degraded in the gut. As a consequence, the only effective route of administration is injection.

18  The supply, in labelled glass ampoules, was sufficient for the team.

19  Dr Jim Puffer, a clinician to the US Olympic Team, estimates that, on anecdotal evidence, up to 30 per cent of Olympic athletics are taking performance-enhancing drugs.

20  Quoted in *Inside Sport*, June 1992.

CHAPTER 13

1   New South Wales Treasury.

2   KPMG Peat Marwick in association with the Centre for South Australian Olympic Studies.

3   M. Bailey, Travel and Business Analyst, Hong Kong.

4   New South Wales Treasury, p 16.

5   KPMG, Executive Summary, p 3.

6   KPMG, Executive Summary, p. 3.

7   Carmody, *Comparison of Sydney with Seoul 1988*.

8   KPMG, Executive Summary, p 3.

9   Australian Tourist Commission Evaluation Report.

10 Garrigosa, *Presentation to Tourism New South Wales Tourism Olympic Forum.*

CHAPTER 14

1 De Coubertin, *Olympic Memoirs.*
2 Fitzpatrick and Pavillard, 'Rewarding the risk: The success of the Olympic Arts Festival', p 66.
3 Holgate, 'Games no good for arts giants'.
4 Miller, *Olympic Revolution*, p 47.
5 Olympic Message (1985), March, p 14.

CHAPTER 15

1 Ritchie, *Mosman Council*, p 11.
2 Moore, 'Paralympics Threats'.
3 Landry, 'Paralympics Games', p 125.
4 Sainsbury, 'Paralympic Villages', p 173.
5 Bariga, 'The role of the media', p 1.
6 Ritchie, *Mosman Council*, p 11.
7 Sainsbury, 'Paralympic Villages', p 173.
8 Steadwood, 'The Olympic/Paralympic Movement', p 2.
9 Landry, 'Paralympic Games', p 124.
10 Landry, 'Paralympic Games', p 128.
11 Beasley, 'The Paralympic Village', pp 105–9.
12 Beasley, 'The Paralympic Village', pp 105–9.
13 Landry, 'Paralympic Games', p 128.

CHAPTER 16

This chapter was first presented at a Conference of the Centre for Olympic Studies, University of Western Ontario, 1–3 October 1998 and was first published in the Centre's Proceedings.

1 Howell and Howell, *Aussie Gold*, p 6.
2 Howell and Howell, *Aussie Gold*, p 17.
3 Findling and Pelle, *Historical Dictionary*, p 13.
4 Howell and Howell, *Aussie Gold*, p 17.
5 Findling and Pelle, *Historical Dictionary*, p 42.
6 Müller, *Coubertin and Olympism*, pp 69–70.
7 Renson, *The Games Reborn*, p 71.
8 Findling and Pelle, *Historical Dictionary*, p 42.
9 *Atlanta Journal and Constitution*, 7 November 1997.
10 Bagnall, 'Hell of a village', p 46.
11 *Atlanta Journal and Constitution*, 13 November 1997.
12 Wilson, 'What is an Olympic city?', p 616.
13 Weirick, 'A non-event?', pp 80–3.
14 *Atlanta Journal and Constitution*, 13 July 1997.
15 Davison, 'Welcoming the world', p 65.
16 Moragas and Botella, *The Keys to Success*, p 264.
17 *Atlanta Journal and Constitution*, 13 July 1997.

CHAPTER 17

1 Walker, 'Cost of the Games'.
2 O'Neill, 'How the Olympics will slug taxpayers'.
3 SOCOG media release, 14 January 1999.
4 Moore, 'Reveal Olympic deals'.
5 O'Neill, 'How the Olympics will slug taxpayers'.
6 Moragas, *The Keys to Success.*

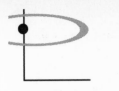

# BIBLIOGRAPHY

Aamo, T. O. and Guldberg, H. C. (1995), 'The doping rules: A set of rules in good Olympic spirit? (see comments)', *Tidsskr Nor Laegeforen*, vol. 115, pp 2120–5.

Albany Consulting Group (1997), *Social Capital in the Olympic City*, Green Games Watch 2000 Inc.

Allen, J. (1995), 'Crossing border: Footloose multinationals?', in J. Allen and C. Hamnett (eds), *A Shrinking World?*, Oxford University Press, London, pp 55–102.

Allison, J. and Keane, J. (1998), 'Position in the new economic landscape', in B. Gleeson and P. Hanley (eds), *Renewing Australian Planning: New Challenges, New Agendas*, Urban Research Program, Research School of Social Sciences, Australian National University, pp 23–45.

Anderson, J. (1990), 'The "new right" enterprise zones and urban development corporations', *International Journal of Urban and Regional Research*, vol. 14, pp 468–89.

Atkinson, G. (1984), *Australian and New Zealand Olympians*, Five Mile Press, Melbourne.

Audit Office of NSW (1999), 'The Sydney 2000 Olympic and Paralympic Games — Review of Estimates', Audit Office of NSW, Sydney.

*Australians: A Historical Dictionary* (1987), Fairfax, Weldon and Syme, Sydney.

*Australians: A Historical Library* (1987–8), 10 vols, Fairfax Weldon and Syme, Sydney.

Bagnall, Diane (1993), 'Hell of a village', *Bulletin*, 9 November.

Bailey, M. Travel and Business Analyst, Hong Kong. See, for example, N. Cockerell (1997), 'Big event blues', in *Issues & Trends*, Pacific Asia Travel Association, San Francisco, March.

Ballard, Geoffrey (1997), *Nation within Nation: The Story of Olympic Village Heidelberg: Olympic Games — Melbourne*, Allanby Press, Melbourne.

Bariga, J. (1998) 'The role of the media in the promotion of sport for the disabled', ONCE Foundation, Madrid, www.ibsa.es/rules/doc/imesa2.txt, 10 February, p 1.

Beasley, K. A. (1997), 'The Paralympic Village: A barrier-free city', *Olympic Villages: One Hundred Years of Urban Planning and Shared Experiences*, IOC, Lausanne, pp 105–9.

Beder, S. (1994), 'Sydney's toxic Green Olympics', *Current Affairs Bulletin*, vol. 70, no. 6, pp 12–18.

Bell, A. (1998), 'Public participation in local government', Sydney, BSc Honours thesis, School of Geography, UNSW, Sydney.

Black, J., Burrows, P., Dobinson, K. and Woodhead, B. (1994), 'Homebush Bay Corporation Transport Advisory Group Report on a Review of the Draft Transport Infrastructure Strategy Direction for Homebush Bay', a Report to the Homebush Bay Corporation, August.

Blainey, G. (1995), 'The rise of the sporting hero', *Quadrant*, vol. 39, nos 1–2, January/February, pp 9–12.

Blue, Adrianne (1987), *Grace Under Pressure: The Emergence of Women in Sport*, Sidgwick & Jackson, London.

Booth, Douglas and Tatz, Colin (1994), 'Swimming with the big boys?: The politics of Sydney's 2000 Olympic bid', *Sporting Traditions*, vol. 11, no. 1, November, pp 3–23.

Bowers, L. D. (1998), 'Athletic drug testing', *Clinical Sports Medicine*, vol. 17, pp 299–318.

Boyle, M. (1997), 'Civic boosterism in the politics of local economic development: "Institutional positions" and "strategic orientations" in the consumption of hallmark events', *Environment and Planning A*, vol. 29, pp 1975–97.

Bradley, J. (1995), 'Inventing Australians and constructing Englishness', *Sporting Traditions*, vol. 11, no. 2, May, pp 35–60.

Brohm, Jean-Marie (1978), 'The Olympic opiate', in Brohm, *Sport: Prison of Measured Time*, Ink Links, London, pp 102–15.

Broome, R. (1996), 'Theatres of power', *Aboriginal History*, vol. 20, pp 1–23.

Burkhardt, A., Toohey, K. and Veal, A. J. (1995), *The Olympic Games: A Bibliography*, UTS, Sydney.

Burnosky, R. L. (1994), 'The history of the arts in the Olympic Games', unpub. MA thesis, American University, Washington, DC.

Buzacott, S. (1996), Planning Homebush: A potted history', *Architectural Bulletin*, 16 March.

Cahill, Janet (1991), *Running Towards Sydney 2000: The Olympic Torch & Flame*, Walla Walla Press, Sydney.

Carmody, G. (1993), *Comparison of Sydney with Seoul 1988*, Access Economics, Canberra.

Cashman, Richard (1994), *Paradise of Sport*, Oxford University Press, Melbourne.

Cashman, R. and Hughes, A. (eds) (1998), *Mosman Council: Forum on the Impacts of the Olympics*, Centre for Olympic Studies, Sydney.

Cashman, R. and Hughes, A. (eds) (1998), *The Green Games: A Golden Opportunity*, Centre for Olympic Studies, Sydney.

Catlin, D. H. and Murray, T. H. (1996), 'Performance-enhancing drugs, fair competition, and Olympic sport (see comments)', *JAMA*, vol. 276, pp 231–7.

Charlesworth, J. and Cochrane, A. (1994), 'Tales of the suburbs: The local politics of growth in South East England', *Urban Studies*, vol. 31, pp 1723–38.

Clark, M. (1995), *A Short History of Australia*, 4th rev. ed., Penguin, Ringwood.

Clarke, F. G. (1992), *Australia: A Concise Political and Social History*, Harcourt Brace Jovanovich, Sydney.

Clarkson, P. M. and Thompson, H. S. (1997), 'Drugs and sport: Research findings and limitations', *Sports Medicine*, vol 24, pp 366–84.

Coakley, Jay (1997), *Sport in Society: Issues and Controversies*, 6th ed., McGraw-Hill, New York.

Cochrane, A., Peck, J. and Tickell, A. (1996), 'Manchester plays games: Exploring the local politics of globalisation', *Urban Studies*, vol. 33, no. 8, pp 1319–36.

Costello, L. N. and Dunn, K. M. (1994), 'Resident action groups in Sydney: People power or rat-bags?', *Australian Geographer*, vol. 25, no. 1, pp 61–76.

Commonwealth of Australia (1991), *Ecologically Sustainable Development Transport Working Group*, Australian Government Publishing Service, Canberra.

Cox, K. (1997), *Space of Globalization; Reasserting the Power of the Local*, UCL Press, New York.

Daniels, P. and Moulaert, B. (1991), *The Changing Geography of Advanced Producer Services*, Belhaven, London.

Davison, Graeme (1997), 'Welcoming the world: The 1956 Olympic Games and the re-presentation of Melbourne', *Australian Historical Studies*, no. 109, October, pp. 64–77.

De Coubertin, P. (1997), *Olympic Memoirs*, IOC, Lausanne.

De Pree, Hugh (1986), *Business as Usual*, Herman Miller Inc, Zeeland, MI.

Dicken, P. (1992), *Global Shift: The Internationalization of Economic Activity*, 2nd ed., Paul Chapman Publishing, London.

Earth Council (1997), *Sydney 2000 Olympic Games: Environmental Performance of the Olympic Co-ordination Authority*, Review 1, December 1996, 23 July.

Farrell, F. (1990), *Themes in Australian History*, UNSW Press, Sydney.

Findling, J. E. and Pelle, K. D. (eds) (1996), *Historical Dictionary of the Modern Olympic Movement*, Greenwood Press, Westport, CT.

Frank, W. H. and Berendonk, B. (1997), *Clinical Chemistry*, vol. 43, pp 1262–79.

Freestone, R. (ed.) (1998), 'Urban impacts of Olympic Games', UNSW Planning Studies No. 2, Working Paper 96/1, School of Planning and Urban Development, UNSW, Sydney.

French, S. and Disher, M. (1997), 'Atlanta and the Olympics: A one year retrospective', *APA Journal*, Summer, pp 379–92.

Fuller J. R. and LaFountain, M. J. (1987), 'Performance-enhancing drugs in sport: A different form of drug abuse', *Adolescence*, vol. 22, pp 969–76.

Furrier, P. and Waitt, G. (forthcoming), 'Sharing the spirit? Socio-spatial polarisation and expressed enthusiasm for the Olympic Games', *Pacific Tourism Review*, vol. 4, no. 1.

Gabra-Liddell, M. (1994), *Alessi: The Design Factory*, Academy Editions, London.

Garrigosa, A. (1997) *Presentation to Tourism New South Wales Tourism Olympic Forum*, September.

Gertler, M. (1997), 'Between the global and the local: The spatial limitations of productive capital', in K. Cox (ed.), *Space of Globalization; Reasserting the Power of the Local*, UCL Press, New York, pp 45–63.

Gillen, Paul (1994/95), 'The Olympic Games and global society', *Arena*, New Series, no. 4, pp 5–15.

Good, D. (1998), 'The Olympic Games' Cultural Olympiad: Identity and management', unpub. MA thesis, American University, Washington, DC.

Gorb, P. (1990), *Design Management Papers*, London Business School, London, p 745.

Gordon, H. (1998), 'Olympic legends', *Journal of Olympic History*, vol. 6, no. 2, pp 17–21; and vol. 6, no. 1, pp 14–16.

Gordon, Harry (1994), *Australia and the Olympic Games*, University of Queensland Press, St Lucia.

Guttmann, Allan (1984), *The Games Must Go On: Avery Brundage and the Olympic Movement*, Columbia University Press, New York.

Guttmann, Allen (1992), *The Olympics: A History of the Modern Games*, University of Illinois Press, Urbana, IL.

Guttmann, Allen (1994), *Games and Empires: Modern Sports and Cultual Imperialism*, Columbia University Press, New York.

Hall, P. and Markusen, A. (eds) (1985), *Silicon Landscapes*, Allen & Unwin, Sydney.

Hall, T. and Hubbard, P. (1998), *The Entrepreneurial City: Geographies of Politics, Regime and Representation*, Wiley, London.

Hamilton, W. (1991), *Serendipity City: Australia, Japan and the Multifunction Polis*, ABC Enterprises for the Australian Broadcasting Corporation, Crows Nest.

Hanna, Michelle (1997), 'Reconciliation in Olympism: The Sydney 2000 Olympic Games and Australia's indigenous people', BA Theory Hons thesis, UNSW, Sydney.

Hardy, K. J., McNeil, J. J. and Capes, A. G. (1997), 'Drug doping in senior

Australian rules football: A survey for frequency', *British Journal of Sports Medicine*, vol. 31, pp 126–8.

Hargreaves, Jennifer (1994), *Sporting Females: Critical Issues in the History and Sociology of Women's Sport*, Routledge, London, p 209.

Hartz, L. (ed.) (1964), *The Founding of New Societies*, Harvest, New York.

Harvey, D. (1989), 'From managerialism to entrepreneurialism: The transformation in urban governance in late capitalism', *Geografiska Annaler*, 71B, pp 2–17.

Henniker, G. and Jobling, I. (1989), 'Richard Coombes and the Olympic Movement in Australia', *Sporting Traditions*, vol. 6, no. 1, November, pp 2–15.

Herod, A. (1991), 'Local political practice in response to a manufacturing plant closure: How geography complicates class analysis', *Antipode*, vol. 23, pp 385–402.

Hillier, H. (1989), 'Impact and image: The concentration of urban factors in preparation for the 1988 Calgary Winter Olympics', in J. Syme (ed.), *The Planning and Evaluation of Hallmark Events*, Avebury, Hants, pp 288–309.

Hirst, P. and Thompson, G. (1996), *Globalization in Question: The International Economy and the Possibilities of Governance*, Polity Press, Cambridge.

Hoberman, John (1995), 'Toward a theory of Olympic internationalism', *Journal of Sport History*, vol. 22, no. 1, pp. 1–37.

Holgate, B. (1998), 'Games no good for arts giants', *Australian*, 7 May.

Hoogvelt, A. (1997), *Globalisation and the Postcolonial World. The New Political Economy of Development*, Macmillan, London.

Howell, Reet and Howell, Max (1988), *Aussie Gold: The Story of Australia at the Olympics*, Brooks Waterloo, Melbourne.

Huey, John (1996), The Atlanta Game: How Atlanta stole the Olympics', *Fortune Magazine*, 22 June, pp 24–40.

Hunt, A. (1994), 'Providing and financing urban infrastructure', *Urban Policy and Research*, vol. 12, pp 118–22.

Huxley, M. (1991), 'Making cities fun: Darling Harbour and the immobilisation of spectacle', in P. Carroll (ed.), *Tourism in Australia*, Harcourt Brace Jovanovich, Sydney, pp 141–52.

Imrie, R. and Thomas, H. (1995), 'Urban policy processes and the politics of urban regeneration', *International Journal of Urban and Regional Research*, vol. 19, pp 479–94.

International Olympic Committee (1993), *The Olympic Movement*, IOC, Lausanne.

International Olympic Committee (1993–98), *Olympic Marketing Matters: The Olympic Marketing Newsletter*, issues 1–13.

International Olympic Committee (1997), *Olympic Charter*.

Jackson, Daryl (1992), 'Olympic village competition', *Architectural Bulletin*, August, pp 5–12.

Jaensch, D. and Teichman, M. (1979), *The Macmillan Dictionary of Australian Politics*, Macmillan, Melbourne.

James, P. (1997), *Environmental Performance Review Report Olympic Co-ordination Authority: Compliance with the Environmental Guidelines for the Summer Olympics*, Green Games Watch 2000 Inc., Bondi Junction.

Jobling, I. (1988), 'The making of a nation through sport', *Australian Journal of Politics and History*, vol. 34, no. 3, pp 160–71.

Karskens, G. (1997), *The Rocks: Life in Early Sydney*, Melbourne University Press, Melbourne.

Kerkin, K. (1998), 'Towards democratic planning?: Negotiating change in St Kilda, Melbourne', *Urban Policy and Research*, vol. 16, pp 293–300.

Kidd, Bruce (1984), 'The Myth of the Ancient Games', in A. Tomlinson and G. Whannel (eds), *Five Ring Circus: Money, Power and Politics of the Olympic Games*, Pluto, London, pp. 71–83.

Kiernan, Ian (1998), 'Opportunities for education', in Cashman and Hughes (eds) *The Green Games*, pp 71–6.

Kleiner, S. M. (1991), 'Performance-enhancing aids in sport: Health consequences and nutritional alternatives', *Journal of American College Nutrition*, vol. 10, pp 163–76.

KPMG Peat Marwick in association with the Centre for South Australian Olympic Studies (1993), *Sydney Olympics 2000: Economic Impact Studies*.

Krüger, Arnd and Riordan, James (eds) (1996), *The Story of Worker Sport*, Human Kinetics, Champaign, IL.

Laudry, F. (1995), 'The Paralympic Games of Barcelona '92', in Miquel de Moragas and Miquel de Botella (eds), *The Keys to Success*, Centre for Olympic Studies, Barcelona.

Lawrence, Geoffrey and Rowe, David (1984), 'The Olympics as popular culture', *Arena*, no. 69, pp 26–9.

Le Heron, R. and Pawson, E. (1996), *Changing Places: New Zealand in the Nineties*, Longman Paul, Auckland.

Leiper, N. (1997), 'A Town like Elis? The Olympics: Impact on Tourism in Sydney', *Proceedings of Australian Tourism & Hospitality Research Conference*, Sydney, 6–9 July.

Leiper, N. and Hall, M. (1993), 'The 2000 Olympics and Australia's tourism industries', paper for House of Representatives Committee.

Leitner, H. (1990), Cities in pursuit of economic growth: The local state as entrepreneur, *Political Geography Quarterly*, vol. 9, pp 146–70.

Leitner, H. and Garner, M. (1993), 'The limits of local initiatives: A reassessment of urban entrepreneurialism for urban development', *Urban Geography*, vol. 14, pp 57–77.

Lenskyj, Helen J. (1996), 'When winners are losers: Toronto and Sydney bids for the Summer Olympics', *Journal of Sport and Social Issues*, vol. 24, November, pp 392–418.

Lenskyj, Helen (1997), 'The case against Toronto's bid for the 2000 Olympics', *Policy Options*, May, pp 16–18.

Lenskyj, Helen (1998), 'Green Games or empty promises? Environmental issues and Sydney 2000', *Global and Cultural Critique: Problematizing the Olympic Games*, Centre for Olympic Studies, University of Western Ontario, London, Canada, pp 173–9.

Levitt, S. H. (1990), 'The 1984 Olympics Arts Festival: Theatre', unpub. PhD thesis, University of California, Davis.

Ley, D. and Olds, K. (1992), 'World's fairs and the culture of consumption in the contemporary city', in K. Anderson and F. Gale (eds), *Inventing Places: Studies in Cultural Geography*, Longman Cheshire, Melbourne, pp 178–93.

Luck, P. (1981), *This Fabulous Century*, Circus, Melbourne.

MacAloon, John J. (1981), *This Great Symbol; Pierre de Coubertin and the Origins of the Modern Olympic Games*, University of Chicago Press, Chicago.

McGeoch, Rod and Korporaal, Glenda (1994), *The Bid: How Australia Won the 2000 Games*, William Heinemann, Melbourne.

McGrew, A. (1992), 'Conceptualising global politics', in A. McGrew and Lewis (eds), *Global Politics*, Polity Press, Cambridge.

McGuirk, P. M., Winchester, H. P. M. and Dunn, K. M. (1996), 'Entrepreneurial approaches to urban decline: The Honeysuckle redevelopment in inner Newcastle, NSW', *Environment & Planning A*, vol. 28, no. 12, pp 1815–41.

McGuirk, P. M., Winchester, H. P. M. and Dunn, K. M. (1998), 'On losing the local in responding to urban decline', in T. Hall and P. Hubbard (eds), *The Entrepreneurial City: Geographies of Politics, Regime and Representation*, John Wiley, London, pp 107–29.

McKenzie, R. B. and Lee, D. R. *Quicksilver Capital: How the Rapid Movement of Wealth has Changed the World*, Free Press, New York.

McLuhan, Marshall (1964), 'The medium is the message', *Understanding Media*, Routledge and Kegan Paul, London, pp 6–21.

Marzano, Stefanno (1993), 'Flying over Las Vegas', unpublished conference paper, September.

Miller, D. (1992), *Olympic Revolution: The Olympic Biography of Juan Antonio Samaranch*, Parikow, London.

Molony, J. (1984), *Eureka*, Penguin, Ringwood.

Moon, B. (1998), 'Reforming the Queensland land-use planning legislation', *Australian Planner*, vol. 35, pp 24–31.

Moore, Matthew (1998), 'Reveal Olympic deals', *Sydney Morning Herald*, 2 December.

Moore, Matthew (1998), 'Paralympics Threats', *Sydney Morning Herald*, 12 June.

Moragas, Miquel de and Botella, Miquel (eds) (1995), *The Keys to Success: The Social, Sporting, Economic and Communications Impact of Barcelona '92*, Centre for Olympic Studies, Barcelona.

Müller, Norbert (ed.) (1998), *Coubertin and Olympism: Questions for the Future*, International Pierre De Coubertin Committee, Strasbourg.

Neuhart, John, Neuhart, Marilyn and Eames, Ray (1989), *Eames Design*, Thames & Hudson, London.

New South Wales Treasury (1997), *Research and Information Paper: The Economic Impact of the Sydney Olympic Games?*, produced in collaboration with the Centre for Regional Economic Analysis, University of Tasmania, November.

Nicholas, F. W. and J. M. (1989), *Charles Darwin in Australia*, Cambridge University Press, Melbourne.

Nocelli, L., Kamber, M., Francois, Y., Gmel, G. and Marti, B. (1998), 'Discordant public perception of doping in elite versus recreational sport in Switzerland', *Clinical Journal of Sport Medicine*, vol. 8, pp 195–200.

Ohmae, K. (1990), *The Borderless World*, Collins, London.

Olympic Co-ordination Authority (1995), *Homebush Bay Development Guidelines: Volume 1: Environmental Strategy* (working document).

Olympic Co-ordination Authority (1997), *State of the Environment 1996*, Sydney.

O'Neill, John (1995), 'How the Olympics will slug taxpayers', *Independent Monthly*, September, pp 28–30.

Paddick, Robert J. (1994), 'Amateurism: An idea of the past or a necessity for the future?', *Olympika*, vol. 3, pp 1–15.

Pearson, L. P. (1996), 'Place reidentification: The 'Leisure Coast' as a partial presentation of Wollongong', BSc Honours thesis, School of Geography, UNSW, Sydney.

Phillips, Dennis (1992), *Australian Women at the Olympic Games 1912–1992*, Kangaroo Press, Sydney.

Property Services Group (1992) *A Transport Strategy for Homebush Bay, Sydney: Property Services Group*, Urban Redevelopment Division, Sydney, Edition 3, July.

Proudfoot, P. (1996), *Seaport Sydney: The Making of the City Landscape*, UNSW Press, Sydney.

Pusey, M. (1992), *Economic Rationalism in Canberra: A Nation Building State Changes its Mind*, Cambridge University Press, Melbourne.

Radford, P. F. (1990), 'Recent developments in drug abuse and doping control in sport', *Journal of the Royal College of Surgeons Edinburgh*, vol. 35, pp S2–6.

Renson, Roland (1996), *The Games Reborn: The VIIth Olympiad — Antwerp 1920*, Pandora, Ghent.

Rich, D. C. (1982), 'Structural and spatial change in manufacturing', in R. V. Cardew, J. V. Langdale and D. C. Rich (eds), *Why Cities Change: Urban Development and Economic Change in Sydney*, George Allen & Unwin, Sydney, pp 95–113.

Ritchie, B. and Lyons, M. (1990), 'Olympulse VI: A post-event assessment of resident reaction to the XV Winter Games', *Journal of Travel Research*, Winter, pp 14–23.

Rivenburgh, Nancy K. (1995), 'Images of others: The presentation of nations in the 1992 Barcelona Olympics', *Journal of International Communication*, vol. 2, no. 1, pp 6–26.

Rothenbuhler, W. Eric (1988), 'The living room celebration of the Olympics', *Journal of Communication*, vol. 38, no. 4, Autumn.

Rowe, D. and Lawrence, G. (eds) (1998), *Tourism, Leisure, Sport: Critical Perspectives*, Hodder Education, Sydney.

Rowley, C. D. (1970), *The Destruction of Aboriginal Society*, ANU Press, Canberra.

Rydin, Y. (1998), 'The enabling local state and urban development: Resources, rhetoric and planning in east London', *Urban Studies*, vol. 35, pp 175–91.

Sainsbury, T. (1997), 'Paralympic Villages', in *One Hundred Years of Urban Planning and Shared Experiences*, p 173.

Searle, Glen (1996), *Sydney as a Global City*, Department of Urban Affairs and Planning, Sydney.

SHOROC (1997), *Proceedings of the SHOROC Conference*, Attachment 4, SHOROC Regional Organisation of Councils.

Short, J., Benton, L., Luce, W. and Walton, J. (1993), 'Reconstructing the image of an industrial city', *Annals of the Association of American Geographers*, vol. 83, pp 207–24.

Simson, V. and Jennings, A. (1992), *The Lords of the Rings: Power, Money and Drugs in the Modern Olympics*, Simon & Schuster, New York.

Slater, John (1998), 'Changing partners: The relationship between the mass media and the Olympic Games', in Robert K. Barney et al., *Global and Cultural Critique: Problematizing the Olympic Games* (Fourth International Symposium for Olympic Research), University of Western Ontario, London, Canada.

SOCOG (1998), 'Nova, Troy and Tanya join call for 50,000 volunteers for Sydney Olympic and Paralympic Games', *News Release*, 9 October.

Sproats, K. (1997), 'Local government and the Sydney 2000 Olympic Games', *Urban Futures*, vol. 22, pp 37–40.

Stanner, W. E. H. (1977), 'The history of indifference thus begins', *Aboriginal History*, vol. 1, no. 1, pp 3–26.

Steadwood, R. (1998), 'The Olympic/Paralympic Movement — Normalization through Sport', ONCE Foundation, Madrid, 10 February, www.ibsa.es/rules/doc/imesa1.txt, p 2.

Stimson, R. (1995), 'Processes of globalisation, economic restructuring and the emergence of a new space economy of cities and regions in Australia', in J. Brotchie, M. Batty, E. Blakely, P. Hall and P. Newton (eds), *Cities in Competition: Productive and Sustainable Cities for the 21st Century*, Longman, Melbourne, pp 58–87.

Taylor, P. J. Watts, M. J. and Johnston, R. J. (1995), 'Remapping the world: What sort of map?', in R. Johnston, P. Taylor and M. Watts (eds), *Geographies of Global Change: Remapping the World in the Late Twentieth Century*, Blackwell Publishers, Cambridge, MA.

Thompson, Alan (ed.) (1996), *Terrorism and the 2000 Olympics*, Australian Defence Studies Centre, ADFA, Canberra.

Towndrow, Jennifer (1993), 'The sites that got the Games', *Australian Business Monthly*, November, pp 120–3.

Turner, L. and Hodges, M. (1992), *Global Shakeout. World Market Competition: The Challenges for Business and Government*, Century Business Books, London.

US State Department (1992, 1996), *Patterns of Global Terrorism*.

Vamplew, W. et al. (eds) (1994), *The Oxford Companion to Australian Sport*, Oxford University Press, Melbourne.

Vamplew, W. and Stoddart, B. (eds) (1994), *Sport in Australia: A Social History*, Cambridge University Press, Melbourne.

Verdier, Michelle and the ITU (1996), 'The Olympic Games and the media', *Olympic Review*, vol. xxv, no. 9, June/July, pp 57–63.

Video on 'The ancient Olympics' (1996), The Institute for Mediterranean Studies and New Step Promoters, Cincinnati, Ohio.

Walker, Bob (1996), 'Cost of the Games', unpublished paper, Centre for Olympic Studies, UNSW, Sydney.

Ward, K. G. (1997), 'Coalitions in urban regeneration: A regime approach', *Environment and Planning A*, vol. 29, pp 1493–506.

Ward, Peter (1996), 'Have we blown it already?', *Australian Magazine*, 21–22 September, pp 10–18.

Ward, Russell (1965), *The Australian Legend*, Oxford University Press, Melbourne.

Ware, C. (1998), 'The communication strategies employed by Olympic transport authorities for the Sydney 2000 Olympic and Paralympic Games', unpublished BE (Civil) thesis, School of Civil and Environmental Engineering, UNSW, Sydney.

Weirick, James (1996), 'A non-event? Sydney's Olympics', *Architecture Australia*, vol. 85, no. 2, March/April, pp. 80–3.

Wells, Jeff (1998), *Boxing Day: The Fight that Changed the World*, HarperCollins, Sydney.

Wenn, Stephen R. (1993), 'Lights! Camera! Little Action! Avery Brundage and the 1956 Melbourne Olympics', *Sporting Traditions*, vol. 10, no. 1, November, pp 38–53.

Wenn, Stephen R. (1995), 'The Olympic Movement and television', *Olympika*, vol. 4, pp 1–23.

*When was That?* (1988), Ferguson, Sydney.

Whitson, D. and Macintosh, D. (1993), 'Becoming a world-class city: Hallmark events and sport franchises in the growth strategies of Western Canadian cities', *Sociology of Sport Journal*, vol. 10, pp 221–40.

Wilks-Heeg, S. (1996), 'Urban experiments limited revisited: Urban policy comes full circle', *Urban Studies*, vol. 33, pp 1263–79.

Wilson, Helen (1996), 'What is an Olympic City? Visions of Sydney 2000', *Media Culture and Society*, vol. 18, pp. 603–18.

Winter, I. and Brooke, T. (1993), 'Urban planning and the entrepreneurial state: The view from Victoria, Australia', *Environment and Planning C*, vol. 11, pp 263–78.

Yates, F. A. (1969), *Theatre of the World*, Routledge & K. Paul, London.

# INDEX